BE STILL

AND LET GOD BE GOD

*Writings about
self-improvement,
discovery, and
one's relationship with God*

Robert Paul Baeyens

Deep/River
B O O K S

BE STILL

© 2010 Robert Paul Baeyens

Scripture quotations are taken from the *New American Standard Bible*, copyright © 1960, 1962, 1963, 1968, 1971, 1972, 1973, 1975, 1977, 1995, 1997 by The Lockman Foundation.

The devotional in chapter 20 is reprinted by permission of Unity, publisher of *Daily Word*®.

Deep River Books
Sisters, Oregon
http://www.deepriverbooks.com

ISBN: 1-935265-12-1
ISBN: 978-1-935265-12-2

Library of Congress: 2010924401

Printed in the USA

Cover design by Juanita Dix

TABLE OF CONTENTS

FOREWORD AND DEDICATION

Dedicated to my sister, Lori (Baeyens) Hubert

*"In the beginning was the Word, and the Word was with God, and
the Word was God.
And the Word became flesh, and dwelt among us ..."*

JOHN 1:1, 14

MY REASON FOR WRITING was to explore and solidify the best philosophy by which to live my life. To find answers to questions we all have. To find purpose and, ultimately, happiness with the free gift of life given to us all. But also to wonder—for what reason and to what end? And then to make it all meaningful.

I have continued to write about my own personal discoveries over a ten-year period. Yet, every day I discover something new to consider, and then I'm compelled to write again. If I were asked, "When you leave this earth, what would you want to hand down to your children and your grandchildren?" It would be these writings. They are me. They encompass my mind and my experiences, my mistakes and my lessons during my forty-nine years.

Until now, no one else has read them and few know I write at all. My words are not dazzling, but in laymen's terms. I am no one special, merely a man who wants to discover how to walk through life to the best of his ability and to be the best husband, father, son, and friend to those around him. Most of all, I want my God to be proud of me. And yet I realize He has so much reason, even the proof, to turn away from me and allow me to suffer what I really do deserve. I feel the burden of wanting God to be gracious to me, but at the same time I know I am unworthy of what I expect. There is something wrong with this, something I had to figure out. Selfishness does not deserve grace, and my soul knows this. How can I justify wanting so much when I've offered up so little? Why doesn't God give up on me? What could I possibly offer Him to keep His interest in me? I felt it essential that I learn to appreciate God in a new way and see Him through new eyes. But how does one go about doing this, and for what purpose?

The Bible verse quoted above is the opening statement from the apostle John in the fourth book of the New Testament, "The Gospel According to John." This is a powerful statement. It has been said the ultimate plan for all of us is answered in that one statement by John, on whether or not it is true. From the beginning of mankind, this question has been asked and pondered by countless civilizations. Many were built or destroyed over their beliefs in a higher power or lack thereof. And, still, nobody can prove or disprove whether God exists. If this one simple question could be answered and proven either way, then mankind would certainly be significantly changed. Does one have to believe in God in order to be happy? Is there meaning to life without God at the center of all things? And, most crucial, should we act differently during our walk through life based on how we answer these questions?

Once we establish our belief, how do we then live life to the fullest based on that belief? How can we maximize our happiness and at the same time walk morally, ethically, and for the improvement of society and mankind? Whether or not one believes in God, it is undeniable we should make this our common goal. Since every man and woman is made up of numerous details, their past experiences and cultures, along with constantly changing times and conditions, how do we coexist with one another in harmony? Is one philosophy the best, or is a blend of different philosophies necessary in striving for that goal?

My intention in these writings is to answer these and other questions in order to live life to the fullest and to be our best possible person for our own sake as well as the sake of others. It is more than a mystery in need of a solution. It is a duty and should be every man's and woman's responsibility. To make no choice is to make a choice for complacency, as so many do. That is irresponsible to oneself and to society. The challenge is for every person to stand up and choose and then to live life to its fullest based on that choice.

One thing is for certain—either there is a God or there is not. Fair enough? Let's start with that.

Every chapter in this book begins and ends with a quote, one that has deeper meaning than at first glance. Some are biblical quotes and some are from men and women of great scholarly and philosophical minds. These writings have been separated into their perspective three parts about man, God, and choices, so some of the quotations are from humans and some are from God and some are about choices. Yet they all have one thing in common—they have a sense that there is more than just *self* at the core of humanity—that someone or something is bigger than us all.

Therefore, it is my intention to help you think beyond your normal surroundings and to look inward and be honest with yourself, to discuss topics that can be uncomfortable, to challenge yourself, and to commit to taking a stance. We all need to know whether or not we are actually in control. Is there a God with an ultimate plan for us? Or not? Is there a choice to be made that affects us for eternity? Or not? Or are there multiple paths to an eternal existence? In the end, I simply challenge the reader to make a choice as to what philosophy will guide his or her steps in life. To not make a choice is the equivalent of having one made for you. Let that not be the way of man or woman.

> *"Reason is the greatest enemy that faith has: it*
> *never comes to the aid of spiritual things,*
> *but—more frequently than not—struggles against the divine Word,*
> *treating with contempt all that emanates from God."*
>
> MARTIN LUTHER

These writings started because of a phone call to my sister, Lori, over ten years ago. That call changed my course in life. I believe God was speaking to me through her that night, just as He was thirty years ago when she brought me to Christ. She has been my spiritual compass, and I cannot imagine what my life would have been like without her. These writings are dedicated to her and are because of her. I love you Lori.

Additional Dedications

To my wife, Susie, and to our three children, Paul, Sean, and Bree

To my friend and pastor, Rick Rzeszewski

To my friend and spiritual guide, Meg Brazil

To my friend and spiritual teacher, Brian Chung

To my mother, Merle (Baeyens) Foster

To my father, Tom Baeyens

PART I

ABOUT MAN

Chapter One

BE STILL—
REGARDING MAN'S NATURE

"Cease striving and know that I am God ..."

PSALM 46:10

Thursday, September 24, 1998

"Be still, for I am God." Those were the words my sister shared with me the night before last—the words that have resonated in my head for two days now. There I lay—hooked up to an electrocardiogram machine, my Levi's rolled up to my knees, my shirt off, staring at countless little electrodes taped to my arms, legs, and chest, and thinking, *My God, what has happened to me?*

Before the EKG, I'd been given a questionnaire about depression. When the doctor came back into the room, I handed her the completed form and said, "I was very honest in answering these questions as to how I feel right now, and I can't believe my answers. It's as if someone else filled it out. That's not me!"

You could never have convinced me it was possible for me to ever feel the way I felt. It was as if my father had passed away again. What had gone so terribly wrong? Why didn't I see it coming? The more important question would become, "Can I learn from this and prevent it from happening again?"

The doctor left briefly, then returned to review the EKG. The chest pain I'd experienced the night before was not a heart attack but merely a pulled muscle. Here I was—at thirty-seven I had accomplished numerous goals in my life. I had married a beautiful, intelligent, wonderful woman; we were raising three children; I had earned a place of financial success; and I had everything going for me. But, somewhere along the way, I had taken a detour, one I didn't recognize and one I would later discover as a meaningless and harmful path. Now, for the first time in my life, I was in a state of depression. If you've never been depressed, it's an awful place to be.

Two nights before when I called my sister—even though I was in Southern California and she was 2,500 miles away in Boone, North Carolina—it was the closest, most emotional, most heartfelt and needed talk of my life. Lori, just shy of forty, seemed to have all the right answers. By the end of our talk we were both in tears, myself because of self-pity and she because she loved me so much. If only I could have recorded her incredible words. They filled my soul like when the emptiness is removed by a new found love. Like the feeling when you hear something a certain way at the right time from the right person—you know it's right.

Those words, "be still, for I am God," have been with me since that day, but with a completely new meaning. Isn't it interesting how, when you're reading a book, it's not the whole book that leaves an impact on you, even if you have really enjoyed it. Often it is only a paragraph, and with me usually a single sentence that captures my heart and in some way changes me. It is that "light-bulb" moment, that "ah ha" snapshot in time when you stop reading and stare into the awakening of a new perspective on life, and you are changed forever. Many great men and women have said a single moment in time set them on their path of greatness. At that time they might not have seen it unfolding, and yet that moment changed the course of their lives and pointed them down a path whereby their greatness was achieved.

For me, during that September night in 1998 on the phone with my sister, those six words changed me forever. I can honestly say that almost every day they come into my mind, and they have certainly made my life better. It's incredible to think six words can completely change a person's life. But they have done that for me. They have given me back the perspective I had lost.

Let me take you back almost twenty years earlier so you will better understand my relationship with Lori.

May 22, 1978

I'm walking down the steps after my second-period physics class, when I look up and see my sister standing there waiting for me at my high school in Long Beach, California. She says, "Hi Baey!" It's short for our last name, Baeyens, and a nickname we used for each other. Her voice is quiet, soothing, and sympathetic. Now, this is an odd experience for me because she had graduated from high school two years ago—so my mind is quickly trying to figure out what's going on.

Did something happen to someone? Is she preparing me for bad news? I'm very worried all of a sudden. I respond before she can answer, "Lori, what are you doing here?"

"I came to see you," she said.

"Is anything wrong?" I ask.

"No," she calmly replies, then adds, "Can I talk to you?"

I said, "Sure, what's up?" It's the school's nutrition break time—little did I know the next ten minutes would change my life.

"I had a dream about you last night. And in my dream you died. And I cried, and a great sorrow came over me when I woke up because I didn't think you would be going to heaven, and I would never see you again."

I always knew my sister loved me, but I didn't really know how much until that day. It felt great to have someone so concerned about me. Not that my parents weren't concerned, and, believe me, they had plenty to be concerned about a seventeen-year-old boy discovering life. But Lori was really disturbed. She made a special trip that very morning after her dream. She didn't know my schedule, but she had to find me. It was urgent to her. So, she went to my high school, found out where I was, and waited for me. I was the most important thing in her life that day.

I've looked back many times and thought of how brave she was. What if I didn't accept what she had to say? What if I rejected everything she was feeling? Success for her that day would only come from something beyond her control. And she knew that going in.

She said, "Do you know if you are going to heaven when you die?"

"I think so," I said, pausing for a moment. "You know I believe in God."

"Well, according to the Bible, that's not enough."

I was curious. "Well, tell me, what it does say?"

"It says 'that God has given us eternal life, and this life is in His Son. He who has the Son has the life. He who does not have the Son of God does not have the life. These things I have written to you who believe in the name of the Son of God, so that you may know that you have eternal life' (1 John 5:11–13). That's pretty straightforward wording, isn't it?"

"Yes," I said, "but how do you know if you have the Son or you don't have the Son?"

Uh huh, a question for a book in itself and quite possibly the question of all religions: Do you really meet the standard of the religion, any religion, necessary to become worthy of its rewards? We'll come back to this.

She continued, "Ultimately, it is up to God whether or not He accepts you into His heaven, but my understanding is that you must love Him with all your heart and have faith that He came to earth 2,000 years ago in the form of a man, His Son Jesus, and that He lived and taught as the Bible describes, and that He was crucified and then rose three days later, opening a pathway to heaven for us to be with Him for eternity. If we trust in Him alone and let Him into our hearts as our Savior and forgiver of our sins He will give us the free gift of eternal life." Then she told me, "Once you have been given eternal life, it will never be taken away."

Wow, I thought to myself, *I can have eternal life and still have a beer at the Friday night band party.* This sounded too easy. What she said made sense to me, and I knew my sister knew the Bible because she was majoring in biblical studies, so I accepted her word as the truth about God's Word. "Okay," I said, "what do I need to do?"

"You need to pray with me and open your heart to the things I'm going to say and have you also say. Listen as I pray."

Now, let me paint the picture here. We're standing under a tree on the grass not thirty feet from the steps I just walked down. Classmates are walking by. And being the type who is always concerned about what other people are thinking of me, I am a little embarrassed someone I know might see me with this older, unknown girl, who's holding her hands on my shoulders, eyes closed, saying a prayer. But all of that was dwarfed by how much I knew she cared about me at that moment. So, I closed my eyes and I listened carefully.

She began to pray, and I prayed with her, "Father, thank you for my brother and his willingness to accept your Son into his life today to be his Savior." She continued, and, in a few short moments, I was a Christian.

"Be still, and know that I am God." Arguably, these are some of the most profound words in the entire Bible. Why? For two reasons: One, it comes passionately straight from the mouth of God. Okay, maybe that's two reasons already—coming straight from God and being passionate at the same time. But, secondly, it is a very direct and precise statement He is making—that He is the one and only God, that He is in control of everything, and that mere man is nothing without Him. It doesn't say, "Be still and know that I am one of the Gods." It doesn't say, "Be still and consider that I am powerful and could probably influence things." It says, "'Cease striving, and know that I am God.' Stop what you are doing, be still, don't move, and look up to My heaven and know in your heart that I am the Creator of it all—that it is all within My power to do whatever I choose, and it will happen exactly as I have designed it to happen. And you are part of that design."

To me, that's incredible. And to me, if that is true, and I believe with all my heart it is, then it must be respected and followed above all things. But God goes one step further: "My child, I give you free will to do what you want to do. To show respect for Me only if you want to respect Me, and to do what is right only if you want to do what is right—and also to reap the rewards if you make the choice for Me. But it is your choice." We'll talk about what *right* means in Part Two, worthy of its own chapter.

Now, I wonder, were things set in motion by His plan for my sister to be there that day? Was I put into an emotional state by His almighty hand in preparation for her arrival to tell me His Word and my heart to be open? Was it His plan to have my sister's dream? Did He plant it in her? Was it all part of His plan, or did I have total free will to reject Him that day? This could be argued by the greatest of scholars. What do I think? He knows me inside and out and He intimately knows my nature. He could have easily dangled the right carrot at the right time to get the right result. But if you go down that path, why not just use His supernatural power in the first place and create a heaven with perfect creatures already in place? Why make them—I won't use the word *earn* since I don't believe you can earn heaven—but why make them choose, and why give them free will if You are going to force the choice on them? That makes no sense at all. Certainly God does not want puppets on strings. I truly believe He created a situation for me and then let me make the choice. It is the same choice you have right now. It is always there—until the day you die. The sinner on the cross next to Jesus is proof that God is merciful right up to the very last second. If you have a heart for Him, He has an ear for you.

But let's come back to religion at a later time. I believe inspirational writing should be interesting and beneficial to many people from many walks and beliefs. It should make one think at a deeper level, a level that makes one look inward. These writings were solely written for my own benefit at first—to force me to look inward and be honest with myself, and hopefully to discover truths about myself and the world around me. My goal was to find peace of mind with my surroundings and to grasp a philosophy that made sense and would bring lasting contentment and a steady direction for my life. At some point while writing, I began considering the value of sharing, the value of what could be learned if all of us made known our own personal discoveries to each other. I also realized it was essential I pass my greatest lessons in life down to my children. This book is my effort to do just that, and, hopefully, to influence others to do the same—for the benefit of all.

I'm going to begin with the bottom line, and here it is: We must learn how to let God be God. That is at the core of all of this. We must discover how to be still, to cease striving, to clear our heads, to calm our minds, and let God do what He does best—integrating all of life's mysteries into His perfect plan. How we choose to be a part of that plan is up to us. God has placed His invitation right in front of us. The only question is: How will you and I respond to it?

To open this book with a testimony of my religion and how I became a Christian may come across as aggressive and probably not the best way to grab the interest of the doubting. But my goal is not to try to turn you into a Christian. That can only come from a higher source. My goal is not to entertain you but rather to grab your heart by being honest. Our collective goal should be to find truths we all seek, while remaining honest throughout the entire discovery. Interest always follows open communication of the heart. One misconception of having opened with my testimony is it can come across like I am some kind of self-righteous saint whom God found favor in and wanted to save. Nothing could be further from the truth. First of all, I want you to know I am no saint. I have done things I know God has smiled at, but I have also done things I am too ashamed to admit openly in this book, and surely God has seen it all and will stand in His own judgment of me, along with all of His creation.

I do not stand on the far end of the religious right. I try not to judge other's shortcomings, and I hope they do the same for me. I do, however, judge other's actions, and I hope they will also do the same of my actions. To judge one's actions is to be responsible. There is no sin in this type of judgment. How can one make sensible decisions as to what is right or wrong if there is no judgment of actions? Good and evil are only good and evil because man judges other's actions and, hopefully, looks to a universal authority of good and evil. However, I know this is not the case. This will be covered in depth in Part Two.

What is important now is to know that the mind works best when it is clear. It can judge properly when it uses logic balanced with an innate, God-given feeling, not one's own feeling but the sense of right and wrong our Creator has built into every one of our souls. To tap into this inner gift of knowledge is to have wisdom from a higher source. It comes from being still—the act of stopping, calming one's mind, and getting in touch with God. You will see things differently from this place—a place I hope to help you visit. This is a place of great strength and great power because it is His power and He offers it to you when you are "still" with Him. It can be life-changing, and it can be done in mere minutes if not seconds.

Let's explore different aspects of life's experiences and the philosophies that can help us understand how to get to that place of being still and tapping into a greater power and peace of mind.

"... that we may have confidence in the day of judgment ..."

1 JOHN 4:17

Chapter Two

FROM TRAGEDY TO TRIUMPH

"Trust in the Lord with all your heart
And do not lean on your own understanding.
In all your ways acknowledge Him,
And He will make your paths straight."

PROVERBS 3: 5–6

HIS MOTHER DIED WHEN HE WAS NINE. His father was illiterate and often beat him. His younger brother and older sister died. His first love interest died. His wife suffered from mental illness. He had numerous career failures, a midlife crises, and suicidal bouts of depression. Two of his children also died. His business partner had this to say about him: "When he began speaking, his voice was shrill, piping, and unpleasant. His manner, his attitude, his dark yellow face wrinkled and dry, his oddity of pose, his diffident movements— everything seemed to be against him, but only for a short time." Eventually, Abraham Lincoln's life would be known not only for tragedy, but also for triumph. One man with a cause, the right cause, can change the world.

Lincoln served one term in the House of Representatives, then returned to Springfield, Illinois, in 1848 to practice law. With only two years of formal schooling, he had read numerous books and educated himself into his law degree. Lincoln probably would have faded away if it were not for the Kansas–Nebraska Act in 1854 that allowed settlers in those areas to determine if they would allow slavery. Lincoln, believing slavery was immoral in every way, realized this act would once again open the door wider to something he deeply felt was wrong. He despised slavery and thought it violated the core of the Declaration of Independence. The passage of this legislation propelled Lincoln back into politics. It was this intense passion for something he believed in that made him great. And it was his resolve to correct this legislation that became his cause. His law partner, William Herndon, also said of Lincoln, "His ambition was a little engine that knew no rest." [1]

[1] Christopher L. Tyner, "President Abraham Lincoln Simplicity Helped Make Him the Greatest Communicator," Los Angeles, CA: *Investor's Business Daily, Inc.* (February 20, 2001).

The question of the moment is whether or not I will resolve to make something of value my cause in life. Or will I only talk about it until the day I die? Shouldn't all of us take up a cause for something we truly believe in—even if it is small—as long as we put our whole heart into it? To sit under the umbrella of protection others have provided for us is one thing. To stand up for a cause that protects others is quite another. So, what about my little life? What will I do? What will you do?

Timing couldn't have been better than the present as I write this chapter because I've been struggling especially hard this past week. I have come to a crossroads and must make a decision in my life. But I'll come back to that later.

First off, I've come to the end of a twenty-year career, by choice, and I've decided to move on and do something different with my life. This took a few of years of deep thinking to actually decide to make the move and go through with it. But I made the choice, and it has been about eight months since I made the change. And I'm happy I did because I love my new life; however, change is never easy.

I am, or I should say was, a building contractor, who built up a business by at first doing small remodels—mostly bathrooms, kitchens, and small additions. Then opportunities came along for other types of construction. Eventually, I established a reputation for trying about anything anyone would throw at me, and performed jobs for well-known companies such as Pepsi, Best Foods, U.S. Filter, W. R. Grace, and Avery Dennison. I had good clients and I built a solid reputation, but I never really felt like I hit the jackpot—the kind of contract that could set me for life. I pretty much worked all the time, six days a week, ten hours a day. Aside from my family, my business success was always at the top of my priority list.

There is, however, what I call a *luck* factor that I believe does play into the equation of life. Many may argue luck is a byproduct of hard work and persistence. For the most part, I believe this is true. But being prepared in the right place at the right time with the right mindset is what sets apart the successful from the struggling. And being ready and willing to act on *luck* when it shows itself is also a necessity. Just like Lincoln, there's a time and a place when a man or woman must know it is time to act. The time to stand up for something and give it your all—a time to change one's life. Let's explore the possibility of helping along the components of *luck* so we are prepared for it and can maximize it in order to help ourselves and increase our happiness when it comes our way. Tragedies are all around us if we look for them. Triumphs must be sought out.

I missed out on what may have been the *luckiest* opportunity in my business life on June 5, 1992, the day my dad died from an electrocution accident. He was sixty-two and I was thirty-one at the time. I had been operating a plumbing business and had earned my general contractor's license and started doing small remodels, but I was tired of it all and wanted more challenge and more money and more success than these businesses could ever offer me, or so was my thinking. I sold the business for peanuts and told my potential remodel clients I was no longer available.

My father, who was an engineer for the city of Long Beach in Southern California and who'd taught me every mechanical thing I knew, had come across an opportunity for us to have a contract with an oil company by the name of Tidelands Oil Production. The port of Long Beach needed to lay new petroleum piping throughout the harbor area, and my father was best friends with the head engineer at Tidelands. Dad had the reputation of being able to solve problems—any problems—so we pretty much had the guaranteed hidden handshake of getting this huge contract. I said, "Is this for sure, Dad?" and he said, "It's for sure! Do what ever you have to in preparation for this." That was good enough for me. If my father said it was going to happen, you could bet your life on it. And I did. That is why I made such a drastic change.

I sold my plumbing business to my office manager and completely changed directions. I studied for my C-34 pipelining license, which would allow me to contract this type of work in the public streets. I passed the test, got the required insurances, and had everything ready to go. It was going to happen. Finally, my big break after so many hard-working years—nothing was going to stop me now.

One month later Dad died. As far as I was concerned, on June 5, 1992, so did I.

My father was my best friend. He was the one person in my life I knew would always be standing there for me—no matter what. Later, I would come to realize my mother played as much a part in who I was as did my father, but at that time my father was everything to me. He was my mentor, my closest friend, and my entire financial future as well. On that day in June it all went away. Just like that—gone. I tried to save the contract with Tidelands, but I was simply another young nobody without the essential experience. It was my father they wanted and trusted. And even his best friend couldn't take such a big risk on just me. They trusted Dad, and he trusted me. Success by association. And now tragedy by association. Everything seemed gone. I was lost and emotionally devastated. What was I going to do?

I will always remember an important lesson I learned when I was eight years old. I had my appendix removed that year, as a third grader. There I was— laid up in a hospital bed eating ice cream and watching "Get Smart" on the television. And no, they weren't reruns. My parents were standing next to me when the doctor walked in. I remember saying thank you to him and asking him how long the operation took and how hard it must have been to remove my appendix. I'll never forget what he told me next. He said, "I can teach you how to take out an appendix in four minutes." And I said, "Really?" He said, "Yes, but it will take me four years to teach you what to do if something goes wrong."

Now, that's the lesson. Life is easy when things are going your way. It's the person who figures out how to be successful when things aren't going their way who rises to the top. There are many people who can do their daily jobs just fine, but the really successful ones are those who can shine when things are going wrong. It is the same with life in general. How does one shine when things are going wrong?

Things have never gone more wrong in my life than when I lost my father, and I hope it stays that way. I really was a broken man. But I still had to make a living to support my family. I went back to bathroom and kitchen remodels, and I was miserable. Susie, my incredible wife, put up with my whining for a year, and then one day she said, "You must get over it!" But for a full year she stood by my side and never uttered a negative word. I think I did need to hear those words though. I was in a funk for an entire year. My ambition had left me. I didn't really see the point in anything. I had two young children at the time, and I did a good job of concealing my lack of ambition and negative attitude toward life when I was around others, but my wife knew I was a changed man. After she said, "You must get over it," I was changed again. And from then on I decided to *get over it*.

Funny how things work sometimes. I hadn't gone to church since Dad's passing. What was the point? But deep inside, knowing I must change again, I prayed to God for help. I prayed for the strength to get a grip again and move on. God had already started His plan in motion. I just didn't know it. But with His plan I wouldn't have my father, I'd be on my own.

Before Dad died, he had helped my wife's younger brother, Sean, to get a job with Tidelands as an engineer. Sean was right out of college. I used to pay him eight bucks an hour to run demolition on my remodeling jobs before he graduated from college. Those days were over now. He had a real job. One day Sean called me and said, "I'm golfing on Saturday with my boss, and there's an opening. I think you'd really like each other, and there may be an opportunity for you to bid on some work for us again." I wasn't the type to schmooze on the golf course, but I accepted his offer and we played eighteen holes that day. The topic of work never came up until the nineteenth hole after the game. For you non-golfers, the nineteenth hole is what they call the clubhouse.

Ron was Sean's boss. He asked me about my work, and we talked briefly. Then he said, "How would you like to bid on hydrostatically testing our oil derricks?" I said, "What?" He explained how they were going to have five companies bid on testing 900 oil derricks by flushing 1,000-foot-long underground pipes with water and pressurizing them to 300 pounds per square inch to see if they leaked. If they leaked they would need to be excavated and new piping sections welded to replace the bad sections.

I took about half a second and said, "I'd be interested." I didn't know what I was talking about, but that's pretty much me. I've always liked challenges and certainly hated remodeling houses enough that I would have tried just about anything, so why not blowing up underground pipes?

The next Monday I met with Ron. The problem was I would have to be prepared in three weeks to test the procedure. That didn't stop me. I called a lifelong friend of mine, Marcus, who worked for a company that designed wastewater treatment equipment, and he helped me design and build a mobile pumping and testing rig. I had motors and pumps flown in—one from San Francisco, one from New York—you get the picture. Two weeks later I had spent over $20,000, at the same time having a custom trailer built to house the contraption. We assembled the thing in Marcus' garage in Moreno Valley, California. I practiced how to operate all the levers and valves on my driveway and in my sleep for days before the big test. Of course, the neighbors thought I was nuts, and they were half right.

I'll never forget the big day. I took two men from a framing crew of a remodel I was doing at the time, and we trailered the rig down to the harbor, where they took us out to an oil derrick called M-300. It was one of Mobil's derricks that Tidelands was under contract to maintain. M-300 was a piece of junk, I would find out later. It hadn't been in operation for years. The foreman had basically set me up for failure. It was hard to gain access to even test this thing, and it was pretty much going to be a disaster in his eyes. You see, another company, one of his buddies, was up against me for the contract. We each had come up with different solutions, our custom rigs, as to how we were going to test these things. Pumps that can deliver a lot of water can't pressurize up to 300 psi. And once the lines were filled with water (this was so in case they leaked it wouldn't be leaking oil into the ground systems, punishable by big fines) the pressure had to be maintained while converting over to a high-pressure pumping system that was low volume. Basically, it was complicated even though it wasn't rocket science. We each had our own custom designs. Little did I know, all the big executives would be there for the debut of the different systems. It was my turn and I was on show. It was now or never, and I was the only one who knew how to operate the thing. Except for my helper's moral support, I was on my own, and I was very nervous.

The most beautiful thing happened. It worked like a charm. Even I was impressed. The Tidelands' foreman was dumbfounded. It did everything it was supposed to, and I was in. Three out of the five companies made the cut, and I was one of them. The other two were big companies with multi-millions in equipment and hundreds of employees. I had invested about $25,000 and had three employees, none with any oilfield experience. But we pulled it off that day. I still smile when I think about it. That's what I live for. It is times like those that make a hundred failures in life all worth it.

Now, was it *luck*? Yes and no. I call it luck that the opportunity came along and luck that the right potential components were in place if everything went perfectly. By that I mean that I had access to the kind of people who could help me build the thing and the competing companies weren't so much better that I didn't stand a chance. So, if I did everything right, the potential for success was already in the cards. But the part that wasn't luck was this: I had previous experiences, as small as they may have been, in solving mechanical problems with my past businesses. Looking back, there is no doubt my father had prepared me properly for this challenge. In addition, the innate risk nature of my personality, the desire for something new in my life and for a challenge, and the fact that

I had some money saved up—those things made *luck* able to run its course and give it the best chance for success. It doesn't happen very often, but when it does you can take advantage of it if you recognize it and you know the time is right to go for it. In my eyes, trying and failing is better than failing by not going for it. Failing just adds one more experience to the *luck factor* waiting for the next round. And it's a mistake that won't be repeated. On the other hand, it might not fail at all and you might be a great success.

The oilfield contract lasted two years. I hired a welder and a backhoe operator, and I taught Brian, one of my carpenters, how to be a pipefitter and run the crew. Within a year I was bidding on a tank farm move against these other big companies. I had much lower overheads and basically could outbid them, but I couldn't handle all the work. I was being awarded large monthly contracts and had thirteen employees, two of whom just directed traffic through the construction area. I bid on constructing two electrical substations that powered their nine hundred oil derricks, and I was awarded that contract, which led to three more buildings. This all lasted for a year, and I worked like a dog. It was too much of a good thing—great money, great success, and great opportunities, but I was wearing out. By the end of the tank farm move, I was physically and mentally drained.

One morning, I was overseeing the pouring of a dozen concrete foundations when I realized a bid was due in two hours. One of the substations was being built one-fourth mile away, and at the same time Brian was running twelve guys in the tank farm move. I took a ten-minute break with my calculator, scribbled down (only hand written) a bid for this tank foundation job that was due, and walked into one of the site trailers and borrowed their fax machine to send it to their corporate office a mile away. An hour later, while I was still on the same job, a Tidelands' employee walked out to me and said, "You got that bid you sent over. When can you start?" It really was that crazy. But it was too much, and when it ended, it was probably a good thing. You can't do much with the money if you're dead. I guess learning to be a better delegator is not my strong suit. I've always been too much of a micromanager. Sometimes a simple quote can say it much better then I can:

"A good manager is not a person who can do the work better then his men; he is a person who gets his men to do the work better than he can."

FREDERICK SMITH, FOUNDER OF FEDERAL EXPRESS

Soon they had me bid on taking over all their maintenance, but the bid was awarded to one of their longtime loyal companies and I was done. I got word on my birthday and had to tell a dozen guys they were out of work. We all knew it would eventually end. Fortunately, I still had the oil-derrick-testing crew going strong.

During that time, my wife's aunt came to me and asked if I would help her sell her home. I was a real estate major in college and had obtained my broker's license years ago, with the intention of buying property and developing it. I really had only used the license once or twice a year, assisting family and friends for a small fee. When Susie's aunt approached me, I recognized her home was in an area zoned for apartments. I made an offer for the amount she wanted, closed the deal with her, and started plans to build the apartments. Here's one lesson in life: The more you have going, the more opportunities you have for success, but also the more that can go wrong. Here I was, trying to be smart and reinvest the oilfield money into apartments and all was going well...until...

Like my father's death, disaster can strike quickly in life and at any time. When all is going too well, watch out—the devil's right around the corner, and he's got his eye on you. That is when prayer is especially important. Pray that God lets you continue on your peaceful, happy path, and make sure you always appreciate where you are. I got the call from Brian that morning. He was at the oilfield. Usually the call meant my backhoe man was late, and they never knew if he was coming in or not. But this morning was different—it was really bad news—there had been an explosion on one of the docks where we had been digging to make a repair. We were digging next to a high-voltage conduit that powered a transformer station. No one was hurt, and that was a blessing in itself, but the fence had melted completely through. You could drive a car through the opening. When I arrived, there were fire trucks, an ambulance, and all the white-shirt executives from the oil company, along with some harbor officials. There was no doubt we were finished, but I was also concerned that the lack of power on the whole pier would cost millions of dollars in lost commerce, and the potential lawsuits could be fatal.

The week before this I had sustained the largest loss in the stock market I had ever experienced. Just when I thought things couldn't get worse…

In between the stock losses and the explosion I had gotten word from my building designer that the city would not allow me to build four units on my newly purchased property because of parking restrictions, and my plans, at that point, were worthless. I could still build three units, but the downgrade would make the investment much less desirable. During the same week, one of my past clients, W. R. Grace, announced they were filing Chapter 11 bankruptcy. The plant manager called to tell me the $23,000 in receivables they owed me would not be coming for a long time—probably never—but they'd try to make it up to me somehow.

Trust me, this was a bad week. I couldn't take any more. I was like Job, the biblical character Satan had his way with. I remember saying to myself, "I'm Job; what's next? I've walked through the gates of hell—where?" It was definitely the worst financial week of my life. Like my father's sudden death, I remembered things can change in an instant—with your finances, with your health, with anything. Don't think it can't. So, be humble if for no other reason. But things can change for the better in an instant also, and this bad week would teach me a life lesson in how quickly God can change things. Turning tragedy in triumph happens when you trust God to take control and have faith He will do what's best for you. I was either the luckiest man on earth that week or God was teaching me to "be still" and let Him drive the plan. And, just for the record, I don't think it was luck. If we can learn to do this one thing—to put everything back into God's hands and say, "God, I'm going to let You be God and trust Your plan for me," He will do miraculous things in our lives.

The morning after the explosion, we found out another contractor had caused the short circuit at the transformer station. I couldn't believe it. We were digging right next to the thing—I thought it had to be us. It wasn't.

The next week W. R. Grace needed a pump system replaced that had caused a shutdown in one of their critical products. It would cost them a lot of money if my crew wasn't there the next morning at six o'clock to start on the problem. They had very restrictive rules about not being able to allow contractors onsite who hadn't gone through their safety programs, and I had all the proper insurances in place beforehand, giving me an advantage. Even though I hated to do it, I acted. I told the plant manager to have corporate do an end run around the bureaucracy that had my receivables tied up in Chapter 11 and wire my bank the money they owed me. If they went to bat for me, I'd have my crew there the next morning bright and early. They caved, I got paid and also established a money upfront method of doing future business with them if they wanted me to perform the work.

The following week, with a new confidence, I put my efforts back into the apartment building plans and came up with a design that would extend the existing house and accommodate the additional living space needed to make the investment work. We redrew the plans, pulled the permit, and built the building in such a way as to make the city happy while achieving the original goal.

I reinvested the money that remained after my significant losses in the stock market, and it turned around within a month. I was on a roll—nothing would stop me now. Wait, isn't that what got me in trouble in the first place? Exactly! You can't think that way. But you can thank God when tragedy turns into triumph. And I did—over and over again.

Here's the bottom line—yes, too much of a good thing can be a bad thing. If nothing else, you'll think it's the norm, and we all know it isn't. It's not that I did great things that got me out of the trouble, it was that I did everything I could to the best of my ability, while at the same time knowing in my heart the outcome was dependent upon the divine plan of our Creator. When we put things back into the hands of God and trust His plans over our plans, we gain the perspective and confidence essential to success.

If you want to believe in luck, that's fine. But you're not going to be lucky your entire life. You will, however, have God as an overseer—at all times, at every moment, for your entire life—whether or not you choose to accept it. If you don't believe that, then play the luck game.

When you pray, God listens. He doesn't always respond immediately. Remember, it's not in your timing, it's in His. God played the big role in my situation because I handed it over to Him. It was very obvious to me that, by myself, I wasn't going to come out of all those bad situations standing up. But to God the little things in life are nothing. He handles a trillion of those little things at once and He does it quite easily. If He wants something to happen, it's going to happen. But what I learned is that we must try our hardest to do our very best when the chips are down and things seem bad. You'll know you did your very best and the outcome is the best it can be. Look at every bad thing that happens as an opportunity for success in the end, even if the success is only the learning experience. That last line is worth repeating—because it has great value in making your next round successful. Don't give up. You don't fail if you're still trying. If you don't quit, you don't fail.

"Let us not lose heart in doing good,
for in due time we will reap if we do not grow weary."
GALATIANS 6:9

Don't be discouraged from trying something new or the same thing over again just because it didn't work out the way you wanted the first time. No great inventor will tell you that any of his successes happened on the first trial. Turn the failure into a success. If not the first time, then the second, or the third, or the tenth. Keep going and keep your eye on the prize. If you want it badly enough you'll get there. If you don't want it badly enough, then you'll quit along the way. One of those two always happens. You have to ask yourself if the price is worth it. If it isn't, don't go for it, and be satisfied with that decision; otherwise go for it, but only if you're willing to go all the way.

Some people never have the problem of setting and trying to reach goals. They just are not interested in setting goals. I guess it's not in their personality. I envy them to some degree. But I've always said that every negative personality trait has an equal positive side that goes with it. And the reverse is also true. So, even though I envy the Type B personality, I wouldn't want to have one. It's simply not me. I'd rather be in the fast lane and lose than to never ride in the fast lane at all and win in the slow lane. Aiming low and succeeding just isn't success to me, and it's not in the cards for my life.

That brings me to my current crossroads—the piano. Now, compared to all the other critical things in life, this may seem trivial to you. And by itself, it is trivial, but the lesson is not. The desire to be good at something that brings enjoyment and balance into your life is important, and for me, there is a lesson to be learned in my love for spending time on the piano.

There is something unexplainable about the piano that I really love—so much that I can't be away from it for long without really missing it. I can't sing particularly well, and I think the piano is a way for me to express passion and feeling. I love the old jazz standards, particularly piano, acoustic bass, and drums. I love the way they tell their story through music. But there's a problem. I'm not talented at the piano. Maybe part of the reason is that I didn't start playing until I was twenty-five years old, and the learning cycle is different for an adult than for a child who grows up with the learning process. But more likely the truth is that I'm just not gifted at the piano.

On the other hand, I was practically born with a wrench in my hand. My parents didn't have a lot, so my father had to fix everything. I never saw a plumber, electrician, or an auto mechanic at our house. My dad could do it all, and I was always by his side learning. I have a great talent for building and fixing things and solving mechanical problems. But I have no passion for it. I have great passion for the piano, but I have no talent for it. I constantly ask God, "Why is this so?" Anyway, it is what it is. But here's my dilemma at forty-six years of age: I felt like quitting at the piano. And I've never quit at anything. But I was tired of not being what I wanted to be with my playing, so I had to really turn inward and ask myself some important questions.

Here's what I've learned. Happiness, with anything you are passionate about, comes in the journey of experiencing the art and not in the reaching of the goal. The goal is about giving the journey a place of reference. The real goal should be the journey itself. Here's how I've come to that conclusion and why it gives me so much happiness and the desire to go forward with my passion for the piano. More importantly, the lesson learned here applies to every other area of my life, and it will to yours also.

The bottom line is I can't live without the expression playing the piano gives my soul. It is like medicine for me. That alone is enough to stay with it forever. But, also, I don't want to quit. Quitting will be failure and not quitting will be my success, even if I'm never the pianist I want to be. By staying with it I'm successful all the time, and I'm on the path that makes me happy and fulfills my soul—the journey. I have other things in my life that are even more fulfilling. My marriage, my kids, my family, my friends, and my faith. I will never quit in any of these areas of my life. These would be my biggest failures of all— that is, if things got tough and I quit. And eventually things will get tough again. That is the way of life, so I must be prepared. Not pessimistic, not cynical, but prepared. So, I will choose to stay the course with my piano and love it for what it does for me. And now I must look for something with even greater purpose— a purpose not just for me but one that can help to improve others' lives. That, I believe is the true essence of contentment.

There is a time and place for everything. Abraham Lincoln acted when he knew in his heart he must act. Now is the time for me to act toward a new life of learning and spending time on things that give back. Creating something always gives back to the creator. Creating something with your heart in it gives back tenfold.

Now, instead of waking up each morning and saying, "Oh God, do I have to do this another day?" I'm not building another home for someone else and I'm not frustrated by flakey subcontractors who are only interested in their day's pay. I'm exploring new opportunities that are exciting, primarily because I don't know where they are going to take me, only that God is saying to me, "Don't continue on the path that was making you unhappy!" And I trust He has a better plan for me—especially when I'm open to Him. Be still and think about it and ask Him for guidance. We don't do this often enough, myself included.

Now, just to let you know, I've come back to this chapter, almost two years after writing it to report that I've taken on another construction job. With two children in college and a new business direction going much slower than I hoped, I've decided this was best for my family. But it is a big slice of humble pie for me, and I am constantly asking God, "Is this what You have planned for me now? Back into construction? And just for the money so I can pay for things? What's the plan here?" It is so hard for me to be patient with this and, again, I'm not happy in my profession. I pray this will be temporary, and I'm keeping my faith in God's plan, not mine. But this is a struggle between impatience and faith. And I'm just a man, one who's getting sick of it, feeling like I want to throw in the towel.

I heard my pastor say something in church last Sunday and it hit home with me in my current situation. He said our prayer to God shouldn't be to get us out of things we don't like, but to get us through them. That is so true. Character is built by getting through tough things, not by getting out of them. The truly noble person is the one who strives to gain character. Character is only strengthened during the journey.

Success comes in the journey itself. Don't spend your whole life going after the goals. They'll come if you don't give up. Concentrate on the journey and the enjoyment of each moment along the journey. No matter what accomplishments or failures you've had, you're a success if you are still at the plate swinging the bat. You're still in the game. So I'm going to take my own advice and hold on to my towel.

Have you ever been to a Little League baseball game or a dance competition and observed the dynamic between the players and the audience? Usually a single kid or a few kids will dominate the game. You know the best when you see them. But, have you ever noticed that the real star of the game is the pitcher who is getting trounced and has tears on his face but stays the course, doesn't give up, and gets through his tough ordeal until the end? I experienced this last night at my daughter's dance competition. A good friend of hers had a solo. She is thirteen years old. About two-thirds of the way through, she forgot some of the routine and had to fake her way until she caught her composure. She was in tears, and the whole audience was pulling for her. I wouldn't have even noticed if it weren't for the look of distress on her face. Her impromptu was actually quite good. But to her it was becoming a disaster. At one point I thought she could take no more and would run off the stage, but she hung in there and got back on track for the ending. I wish she knew she was the star of the night in my eyes. I certainly thought she was, and I know others in the audience had to feel the same way. The star is the person who triumphs over tragedy not the person who is so good they can't help but win.

So, go out and face every day, good or bad, as an opportunity for triumph. Know that good can turn bad quickly, and the opposite is also true. And be prepared. Be ready for *luck* to show itself, to recognize it when it does, and to pounce on it quickly without fear of failure. The failure will come in the lost opportunity if you do nothing. One big success will make ten failures seem inconsequential. See success as an opportunity to be humble and to help others. And see tragedy also as an opportunity. Be positive in your outlook and confident you will be successful. Most importantly, don't give up—don't ever quit—and success will surely find you. Call it luck or call it prepared opportunity, but be prepared to call it something because with the proper attitude, perspective, and readiness you'll get caught in the way of success. But don't forget—it starts with being still and looking upward to God.

"Do not go where the path may lead,
go instead where there is no path and leave a trail."

RALPH WALDO EMERSON

Chapter Three

BE HONEST WITH YOURSELF

"And you will know the truth, and the truth will make you free."

JOHN 8:32

BEING TRULY HONEST WITH YOURSELF will probably be painful. That offers a good excuse not to want to do it. There is a reason this is true. The human mind is so good at protecting itself it will naturally do so without you even knowing. Humans are great survivors primarily because they are intelligent. This intelligence works to protect the mind and the body in much the same way as it automatically injects adrenalin into the bloodstream to heighten awareness and strength when it senses danger. It is not something you plan. It's involuntary and happens almost instantaneously.

That is why true honesty with oneself is usually painful. Our mind's protective ability must be overridden by the same mind's willingness and commitment to intentionally remove the safeguards that want to protect, thus leaving us totally vulnerable. In other words, you must make a conscious effort to be completely honest in admitting your own shortcomings, otherwise your mind will make excuses (which you will buy into willingly) about why you acted the way you did or why you said the things you said.

Who wants to be ashamed of themselves? Is it not easier to let our minds casually suggest: Something was the fault of someone else. I am not to blame. I lied because it avoided the instant pain of revealing the truth. I cheated because I felt cheated. I stole because prices were too high. I went out on my spouse because she was not giving me the attention I desired. I envied my neighbors because I deserve what they have more than they do. I gossiped because the person earned that bad reputation by his actions. And this is probably the granddad of them all—I didn't forgive them because their act was unforgivable.

Well, what about your act and what about my act? I am as unforgivable as the next guy, maybe even more. Sometimes I see another person who appears to be less fortunate than I and I think, *God loves that person just as much as me,* and then I think, *maybe even more*. By this, I mean that God may find greater favor in certain people because of their walk. Let me clarify. I believe God loves each of His creations equally. He is not a God who values us by our works, our looks, or our accomplishments. I do not love one of my three children more than another. But there are times when I find more favor in one then the other, a time when I'm more proud of the one who is thinking of others over the one who is acting selfishly. God also operates in this way. So the question becomes, "Are our plans in line with His plans?" This is what I am talking about when I say He might hold another person in higher regard than me.

One in particular attends the same church as I and leads a Bible study at his home on Tuesday nights. His name is Phillip. I agreed to meet with his study group for six Tuesday nights to teach a class called Evangelism Explosion (EE). You may have heard of it, since it is now in every country in the world. Chapter 28 of this book is dedicated not only to telling you about EE but to give you the greatest gift I can pass along through these writings. A free gift is waiting for you—God wants you to have it—and you can be assured of receiving it. But, now, I'd like to tell you about Phillip.

On the first night, before I began teaching the EE class, the group went around the circle and shared things heavy on their hearts, which we could all pray about. Phillip went last since he was the host. He began to tell us how his landlord was raising the rent $100 per month, his car needed $450 in repairs, and he could barely make ends meet. He and his wife had wanted to own their own home for a long time. With real estate prices sky high, their possibility of becoming homeowners seemed distant at best. He also suffered from ongoing back pain, which was particularly bad that very moment. Phillip was distraught and broken down both mentally and physically.

I felt bad for him, and at the same time I felt guilty about how good things were for me. I had been whining for months about how much I had lost in the stock market, and here was someone with real needs and the uncertainty of how or if they would ever be met. As he finished talking, a strong feeling came over me. I made my feelings known to Phillip right then and there in front of the whole group. It was my turn to begin to teach, but I started out saying, "Phillip, I just know in my heart right now that God is smiling on you and this is why I am sure of it. As you were talking, I couldn't help but think how proud of you He must be. Here you are without a home of your own, but look at what you are doing with what you do have. There are so many people who own their own homes. We could walk up the street right now, and I'll bet that in the first one hundred homes we would not find one who opens his home up every week like you do, to whomever would like to come in and openly celebrate and worship our Creator God. You might not have much, but look what you are doing with what you do have."

A week later, Phillip came to me and told me how much that meant to him. I told him I had just spoken the truth—what I was really feeling. What I didn't tell him was how ashamed I felt. Because I do own my own home, and I was one of those one hundred I had been talking about. He was openly doing more in support of our God than I was, and with a lot less. I made a commitment deep inside myself that night at his house that I would do more and that I would try to help him because I could see the size of his need, and, even more so, the size of his heart. Times like those show me how much more I could be doing and how much more I must do. And, yes, Phillip is one of those people I'm sure God finds more favor in than little old me.

Honesty, like so many things in life, is much easier to aim at someone else. This book was written over a period of ten years. During the last years of writing, one day I was completely honest with myself about something I always knew but never had admitted to myself. Standing in our kitchen with my wife, I said, "I've been doing some soul searching these past few days, and I was very honest with myself and deeply ashamed at what I admitted to myself to be the truth." Susie stopped her work and directed her attention to what I would say next. It was as if she knew some permanent change would come in the next few moments. Then I let it spill: "My happiness is dependent on how much money I make." There was silence. I could feel the knife twisting—the painful hollowness you feel in the center right below your ribcage if you push in hard with your finger. It feels like someone punched you in the stomach and the wind is knocked out. You want to throw up but you're not sick. Just sick at your thoughts of the brutal reality called truth. And now, not only have you realized it, but you have made your soul known to another.

Susie replied, "I think you've always been happiest when you've been making a lot of money. I know that." And she gave examples of different times in our sixteen years of marriage as evidence of her statement. I felt a great relief, partly because of her acceptance for knowing me and loving me for the whole package of who I was, but mainly for the admission in myself in total honesty and in voicing to my soul mate what I was building my own personal happiness around.

My next words were, "That is going to change from this day on. I'm not going to base my happiness on my financial condition anymore." Just saying it and realizing I was committed to this new way of thinking was huge. I felt like I had a new control over my life.

That week I bought the book *Of Mice and Men* by John Steinbeck and started reading. This was something I never did. I never took time to read anything but the *Investor's Business Daily* financial paper. I was making changes. I was reinventing myself. I was living.

Honesty with oneself (this is my definition) is to have a conversation with yourself without worrying about discovering hurtful truths. I guarantee you are going to discover painful truths about yourself. But if you fear this, you will never be honest with yourself and you will never be set free from the dishonesty. And doing nothing, that is, not admitting the truth to oneself, is dishonesty.

That same week, Susie and I went out to dinner with three other couples to a quaint little restaurant. We all met at one of the homes to have hors d'oeuvres and then drive together. One of Susie's best friends, Melanie, was there. Her father had passed away just weeks before, and she had sent me a tape. She knew I had a passion for old jazz piano standards, particularly by an artist named Bill Evans, whose mellow piano ballads are in a league of their own for their ability to tell a story and make you melt in your own personal interpretation of the music. So when she came across one of her father's tapes of Bill Evans she thought of me. I had received the tape from her about a week before the dinner night, but I was determined to let her know how much I enjoyed it and appreciated her thoughtfulness.

At the pre-dinner meeting I thanked her for the special gift and we talked about how her father had loved the music. When we arrived at the restaurant we weren't even through the door when I could hear a very familiar song. It was a Bill Evans piano ballad. But something was different. I could instantly tell it was a live performance. Bill Evans himself had been dead for over twenty years, but this man had his style down to a tee. All through dinner we had conversation, but my ears were constantly being pulled to the music I so loved. He continued to play one Evans tune after another. After a while a knew I must go over to him and not only tell him how much I had enjoyed his playing, but also to let him know how closely I felt his style was matched to the great Evans himself.

The pianist's name was Michael. He was amazed someone who had been listening was moved by the songs, let alone having such a deep appreciation for the artist. I had listened to Evans almost daily for years now. I once told Susie I figured if I listened to Bill Evans every day for two years maybe his style would seep into my own piano playing. So far I'm still waiting. I mustered up the courage to ask Michael if he would be interested in seeing me privately for lessons. I took down his number, called him two days later, and the very next week I was transcribing piano music with Michael at his home.

It is one thing to think of taking an action. It is quite another to make a move toward that action, even if it is not the action itself. If you want to take up a musical instrument, try one lesson. If you want to teach, then offer to teach something you know very well to a small group or even to one other person and do it for free. See if you like it. See if you are talented at it and if it is right for you. If it is, expand on it. If it isn't, then find the thing that is you and take a little step toward that goal. You will be amazed at what outcome may be reached from just the smallest move in that direction. The key word is *start*.

In addition to these actions, I rekindled my writings and made a deep commitment to myself to finish what I started—to put into words what I had experienced and to pass it along to others to help them find their lives again by choosing to control what their happiness relies on. Days later I found myself easily telling people I was too busy for the things I now clearly saw were causing unbalance in my life. Why had it been so hard before to tell people "no"? Because I was always trying to please everyone. It was easier for me to say "yes" and just do it. But this certainly was not practicing honesty with myself or with the other person. If someone truly needed something, I was there for them. But to squeeze in things just to squeeze them in was not giving stability or balance to my life.

What a great feeling of control I had over myself once I started to let others know exactly how I felt—once I was totally honest. "I have a full plate this week, but I would love to see a hockey game with you another time when I'm free." How easy is that? They understand my situation, and I didn't insult anyone. In fact, I've thanked them for asking me, and they walk away feeling appreciated for their gesture. Everyone wins and balance remains intact.

Be honest! Why is this so difficult for us? Let's explore it. First off, we have already talked about the natural pain associated with it. So, we know why it is difficult. But what is causing the pain? Pain is caused by a combination of two conditions happening simultaneously. The first is unfamiliarity, and the second is an attack on something we place value on.

There are also two types of pain—physical pain and mental pain. But both are caused by the two conditions. Physical pain is an attack on the normal comfort zone of your body. But if you stick yourself with a pin in the same place for long enough, you will become comfortable with the familiarity of it and soon it will not register as pain. Talk to people who have to give themselves insulin shots. They are used to it and are not afraid of the routine shot. To them it might be more painful mentally than it is physically because they have become familiar with it.

Circumstances might, however, bring mental discomfort through feelings of victimization: Why me? Why has God chosen to let this fall upon me? Why was my child born with such a condition? Why was I born into poverty? Why did I have an abusive parent? The list is endless. The mental pain is caused by the loss of something we value dearly—an understanding and a feeling of conformity. We want to understand why we were chosen for this hardship, and we want to be accepted and loved for the honest truth of who and what we are. The diabetic may feel God doesn't love him and that is why God has let the condition fall upon him. There is the pain. We want to experience a life free from suffering, to belong, and to feel like something wasn't handed to us we didn't deserve. A man or woman can handle anything if they feel loved and accepted for who they are.

One of my biggest problems has always been trying to wear multiple hats at one time. By a hat, I mean putting on the personality that fits best with the person I'm with. But how comfortable do you think it is for me when I'm at a function with my sister the Christian and my old beer-drinking college buddy and a client friend whose home I'm remodeling? Three hats to juggle in harmony. Good luck, Bob! It is laughable to think I have done this for forty years. Enough. It's painful. It attacks my comfort zone of being able to please everyone at the same time. It attacks my comfort zone by thinking my sister is ashamed as she hears the college buddy talk of foolish past acts, with a couple of cuss words thrown in. It attacks my comfort zone if the client doesn't have trust in me to handle what may be his biggest investment ever. It attacks me because I want them to understand me and accept me for me. So, I wear all of these hats to be something different for each of them. How about being myself for all of them at once? Let them choose to accept me for the real me—or not.

Either way I'm a winner for knowing who will be my true friend or client or a true sibling to me.

I have a friend I met in the seventh grade. On the first day of school we kept seeing each other in our classes, and by the end of the day we discovered we had all our classes together. We became friends, went on to the same high school, and played in the jazz band together. I traveled to New York to visit him in college when he attended Columbia University in the eighties. He married just a couple of years ago at age forty, and I was in his wedding party in a lovely ceremony on a beautiful day in Colorado. About eight months ago I received a startling e-mail from him. He was facing a painful experience and confided in me. He was being totally honest with himself, and let me know his vulnerable but now liberating lifelong secret.

He wrote, "Sit down, because I'm about to tell you something that will blow your mind." The e-mail continued: "I've always felt that I was a woman trapped in a man's body." He continued to pour out the lifetime of guilt, frustration, pain, and shamefulness he had been living with for so long. It finished with, "I might lose my family and friends over this, but I cannot live with the lie any longer."

I felt so bad for him to have lived so long with this burden. I responded back to let him know my feelings, that I would not leave him. We have e-mailed many times since, and he knows I am still his close friend. But there are those, including his family, who have not been so receptive of the news. In subsequent e-mails he told me of his newfound freedom and the incredible happiness he had never felt before. He also shared that suicide had entered his mind on more than one occasion as he lived with his lie.

Self-honesty literally saved his life. I'm happy he is happy now. That is what matters. I feel it is not my place nor do I feel right in judging something I cannot possibly understand. He hasn't hurt anyone. He has only made himself known to all—the real person with all of his hats thrown away—once and for all. And he let me know he wished to be addressed as "she" and by her new name, which I have honored. She now has the peace of mind that comes with total honesty.

The second thing that causes pain, the loss of something we place value on, is more obvious. Men value their jobs. It is how we measure ourselves and find our self-esteem and our sense of worthiness. We want to be good providers for our families. If we suddenly feel a loss of income or net worth, we feel the pain of having lost something we place great value on. Is it right to place such great value on our jobs? Yes and no. Yes, it is the value we place on our jobs that keeps us diligent at being the providers we need to be—in order to put food on the table and raise our families with opportunities to be the next great generation with good morals and values. And no, if we place too high a value on money and success, we can jeopardize the very thing we are trying to achieve. We can miss out on being with our families and miss having the closeness necessary to raise our children properly, all for the sake of more things. Balancing these two sides of the equation is extremely difficult to do smoothly. It is also one of the most important things we must learn to do.

This was one of the hardest things for me to continually balance in my life. It was not easy for me to admit the high value I placed on other people viewing me as a success. It still is important, if I am to be totally honest with myself. But now I see very clearly the path I walk in this regard, and I recognize the telltale signs when I start to wander from it. Do I have a perfect balance in my life now? No. One never does or, at least, not for long. But I can identify who I am, what I'd like to become, and how I can alter my path to go that direction and to feel good about myself for knowing I am doing my best to be this better person constantly. Better for my wife, my kids, my family, and my friends. And better for myself.

Husbands can and do take care of their families while their wives earn the living, so when I talk about jobs it can be the job of raising a family and it can be a man or a woman. And while income isn't the pay for raising the family, the disposition of the children, their morals, and their behavior in society is the payoff. And the self-esteem one derives from being the parent of such great contributions to our society is the reward in itself. Here again is the potential for pain from the loss of something we value. If we feel we are failing at this job of raising our children, we feel pain. These are just two examples of pain caused by the loss of something we place great value on. The greater the value, the greater the pain. The greater the unfamiliarity, the greater the pain.

How can being totally honest with ourselves help alleviate the pain we feel? Here is how: Communicating effectively with ourselves gives us an understanding of why we feel a certain way. And this understanding of ourselves removes the unfamiliarity part of the pain equation. If we are totally honest we will understand how we can change, and we can take steps to protect what we do not want to lose—the thing we place great value on, which is the other side of the pain equation. Or we may discover we can lose this thing we place great value on because it is not worthy of that value, and, again, we are liberated by not worrying about its loss anymore. Both ways we win the battle through total honesty with ourselves.

"Honesty is the first chapter in the book of wisdom."

Thomas Jefferson

How we can practice this honesty with ourselves and others, and how will it liberate us? It can be quite liberating to realize God made each of us a certain way for a certain purpose. Think about it. This removes the worry about why you and I have so many quirky traits. We were made that way. Does that mean we aren't responsible for the stupid things we say or do? I wish, because I have a few times I'd rather forget as my sharp tongue won the battle between stopping, being still, and thinking first, versus blurting out the first thing on my mind. Usually someone gets hurt when we bluntly state our initial thoughts. But it is quite refreshing to realize the reason I am not great at something is because God didn't make me great in that way.

As I've said before, I always wanted to be a great piano player. I constantly see people who were born with the gift. Why not me? Why did God give me a passion for something without the gift? There must be a reason. Maybe He wants me to work harder. Maybe He knows I'm the kind of person who loves going after something and is bored once I achieve it. This could be His way of allowing me to have fun working at it—for a long, long time. I don't know, but I do like knowing He is responsible for what I am good at and what I am not good at. And I'll go one further—He is responsible for who I am, period. He made me. He has a plan for me. He made me perfectly for His plan. Now, I did not say He made me perfect. I said He made me perfectly for a certain plan or task of His. It is my responsibility to find out what that task is and then to decide to do it or walk away from it.

The book of Jonah comes to mind whenever I think of this concept. God said to Jonah, "Pick up and go this way," and Jonah picked up and went the other. Then God said, "Hmm, maybe he needs a little more convincing that I mean it." And so God dealt Jonah a meeting with a whale because God had plans for him and the plans were going to happen whether Jonah wanted it or not.

We should be thankful our incredible God does not just let us go our own way but clearly guides us toward His perfect plan. More often than not, He allows us our free choice to look to Him for direction, or not to, and to go where we think He would like us to go—or not. My prayer is that God would give me clear direction. Because I promise to go that direction if He will touch my heart with His guiding hand. Far greater are those who have gone in the direction they think God is leading them, on faith alone, with much less then I have.

"For we are God's fellow workers; you are God's field, God's building."

1 CORINTHIANS 3:9

This is a partnership with the Almighty. It is a team effort. It is you and Him. How can that fail? And if it is so foolproof, then why am I so afraid? Why are you so afraid? Here is why. It is the fear of pain. It is the fear of the unfamiliar. It is the fear of losing something of great value. And the root cause of all of this is our lack of faith. If we had faith in Him, it would dismiss all the fear. We could confidently go out knowing He is guiding us toward His perfect plan. We would be fearless, and we would triumph. But this is next to impossible for mortal man. Not completely impossible, but it is probably the most difficult of all commitments a man or woman can make. And that is why so few ever make it.

In writing this, I feel the disappointment in myself knowing I am not strong enough to make this all-out commitment. Years ago I knew I could never share my faith properly with another because I simply felt it was not my God-given talent to do so. I believed it was the job of someone much more capable and eloquent, who had the gift of delivering His words like poetry. Later, I discovered I was to become compelled to do just that—to teach a class in how to share the Christian faith. I made a baby step, and it took me somewhere. Who knows, maybe I can become a man who can make a commitment to pick up and go where I think God wants me to go. And this thought of how I have kept my mind open to Him and how He has changed me in the past gives me hope that He will change me again to meet His plan in the future.

Never again will I say I am not meant to do something. That is for Him to decide and to deliver the thought to my mind. At that point I can accept or reject it. And I pray for the power to accept it when I face it. You will come across the same opportunities. And you will have to make your own decisions.

He gives you that great gift, and He is watching to see what you will do with it. Does that feel like a lot of pressure? It should, because it is. The alternative is to go the other direction right now and not feel the pressure. I wonder which one has the greater reward? That is total honesty. It hurts and it liberates. The truth to others is liberating, and the truth to oneself is ten times more so.

> *"The Lord is near to all who call upon Him,*
> *To all who call upon him in truth."*

> PSALM 145:18

Being honest with yourself is the start. Admit you have peculiar little personality traits. Admit you have your vices and little habits. Admit you have many faults. And then know it is God who has made you this way and He will take responsibility in seeing that it works out best for you. After all, it is His plan for you. How about giving Him a chance and seeing if His plan is a good one? All He asks is that you have faith and put your trust in Him. And if you have faith, He will be there for you and you will be a winner. With God on your side you can't lose. Be honest, have faith, don't give up, and look inward and then upward for your divine desire. And you will find it.

Remember, it is in His time, not yours. Trust that His plan will be better than yours and see what happens. A little faith goes a long, long way. God promises that.

"God will not create a desire in you that He will not meet the need in His own time."

RICK RZESZEWSKI
PASTOR OF ORANGE COAST COMMUNITY CHURCH

Chapter Four

PERSPECTIVE DETERMINES HAPPINESS

"Reading makes a full man, meditation a profound man, discourse a clear man."

BENJAMIN FRANKLIN

A STUDY SHOWED OLYMPIC bronze-medal winners were happier than the silver medalists above them. That's because the silver medalists were disappointed with how close they came to the gold, whereas the bronze medalists were glad just to be on the podium. Yes, perspective makes a difference.

Have you ever talked yourself into worrying about something that moments before did not even concern you? Have you ever convinced yourself something was not as bad as you first thought? If you've been around life for a while, you probably answered yes to both. In the first case you made a worrisome situation out of one that had not been. And in the second you cancelled a troubled feeling by deciding it was not worthy of worry in the first place. In both situations your perspective guided your decision. The circumstances remained the same. The only thing that changed was your thinking. Thoughts precede plans, which precede actions, which precede change. Even if you don't change the physical situation at all, you can change the perception of your mental situation or status, and in doing so you change your outlook. Usually a change in outlook will result in a change in the way you address the problem. You have a different solution to the same problem merely because you stepped back and looked at it in a different way.

The first step in getting a new perspective is to stop and "be still," knowing a rash conclusion will be just that, rash. One of the reasons I understand this so well is because of my profession in the construction business. I have to make numerous quick decisions every day that I don't have the time to stop and research. This habit transferred to my personal life—I made decisions too hurriedly without researching them properly. As I continued to make uninformed but avoidable mistakes, I started to realize I didn't have to make these decisions so hastily even though that was my nature. When we are "still" long enough to get the proper perspective on our goals, it allows us the necessary time to process the best way to go about getting the right information, which in turn will lead us in making the best decisions. I can't emphasize this enough. *Be Still* is the title of this book for a reason. I want you to realize how vital this simple concept is. It will change your life. Almost always, being still and stopping to think for a moment will be advantageous. If someone is bleeding to death then put the "be still" on hold for a bit; however, more often than not, it will pay off for you. To "be still" is to let God enter your thoughts and take control of your mind and soul. Let Him in and feel Him for a moment. Allow God to be God. He will give you understanding.

> *"The best and most beautiful things in the world cannot be seen or even touched.*
> *They must be felt with the heart."*
>
> HELEN KELLER

I can't help but think Helen Keller must have had plenty of time to practice the art of being still. Quite possibly, she gained a wisdom we lack because she had no choice, since she was blind and dumb. We do have a choice, and we should choose to do what she had to do—not because we have to—because it will help us.

Chapter 2 emphasized how the right perspective can change tragedy into a triumph. How you react to a good or bad situation will usually determine the outcome. The object here is two things: 1) to have a better understanding of what is happening to you, so that 2) you can react in the proper manner to maximize the situation to your mental advantage. If simply feeling better is the advantage then that is worthy in itself.

Most of the time, we fret about something not worthy of worry in the first place. Stop, be still, and ask, "Is this a big thing or a little thing?" Usually, it's a little thing. A friend said something that bothered you—a little thing. You have a cold—a little thing. Your child skinned his knee—a little thing. You burned dinner, you broke a heel, your car won't start—all little things. A friend or family member was diagnosed with cancer—big. Your child is at the bottom of the pool—big. You received news your father was electrocuted—big. You just lost a loved one, your spouse is having an affair, your child is on drugs—all big. It is up to you to stop, be still, and get perspective on just how important the matter is. It isn't completely black and white, but your thinking process should be. Make clear in your mind what is big and what isn't, and act accordingly. Either something is truly important, unlike like most things in life, or not that big a deal. So, don't worry about it; usually you can't change it anyway. Know the difference, and know how to react with the appropriate response.

You probably realize many things are out of your control. Maybe you think a friend owes you an apology, but it's not forthcoming. Someone may always be late; a loved one might forget things important to you; or somebody makes a hurtful comment. These little things happen and are often unintentional. Love others for the same reason you became friends with them in the first place, and, since you can't change them, let the little things go. Hopefully, they will do the same for you with those quirky little things you do that bother them.

Here are five key points to help keep a good perspective:

1. Know you are not in control of everything and that God's plan will be carried out.
2. Align your plans with God's by asking Him how they fit together.
3. Realize you can always change your outlook on a situation. This allows you to make a new plan, leading to a new action that will ultimately take you in the right direction, the one God has planned for you.
4. Be content with what God has given you and thankful you have so much more opportunity than most people in the world.
5. Aim high, but don't expect unreasonable results.

Sometimes bad things happen to us by chance. We didn't ask for them to happen and we didn't do anything to deserve them, but they happened to us anyway. How do we look at these things? How do we gain proper perspective on things we can't explain? This one is tough—let's explore it.

The key here is to accept the fact that all things are not known to man. This is where having faith in God gives one peace of mind. Even though we don't have the answer now, we can have faith it will be given to us eventually and it will make perfect sense. God had it all figured out long before you and I came along. Trust Him and have faith that everything has a perfect purpose in His plan. Otherwise you're left to make your own sense out of it, in addition to thinking every other person's sense must also have merit—unless you're so self-absorbed that only your answer, out of some six billion, seems to make the best

sense. Don't be stupid. You and I are not that smart. But our Creator is. Trust
that God has a perfect plan.

> *"How blessed is the man who finds wisdom*
> *And the man who gains understanding."*

PROVERBS 3:13

I believe God made man with the innate understanding of good and evil. Why
is it important you consider what I am saying? Because to look at the world
with divine rules in place makes it much easier to find contentment with reality. In other words—it's much easier to accept something as true if, by being
true, it makes for better living conditions either physically or mentally. To believe
God has a master plan and it all will make sense to us one day makes it easier
to accept the unknown.

My attitude for a year after my dad died was, "What's the point?" because
nothing seemed to add up anymore. I wasn't trusting God's plan. I was depending on my own plan, which didn't go the way I thought it should. Of course not,
because God had a different plan for me. Once we accept that God is in control and our plan may be altered by His divine intervention whenever He
chooses, we can then become excited about what He is going to do with us. It
is this new perspective that will bring happiness because now we are aligned
with God's plan for us. Does that mean we should be happy if the outcome is
negative? Yes, if our faith is genuine! Mainly because we accept His plan as superior to ours and trust His outcome has our best interest at its core. Job gained
this perspective, as evidenced in His last words to God: "Therefore I have
declared that which I did not understand, Things too wonderful for me, which
I did not know" (Job 42:3). Sometimes the things we perceive as bad in our
lives are too wonderful for us to understand at the time. If we can learn to think
like this, we will find true happiness.

Here is another important thing to consider: When you or I do something
wrong, I believe we know it before we do it. Or, at least, we suspected it was wrong
and even lied to ourselves about not knowing for sure. We say, "Let's do it and find
out." Almost always, if not always, we learn it was wrong. But we have a conven-
ient little lie that says it's not our fault. We rationalize that since we had never tried
it before, how were we supposed to know it was the wrong thing to do?

I took my share of risks when I was younger, but I always knew right from wrong. That doesn't mean I obeyed right and wrong. To illustrate this, I'll share a personal experience. One of my favorite places is in a little cove called Blue Caverns near the isthmus at Catalina Island. The water is very clear and beautiful, with an abundance of fish. Few people know there are caves under the steep slopes that cascade down to where the mountain meets the water. My boating buddy, Dan, and I owned a twenty-five-foot skipjack boat with a little cabin. The boat afforded us the opportunity to go places untouched by man. Definitely God's country. Blue Caverns was one of those places. Both of us loved to free dive and spearfish. But this night we had scuba tanks and we were going for some tasty lobster. It was lobster season and we had our fishing licenses updated so everything would be legal. A legal lobster must measure three-and-one-fourth inches from the back of the neck to the beginning of the tail. We came across the caves, and it felt as if we were the first ones to discover them. I went in, with Dan following.

One cave led to another, and, since it was pitch-black except for our dive lights, I became worried we might not find our way back out before our air ran out. Suddenly, I was completely drawn in by what I saw next. It would become known as Hercules. The monster-sized lobster appeared to be three feet long. Now, we all know things are magnified in water, but there was no way I could grab this guy with one hand. I immediately curled and turned around to get Dan and motion toward the beast so, at least, he would be able to corroborate the existence of this unbelievable creature.

Dan got a good look at Hercules, his eyes wide just like mine. I motioned for Dan to take my light and dive bag because this was going to take both hands and a lot more. I actually felt a little scared to wrestle with this giant. I didn't know if I could take him. *What if he pulled me back into his dark, little corner?* I thought. But something compelled me to go after him. Turns out he wouldn't let me get close enough to grab him. He kept backing into his hole on the ledge. He would come back out, curious about me, but then back he'd go, repeating the process. At one point I was pinned between the top of the cave and the ledge as it thinned down to only about two feet high. I didn't panic and figured the movements of the current would eventually loosen me. They did. We left without the big guy.

On the way back from the caves we grabbed some small lobsters and, after measuring them on the boat, decided to cook them all even though a few were slightly under legal size. Who would know? They'd be in my stomach twenty minutes later. I knew there was no way we'd get caught. The evidence would soon be gone. I knew it was wrong. And knowing I couldn't get caught made it all the worse. Even when no one else is watching, God is. Although I knew it was wrong, I made the conscious choice to do it anyway.

The next year, I was at the same caverns with another good friend of mine, Glenn. It was daytime and it wasn't lobster season. I was spear fishing that day. I saw a lobster in the rocks and I couldn't grab him. They are real tough to catch in the daytime when they are hiding. But with the help of my spear gun he was no match. It is also against the law to hunt lobster with a spear. Did that stop me? No, I speared the thing. I brought it to the boat, where I noticed it was a female and had an egg sac underneath. I felt bad. There is a reason you don't take lobster out of season—because you can strip the population. By taking one, you kill off the would-be offspring. Yet, to this day, I remember how I knew it was wrong and did it anyway and tainted an otherwise beautiful experience with something I still feel ashamed about. That is not beauty. That is ugliness. Here is the lesson: The satisfaction of the body will certainly be spoiled without the satisfaction of the mind knowing things are right with God. And I believe every person knows the difference.

I gave up diving when Dan moved to Florida with his job. But another compelling reason was another experience I had at Catalina. I had always wanted to spear the illusive white sea bass. A white sea bass over forty pounds is a coveted fish. They are extremely hard to get because they live in deeper waters and are quite skittish. If they even sense your presence, they disappear in a split second. I was with another good friend, Marcus, who only pole fished, so I was diving alone. Usually it is not very dangerous to spear fish while holding one's breath. Most people who drown while spear fishing are the more experienced divers because they take more chances, sometimes ending their lives in what is called a shallow-water blackout. I had experience in diving deep, and that added a level of danger I certainly took for granted. This day was about to teach me a lesson.

It was a beautiful day like most at the island. What could go wrong? I was down about thirty-five feet, holding my breath and hiding in the kelp, when I saw the huge fish (remember water magnifies). If it was an ounce under fifty pounds, I'd bet my life savings. Maybe it was sixty, I don't know. I chased it slowly and deeper and then sideways for a while and then deeper and finally got the shot. The reel on my spear line ran out quickly as the fish darted away injured, with my spearhead in it. Suddenly, I became aware I was completely gassed—in critical need of air. I had been caught up in the hunt. I looked up and could only see water—no surface. I was a long way from getting any air—and I was already hurting. I let go of my five-hundred-dollar spear gun. Now it was all about saving my life. I swam and swam and looked up, and I could barely make out the surface. I was in big trouble. I continued to swim as hard and fast as possible with everything I had.

I looked up again and could see the top now—only another fifteen feet to go. I started losing consciousness as I kicked through to the surface, gasping for air. I was deranged for a full two or three minutes afterwards. I didn't know which way was up; I couldn't speak; I couldn't think or function. It was like I was under a drug, like in a dream. I was semiconscious. I eventually regained complete consciousness and composure and realized how close I had come to death—another ten feet, maybe even five, and I wouldn't have made it. When I look back, I'm thankful God didn't take me that day. I had a wife and three young children at the time. We sold the boat shortly after that.

The Blue Caverns is definitely a place where it feels so right to be still and look at the vast ocean, above and below, and appreciate all of God's creation. I love that place because I connect with my Maker and because I've learned valuable lessons there, like how life is precious. It is His for the giving and His for the taking. It's a place where my life could have been taken and a place where I took life, wrong as it was. I abused my power. Thankfully, our heavenly Father never does that. His taking is always right and part of His perfect plan. We must realize and accept everything is His and He can do what He wants with it. My life and my health and my money and my wife and my children are all His, which He gave to me with great grace and also can be taken away if that be His will. They are all His and only mine as long as He graces me with them. I don't deserve any of it. That is what makes it truly incredible.

I love the book of Job in the Old Testament. Having had great wealth of family and fortune, he was the Bill Gates of that time. But one day the devil came to God. God asked Satan what he thought of His servant Job, who was a blameless man. God said, "There is no one like him on the earth" (Job 2:3).

Satan said, "Does Job fear God for nothing? Have You not made a hedge about him and his house and all that he has, on every side? You have blessed the work of his hands, and his possessions have increased in the land. But put forth Your hand now and touch all that he has; he will surely curse You to Your face." Then God answered Satan, *"Behold, all that he has is in your power, only do not put forth your hand on him"* (Job 1:9–12). To paraphrase, "You can do whatever you want with him, but you cannot take his life." So the devil took away all Job's possessions, his children, and his health. Never in the book's forty-two chapters does Job curse God. Job said, "Naked I came from my mother's womb, and naked I shall return there. The LORD gave and the LORD has taken away. Blessed be the name of the LORD" (Job 1:21).

But, like any mortal man, Job became weary during his trials. We read his words in chapter 21:22–26. "Can anyone teach God's knowledge, in that He judges those on high? One dies in his full strength, being wholly at ease and satisfied;… While another dies with a bitter soul never even tasting anything good. Together they lie down in the dust." Wow, is Job saying God gives His blessings to some and not to others? Maybe it is better to say God gives blessings to some in this life and to others after they leave it. But again, isn't it His to give? And isn't it up to Him to whom He chooses to give? Maybe some without fortune are to have theirs in another time and place and for longer than our little existence on this finite planet. Either way, rich or poor, our bodies will have the same ending—dust. But what of our souls? Thanks to God for having a plan better than that of man and that we're not to understand it all while here on earth. Job didn't understand God's plan either, but He remained faithful to God in acknowledging it was all God's in the first place.

I cannot leave the book of Job without recounting the best part. After thirty-seven chapters, Job has relinquished all to God and wants to die. He wants an answer to it all—for everything to make sense—just as we all do. God finally speaks, and He answers the questions we all have. His answer is long, but it is worth reading. The following is a portion of God's answer to Job.

"Who is this that darkens counsel by words without knowledge?…I will ask you, and you instruct Me! Where were you when I laid the foundation of the earth? Tell Me, if you have understanding, Who set its measurements?…Or who laid its cornerstone, when the morning stars sang together and all the sons of God shouted for joy?…Have you ever in your life commanded the morning, and caused the dawn to know its place, that it might take hold of the ends of the earth, and the wicked be shaken out of it? It is changed like clay under the seal; and they stand forth like a garment. From the wicked their light is withheld, and the uplifted arm is broken. Have you entered into the springs of the sea or walked in the recesses of the deep? Have the gates of death been revealed to you, or have you seen the gates

of deep darkness? Have you understood the expanse of the earth? Tell me, if you know all this."

That would surely have been enough! But God continued speaking: *"Where is the way to the dwelling of light? And darkness, where is its place...? You know, for you were born then, and the number of your days is great!... Can you lead forth a constellation in its season, and guide the Bear with her satellites? Do you know the ordinances of the heavens, or fix their rule over the earth? Can you lift up your voice to the clouds, so that an abundance of water will cover you? Can you send forth lightning that they may go and say to you, 'Here we are'? Who has put wisdom in the innermost being or given understanding to the mind? Who can count the clouds by wisdom, or tip the water jars of the heavens...? Can you hunt the prey for the lion...? Who prepares for the raven its nourishment when its young cry to God and wander about without food?"* (Job 38:2–41). And God finishes with, *"Will the faultfinder contend with the Almighty? Let him who reproves God answer it"* (Job 40:2).

Then Job answered God: "Behold, I am insignificant; what can I reply to You? I lay my hand on my mouth. Once I have spoken, and I will not answer; even twice, and I will add nothing more" (Job 40:4–5). Yes, Job was a wise man. And he understood it was God's plan in God's time and in God's way.

Perspective. Do you see the world as belonging to God? Or do you think you have the answers and the power to do what you want when you want and how you want? And, even if this is so, do you understand that any power you do have is only what He gives you and is temporary? This is the proper perspective. If you don't have this you will struggle with trying to make sense out of the many things in life that are not in God's design for you to comprehend. Perspective doesn't mean you understand everything, it merely means you see and accept things for what they are. It also means you know how important or unimportant something is and that you are where you are today because someone helped you along. You are not where you are solely because of you. At some point, everyone needs the perspective of knowing *who* is ultimately in control.

"The fear of the Lord is the beginning of knowledge."

PROVERBS 1:7

Chapter Five

HAPPINESS REQUIRES BALANCE

*"Your happiness lives in your past, present, and future,
and only in your mind, of which you control."*

ROBERT P. BAEYENS

PERSPECTIVE DOES HELP you achieve happiness. But perspective, although significant, exists only in your mind. Even though that's all it takes to be happy (*being* in your mind), it is much better for that perspective to be based on reality. A person can feel happy on morphine because he's in fantasyland, but his reality may be in an undesirable place even if his mind doesn't know it. Assuming you're living a normal life, your perspective should be based on facts, that is, on your reality. You must implement your perspective into actions—the way you live your life. Perspective is the mortar that holds your plan together. Actions are the execution of that plan. A plan may seem good on paper but will fail if it lacks one crucial ingredient—balance. Balance is any easy concept to understand but one of the hardest to attain and to keep.

Every day I struggle with balance. We all do. Too much of this and not enough of that. I carry on mental conversations all the time. *Should I eat fast food today? Let's see, I did yesterday. Maybe I'll have the burger but skip the fries. Or, better yet, I'll have the fries too, but I'll go to the gym later today to make up for it. But wait, I went to the gym yesterday, and my knee is kind of sore. I know if I work out too hard too many days in a row I usually get sick. Okay, forget the gym, the burger, and the fries. Now, where was I? Oh, yeah, I was hungry.* Sound familiar? Trying to balance the good with the bad, the fun with the not so fun, the work with the pleasure, the role of husband, the role of father, the role of friend, the role of boss, or simply the role of self-preservation.

How do we balance them all at once every single day? The answer is, we don't. But the real answer is that we must try constantly to attain the best balance we can. It's okay to get a little out of balance, especially if we're aware of it. You can even give yourself permission to get a little out of balance; however, realize what you're doing. You might even have a plan of how you will correct the unbalance later. But to ignore this truth is to let an unbalanced life take control of you. In Part Two there's a chapter on "Who's in Control?" For now, with what control you do have over your daily choices, you must choose to live aware of how everything affects other things.

Here is an example of something I struggle with. I feel I need to do something productive everyday in order to maintain balance and feel happy. I also have to do something for enjoyment everyday to be happy. The balance of the two is my perspective of a successful formula. But if I'm on vacation or away from home for a few days, out of my normal circumstances or away from my usual routine, how do I do something productive or how do I give myself permission not do something productive? Here's what I've learned to do. I realize that learning in itself is progress, so if I'm away on vacation then the traveling experience is the productivity. It is the bettering of myself through the new experience alone. And I don't expect anything else. I'm not trying to force the issue. Sometimes rest itself can be productive.

On a recent vacation, my mind's sense of balance came from committing my time to my family and realizing I needed that time solely for that purpose—to be with them and grow with them—and not to be self-absorbed in my own personal betterment, working, reading, writing, or whatever. Since the kids slept in every morning, it gave me the opportunity to get up early, exercise, have breakfast with Susie, and fill another area of balance—maintaining my physical health and some time alone with my wife. I really needed the morning exercise because I would start feeling lazy and tired in the afternoon without some physical activity. I know a person is supposed to rest while on vacation, but my body told me what it needed in order to keep its balance. I worked out every morning for the eight days we were on vacation, and, sure enough, I overdid and started feeling sick about the time the vacation ended. I got out of balance trying to keep the balance. It happens to me too often. This is the hardest part.

Let's define happiness. In order to identify with each other, we must first agree on its meaning. Our purpose is to achieve personal contentment and peace of mind, not only at the moment, but in viewing one's past and in looking forward to one's future. This will be our definition of happiness—contentment of mind with one's past, present, and future.

Your place in life is irrelevant if you love where you are and where you have been and are looking forward to where you will go. These three time periods—your past memories and experiences, your present state, and your future outlook—all contribute to your total view of yourself. They are the basis of your contentment, your peace of mind, your happiness. Does it really matter how much status, money, good looks, or accomplishments you have if you love your past, present, and future life? Who is happier—the person who has very little and is content, or the person who has much and is still not content? Who lives happier—the person who does not appreciate a lifetime of perfect health or the person who battled cancer and now sees every day as a blessing? Does the average person need tragedy or loss to fully appreciate life and be happier? The simple answer is yes. That doesn't mean it is impossible for someone who has not had tragedy or great struggle in life to be happy, but they are the exception. People of depth are usually happier people because they have experienced hardship and it has given them a perspective of what is important and what is not.

Let's look at the three areas of a person's self-image and analyze how they correspond to one's own personal happiness.

YOUR PAST

First, let's look at the past. Obviously, you cannot change actions and consequences that happened long ago. But there are two things you can do regarding your past that will enable you to be happier with it and, thus, happier with your present.

First, you can change your thoughts about your past by changing the present—either by a physical action or by a simple communication. If there is someone or something you wronged, treated badly, or caused harm to, and you are holding on to the guilt of this memory, then you need to let it go. If they are alive or the situation is still ongoing, then you can contact them and confront the current status if it is still possible to make a change. Maybe you damaged or lost someone's property and now have the means to compensate them. Maybe you treated them cruelly or ended a relationship. You still have the opportunity to go to them and apologize and make things right, even if it is only one conversation and you'll never see them again. Even if it wasn't your fault, you'll get the closure you need to be happy about it.

Years ago, I helped my friend Charlie evict a tenant who wasn't paying rent. The tenant agreed to leave. We even paid his transportation and the storage rental for his belongings to help him out. He hired an attorney, decided he had been wronged, even though he was six months behind on rent, and claimed we forced him out. I was also named in the lawsuit, even though I had no interest in the property. It drug on about three years, and the judge awarded him a settlement, which I thought was ridiculous. At the time of the settlement, I asked the other attorney if we could have one last meeting with his client to shake hands and end with some dignity and honor. He declined. I had offered and I was sincere about it so I could walk away with the peace of mind and contentment of having my own honor. You don't have to have a good relationship with someone to feel good about the way you handled a situation with them. You can't force other people to make good decisions—decisions that will free their mind and your mind from the clutter of the past. My sincere offer alone gave me the power to let it go.

The second way to "let it go" is needed if you can't do anything physically to change the situation. Maybe the person you wronged has died. The only way to let go of this type of past guilt has to be in your present mindset. You have to forgive yourself. Making a commitment to do something in the present to help someone else brings healing to the situation. This way you turn a past bad into a present good. If possible, inform the person or his family how the negative situation of the past changed you to become a better person in the present— then you will have peace with your past. Even if no one else ever knows, you will. And you can act on the present and the future knowing you are doing your best to remedy your past mistake.

The past is a mysterious place in one's present mind. Usually it has been altered to either ease some pain or to increase the pleasure of an already good memory. Pictures are great, but nothing compares to a wonderful memory. If you love the arts in any form, then you understand what I'm saying. Poetry, dance, art, wine, music, to name few—the memory of a good experience can't be beat. Often this nice memory happens because of who you are with, as much as the art you are experiencing. But those exceptional occasions are rare. And so are great memories with friends and family, perhaps even more so. It is easy to think the grass would have been greener going down another path. Where would you be now if you had married that other person? If you had taken that other job? If you had started your own business? If you hadn't made that one major mistake? We all have "the path not taken" in our lives. Be happy with the one you did take and that you had the opportunity to take that one. And if you don't like where it has taken you today, then work to change it now.

This brings us to the present. Don't wait. Start planning your change. A failure in a new path you've always wanted to try is not really failure. It is much better to fail in your new path than to assuredly fail by sticking with the old one. You can't win with the old if it has already proven itself over and over to make you unhappy. It has had time to prove to you it is a failure. The new path hasn't had the chance to prove anything. So, you can only increase your happiness by changing. Even a failure on the new path will bring closure about that path, and this will also bring some degree of happiness. You can't lose by changing. You can only win. And if it doesn't work, then change again and again until it does. But don't regret your past. It has made you who you are with its experiences, whatever they were, and they are invaluable for making your present and future happy.

YOUR PRESENT

It might be easier to recognize how to correct the present than the past, but implementing it is not easier. Like correcting your past, you must make an inner commitment to change.

The hardest part of being happy with your present condition is in knowing what it takes to make you happy in the first place. There has to be balance, like everything else. Too much happiness can also cause unhappiness. Sound funny? I believe it is true. Too much personal perfection doesn't build the depth in you that makes you appreciate the little things. And you can't be happy only counting on big events in your life. They don't happen often enough, and even when they occur they are short-lived, and then another big high is needed to get you back to happiness again. Like a drug, it coaxes you into a false sense of what you depend on to be happy in the first place. Too much perfection, too much happiness will leave you with no challenge in life. The lack of challenge breeds boredom and leads to an absence of appreciation and gratitude. Such a person shows no depth of character or the essential qualities that lead to happiness.

When teaching my son Paul how to play chess many years ago, I noticed he looked all around the board trying to make his decision. I would say, "Paul, where's the game?" I meant, where was the last move and what might threaten you based on that move? That's where the game was at the moment. Chess can be compared to life. While we are thinking about our plan for tomorrow, we are not focusing on what is happening today. Paul is like me; sometimes I'm planning ahead so much that I forget to live in the now. I have learned from my son Sean who has, by example, with his soft gentle spirit, taught me and Paul how to better live in the moment. The present is the most important time period because it is unfolding as you breathe.

I've said many times to my children, "Organization is the key to success." Success, or at least the quest for a certain success by setting goals, is essential to happiness. Therefore organizing and writing down a list of human attributes as a guideline is the first step in your pathway to happiness. One of my favorite books on happiness is Dennis Prager's *Happiness Is a Serious Problem.* He has so many great things to say about what it takes to achieve happiness, at least for the average person. After reading his book, I wrote a short list of one-liners that were to be my main focus when I felt myself becoming unbalanced. His book made these clear to me.

1. Be grateful for how much misery you've been spared in the world.
2. Human dissatisfaction as a motivator is a good thing, but do not let it make you unhappy.
3. The joy and meaning of one's work (not success) brings happiness.
4. Fun is temporary; happiness is ongoing.
5. Expectations are not good—unfulfilled they cause pain, and when fulfilled they diminish gratitude.
6. Gratitude is a key to happiness.
7. Understand the insatiable male and female natures: Males desire sexual variety; females desire emotional intimacy. Both are unsatisfiable.
8. Have meaning and purpose in your actions and goals.
9. Nothing lasts forever (good or bad).
10. Find the positive in every negative.
11. Tension is good if you are growing from it. Aggravation is not good.
12. Everything has a price. Know what that price is and decide if you are willing to pay it, or forego the desire.
13. Moderate your vices. Stop if addictive or harmful.
14. Exercise not only your body but your self-control, and keep your goals in sight.
15. Choose friends with good values.
16. Practice your religious philosophy about life.

Incorporating these attributes into your daily life will change your life. Reinvent yourself. It can actually be fun to see the changes in yourself especially when you see the benefits at the same time. It takes a little time and a little practice and certainly a little patience, but the reward is definitely worth it.

All of us need to take the time to open our minds to a world we don't notice. We need to make changes in ourselves. When I apply this concept to my own life, I realize any outcome would bring some happiness just in knowing I had the courage to make the change. I could always go back to what I was doing before, if I had to. So, what would I risk? Not really much if I think about it. What exactly was the risk? Looking bad to my friends or family? My pride, if my new path wasn't successful? Quite the contrary—I was already partly successful just for making the move, and that was evident in how others reacted to it. Everyone would like to make changes to themselves and their lives. And no one will look at you with anything but admiration for the courage to follow your heart and for the courage to act on it.

YOUR FUTURE

Now, how about your future and how to be happy about what you haven't done yet? The great Christian pastor and motivator Joel Osteen, in his book *Become a Better You: 7 Keys to Improving Your Life Every Day*, talks about how God has great plans for all of us. God made us with unique talents that He wants to see us bring to their fullest potential. Joel is absolutely right. God does have great plans for you. Why create something if you don't have a plan for it? God's plan is perfect, and you are a part of it, which means He has made you the very best in the world at something or at meeting some need at some time. He didn't just make you good or one of the best, he made you the best for His purpose. It might be something you will never discover, and that is sad because He wants you to know it and use it. But remember, God gives you free will, and you have to make the choice to discover it and not give up until you do.

I truly believe the road to discovery with God starts with being still and asking Him to come into your life. Tell Him, "God, this is Your plan and I'm excited about it, and I want to be the best at what You have planned for me." And then tell Him, "I will go where You lead me. All I ask is that You give me direction. If You do, I promise I'll follow." And then be ready to follow because God honors that type of prayer from your heart. He wants that relationship with you, and He's not going to turn His back on that prayer. God promises if you have faith even as small as a mustard seed you can accomplish anything through Him.

> *"For truly I say to you, if you have faith the size of a mustard seed,*
> *you will say to this mountain, 'Move from here to there,'*
> *and it will move; and nothing will be impossible to you."*

MATTHEW 17:20

Go, find your potential by searching for it. Here's how to start. Ask yourself, "What it is I do that always seems to work out well for me in the end?" And don't say "nothing." There is something you are good at. It might be listening. It could be the ability to bring people together when they are at odds, to calm down situations. It may be a physical talent you excel at or an intellectual talent, like teaching on a subject you have great passion for. It might be an art, like painting, or playing a musical instrument, or simply being able to appreciate art or music.

I took a class in jazz appreciation in college when I was twenty years old. The teacher loved his subject matter so much we only talked about two tunes the whole semester. That's all we did each day in that class for four months. We listened to the two songs measure by measure and discussed the motivation of the composer and the expression of the instrumentalists. I will always remember those two songs: "Maiden Voyage" by Herbie Hancock and "So What" played by Miles Davis on trumpet. I don't even know if the teacher could play an instrument, but I do know I've never met a more passionate and convincing teacher who left such an impression on me about a subject matter, one most people would never take a second look at. I loved that course and learned so much about the expression of music as an art because of the teacher's passion. He was the best at teaching the appreciation of someone else's art form. He didn't have to possess the talent himself, just the passion to be the best at appreciating it. He obviously had found what God had made him best at, and he was happy with his profession and even happier about thinking he'd be able to wake up every day and pursue it.

Joel Osteen has found his purpose in life—what God has called him to do, what God made him best at. Joel loves motivating people to also be their best at what God has called them to do. Every time I see Joel on television I find myself a half-hour later still glued to him. He's like that Lay's potato chip slogan, "You can't eat just one." If you hear Joel for thirty seconds, you'll still be listening thirty minutes later. You can hear God speaking through him. He is uplifting, and yet he still manages to stay on track about where it all comes from—our heavenly Father.

Here is the answer to being happy about your future that will also make you happy with your present. It's one simple concept: *Look forward to it!* Know that you are constantly looking for the hidden, God-given talent you are the very best at. And know you will find it because you have given yourself over to God as a partner in seeing that talent come to fruition for His purpose and for your happiness. It is you and Him—a team that can't lose. He doesn't promise the road will be easy but that it will be successful if you don't give up and if you keep your faith in Him.

Stop and be still. Spend a little time with your heavenly Partner. Find the good in your daily trials. Practice the human attributes that will help you achieve balance in your life. Be still and let God in. Have the faith the size of a mustard seed and you'll move your mountains...just as He promises.

"Consider it all joy, my brethren, when you encounter various trials,
knowing that the testing of your faith produces endurance.
And let endurance have its perfect result, so that you
may be perfect and complete, lacking in nothing.
But if any of you lacks wisdom, let him ask of God,
who gives to all generously and without reproach,
and it will be given to him."

JAMES 1:2–5

Chapter Six

TEMPTATION

"No temptation has overtaken you but such as is common to man;
and God is faithful, who will not allow you to be tempted beyond what you are able,
but with the temptation will provide the way of escape also,
so that you will be able to endure it."

1 CORINTHIANS 10:13

WHAT IS TEMPTATION, and why is it necessary to understand it? The *Random House College Dictionary* defines temptation as "to entice or allure to do something often regarded as unwise or wrong."

We all know from experience it is human nature to be tempted. Although we face numerous temptations every day, the majority fall into three categories: temptations merely for survival, temptations caused by a person with a medical or psychological condition, and temptations that lure us simply because we think they will make us feel good. We will focus on the last type. To some extent a psychological factor is involved here too because part of what makes us feel good is merely the act of giving into it. This might seem odd, but it is true. Most people, even those who are not quitters, entertain the idea of giving up on certain things because it takes work to constantly keep oneself disciplined. To give into temptation is to surrender to an inner need to escape the effort of keeping the brain in control over the mind's wandering desires. What makes it even more attractive for us is that usually our temptations are secret. This is an important factor, and we'll get back to it.

In this third category, I'm talking about those of us who have the necessities in life but are tempted to acquire more for the sake of selfishness. If you think about it, almost all of our temptations are related to selfishness. It is also part of our human equation to have ambition and to be unsatisfied with our current levels of success. This isn't necessarily a bad thing; in fact it has helped to make humanity better in many ways, but also worse. Even those with exceptional achievements want to reach the next rung on the ladder—to have something to aim for, a reason to wake up in the morning and be excited, to reach their goals or to accomplish the impossible. That's what makes us tick, but often to a fault.

This same quality also makes us vulnerable to temptation. Therefore, temptation, which is the first step (or the first feeling) in the process of making a choice for a wrong, unwise, immoral, or illegal act, is this: *an illegitimate means to a legitimate need.* Another word for committing such a deed is sin. But keep in mind that sin is the act and not the thought, which we'll be talking about next. Others simply call it "knowing what's right and choosing to do the other thing." You can label it whatever you want. The bottom line is that temptation is the feeling of great desire for something, which leads to using a wrong method to obtain it. In other words, we decide to do something we would not like someone else to do, especially to us, since it violates our sense of what is right. Giving into temptation usually causes further harm and not always just to ourselves. Yet, too often, we yield to it. Why? Obviously, we think it is going to feel good, and, since it usually does, we're likely to repeat it. We already know there's a price to pay, and, by giving in, we're obviously willing to pay it. It's like a credit card. It doesn't hurt when you make the purchase, but when the bill shows up it's another story. Those of us who despise the bill are usually much better not using the card in the first place.

This is another area in life where a plan is needed. If we don't talk about these questionable acts we all entertain in our minds and if we don't have a plan to respond to these temptations when we face them, then we're leaving ourselves open to being unprepared when we are most in need of being prepared. But, then again, don't we sometimes purposely decide to remain unprepared so we won't be as accountable when we make the choice to give in? I'm speaking from experience, of which I'm not proud, but, at least, honest. We are all human and we all think of indecent acts in some context. If we didn't, we wouldn't know the difference between right and wrong. To not consider these acts is to not understand them and, thus, to put ourselves and society in a dangerous place. Discussing temptation is a very necessary part of conquering it. And too many people in the world, Christians and non-Christians alike, do not like to face this topic.

Thinking about something that has been tempting me lately, as so many things constantly do, enables me to dissect my own feelings—as long as I remain completely honest, which I intend to do. Soon it becomes apparent to me what has tempted me most recently is a situation I believe is wrong. This is not because the initial act is wrong but because I believe it will lead me to the next stage, where both the decision and the temptation may be too great for me to deny. Am I saying I don't trust myself? Am I saying I can't put myself in a dangerous situation because I'll probably be too weak to make a good choice once I'm in the situation, facing it close up? Yes, that's what I am saying. It feels terrible to admit, and yet I know it is the truth. Most violating acts don't start with the act but with the thought of flirting with the act, to look but not to touch, to smell but not to taste.

This opportunity, for lack of a better word, is innocent at this point, and I use this to convince myself I'm not being bad by entertaining it. However, I also know I'm curious about my own nature, almost as if I want to test myself, to understand my own character. I'm willing to risk facing the harder decision, which could be perilous, in order to satisfy some selfish need. Now, I need to figure out what this need is and why I'm not satisfying it in another way that would make God proud of me rather than flirting with potential harm and dishonoring my God. I've come to the conclusion this little scenario playing out in my head would meet a need I seemingly have for an ego boost—possibly because of some low self-esteem, which is usually not me at all, and possibly even the need for some acceptance.

What's wrong with me? I already have all these things in my life. I have plenty of things that keep my self-esteem, ego, and acceptance at healthy enough levels. As I continue to probe my own heart and mind, it becomes clear the secrecy has something to do with it; otherwise I would immediately stop thinking about it in the first place. But it is not secret from God. Why isn't that enough to dismiss it? This really feels bad. Am I saying I wouldn't want a friend to know what I'm pondering but I don't care that God knows?

This is a light-bulb moment for me. The secrecy gives me the feeling of control and power and also the confidence that if this control or power isn't maintained it won't matter anyway because no one will know. So, now, dishonesty comes into play. And I'm already convinced God is looking the other way. Why? Because He's a forgiving God? That's the first thought that comes to mind. Because I know I have a good heart and I'm not trying to do anything bad? No, because I'm fooling myself thinking God is going to give me a pass to make a borderline decision. That's exactly the answer. It's not borderline. And I know that. I'm lying to myself going into the situation, and, therefore, it is easy for me to lie to God. After all, if I don't spend the time to figure out what is right and wrong, then how can I be accountable to know the difference? Now that's convicting. Yet, there is another answer, the solution—the way out. We have to be honest with ourselves and then come to terms with God about our potential behavior, while at the same time asking Him for the way of escape. The opening verse in this chapter says it all, "… but with the temptation [God] will provide the way of escape also…."

Is God tempting us and then providing the way of escape? No, God allows us to be tempted through our free will, but He always provides the same way of escape. We can go to Him and lay it all out there in front of Him and say, "God, what's the right thing for me to do? What will make You proud?" And then do it, and don't look back at the stupid, little short-term satisfaction you think you missed out on. You gained much more than that. Another of my conclusions here, after thinking about how this all applies to me, is that a person must know himself. We must know our own limitations. These temptations will always be around, so we must know how close we can get to them without them getting to us—not so we can venture to the edge, but so we know the area of safety.

Are there times when it is right to cross the line? If it is selfless in its motivation, can that make it right? Does this always have to be black and white? Here is my answer: It should always be black and white. If it isn't, then there is not a true guideline of right and wrong. The world is filled with trouble because too many people, religions, and governments think they are self-righteous enough to be that authority—to make the code of what is right and wrong. The problem is there are too many disagreements. Again, we need one authority with one code for this to be successful.

Now, it's time for me to get bold with some statements I believe are true. If we took money, sex, and mind-altering substances away, we'd probably eliminate about ninety-nine percent of all temptations. Without the desire for things—all that stuff that's sitting in our homes and garages; without the greed for money, which gives us power and influence; without the desires for sex, physical or emotional; without the influences of even the simple legal drugs, such as alcohol, caffeine, or nicotine, to name a few—there really are not that many other distractions that tend to pull most human beings from walking cleanly through life. What do these things all have in common? They make us feel good for the moment. They change our brain's chemistry. They pull at our longings to take the easy path. They bring pleasure without having to work for it. Sounds like a credit card to me. I understand myself much better when I think in these terms. Especially when I know we were created to think and feel the way we do. We are also made to know better—if we stop to figure ourselves out first.

The largest and oldest business in the world seems to have all three—money, sex, and often drugs going on at the same time—prostitution. And it is also a means by which both men and women have control over something—their own bodies. Another big issue is also related to the control of one's body, the issue of abortion. The fact that so many topics divide so many people should be reason enough to discuss them and, certainly, to know where we stand. If you're not sure, then you need to think about these things so you can be certain. Not knowing your own stance on immorality is immoral.

Life has so many controversial topics. It becomes apparent the answers must come from a higher authority than merely the collective minds of differing societies that make their own laws. I believe God has created each of us with the innate awareness of when these immoral lines get crossed. But since we all think differently, the line is almost certainly at a different place for each of us.

For an example, let's use the topic about how we treat our bodies. I don't make a practice out of judging what others do with their own bodies; however, I do judge what I do with my own. I'm no saint. I have pretty poor eating habits. Some days I sit down to dinner and then realize that I hadn't stopped for breakfast or lunch that day. Other days I quickly drive through a fast-food place for the second time, skipping the fries just to make myself feel better about it. Where are the true lines we should not cross? My unhealthy eating habits are no better than disrespecting one's body in all sorts of other ways. Even though fast food doesn't seem as bad to me as prostitution, it might seem worse for the prostitute who is a vegetarian and looks down on me for the way I eat.

Who's to say whether an act or a temptation is really bad for you? Isn't it all subjective? Where are the lines? Without an authority that has defined it all for us there can be no true answer to this question. God is that authority. The true line is the place where peace with God makes the decision for you. It is a divine feeling He has put into all of us, but it needs the mind to make sense of it, to think about it deeply and seriously, and to find the truths about God's code. Otherwise, we're each making our own personal lines where we think they should be, using our own self-righteous thinking, while placing that same line on everyone else and then judging. That brings chaos.

Where is God's line? That's what we should be asking ourselves. But before we can look to God for answers, we must believe God exists and He is in control of it all. We must first know God is talking to each and every one of us. If only we would be still long enough to listen to Him, to shut up and let God be God in our lives. Without looking to one authority, our one God in heaven, and asking Him for the answers, we will never know if our innate feelings are the true feelings from both our souls and our minds together, collectively with our Creator. Fortunately, we have a source, something we can touch right now that can be our divine guide. It can bridge our human gap of uncertainty and doubt. It is the greatest tool with which to restore our faith in times of weakness. That is why God handed it down to us, communicating through specifically chosen people, a God-given guide to be used while we're here on earth.

Most things come with an instruction manual. God has given us an instruction manual to life—the Bible. When in doubt, go to God's Word for the answers. Interpreting the answers may be another matter, but finding them and reading them is not. This is the first step. Here's what the Bible says about how we treat our bodies: "Do you not know that your bodies are members of Christ? Shall I then take away the members of Christ and make them members of a prostitute? May it never be! Or do you not know that the one who joins himself to a prostitute is one body with her? For He says, 'THE TWO SHALL BECOME ONE FLESH.' But the one who joins himself with the Lord is one spirit with Him" (1 Corinthians 6:15–17).

All you have to do is keep reading this passage and it also reveals God's will regarding other ways you treat your body: "Flee immorality. Every other sin that a man commits is outside the body, but the immoral man sins against his own body. Or do you not know that your body is a temple of the Holy Spirit who is in you, whom you have from God, and that you are not your own? For you have been bought with a price: therefore glorify God in your body" (1 Corinthians 6:18–20).

It amazes me so much can be learned from the Bible in so few sentences. And there are a lot of sentences in the Bible. This is where interpretation and common sense, along with the innate sense of what God is really telling us, is essential. This is where it is left open to argument by those who don't believe in our great God. And, as we know, it is also open to argument between those who do believe in God.

Let's take one sentence from 1 Corinthians 6 above and see how it can be interpreted in different ways. "But the immoral man sins against his own body" (verse 18). One may ask, "Does this mean anything you do to your body is a sin if it is not necessary?" And what is the definition of necessary? Is marking your body with a tattoo a sin? Is piercing an ear a sin? Are braces on your teeth a sin? Do you see where this can go? People will answer differently to all of these questions. There are two problems: First, such thinking is subjective for each individual, and, second, God's Word is interpreted by man, even though His biblical Word is designed to be specific and exact in its meaning. We have imperfect beings trying to interpret what is perfect at its core.

So, how does Bob interpret the biblical answer to the previous question about prostitution and defiling one's body? Remember, I'm only a man interpreting it, but here goes: God made you and me in His image, and He paid a great price for us by giving up His Son on the cross. It is a dishonor to God not to appreciate the free gift of our bodies. It is also a dishonor to lie down with someone else who is not respecting this great gift.

God knows all of our hearts. Ask Him what His divine plan is for you. It is not my place to judge your heart and your relationship with God. But it is His place, so ask Him. Read His Word, take it to heart, and get your answers.

Most of us are trying to be good people to the best of our abilities. We are all in the same boat; that is, we are sinners, we have selfish natures, we usually think of ourselves first, and we hurt others to lessen our own hurt. Only by practice can we better ourselves to the point where we can stop wanting for ourselves and be still and say, "Wait, I'm feeling this, but I should be thinking about that person first. That's what I would want him to do. So I should do it. I wonder what he feels right now. If I can just step out of myself for a moment and try to sense his thoughts and feelings and desires and needs …" If you do this, trust me, you'll be a new person and everyone around you will know it. If it sounds easy, it's not. I blow it all the time. Jesus' words from the Gospel of Matthew are so true for all of us:

"You hypocrite, first take the log out of your own eye,
and then you will see clearly to take the speck out of your brother's eye."

MATTHEW 7:5

Let's not judge others when we have so much self-correcting to do.

If we can keep from needing to escape in the first place, then our temptations won't have power. But we all have our little escapes, don't we? We might be able to fool ourselves into thinking we are good at controlling them, but we're not. Escapes put you and me above everyone else. That's not God's way. It's our way. And I'm just as guilty as the next person

What about taking another's life? What about adultery? Stealing? Coveting? What about lying? There are too many topics—all concerning right and wrong, good and evil—but they all have one thing in common, temptation.

Now, instead of questions, let's get to some answers. First off, I don't have all of them. But, as I've previously stated, I believe the Bible does. Just like the rest of the world, constantly wrestling with how to treat these issues, I can only tell you my opinion.

Since we're all going to interpret the answers to our questions in our own ways, whether biblically backed or not, we need to focus on how to recognize temptation and have a plan of action ready when we feel its presence. We need a defense in place for the times when we know something is wrong but it entices us to make excuses why we should do it anyway. We convince ourselves it will be all right even though deep in our souls we know it isn't—that's when we need an immediate response that fights back and says, "Stop and think first." So, here it is again—be still and look to God for the answer on how to proceed. Ask yourself, "Who am I hurting, and why is it worth it?" And even better, "Would I do this thing knowing someone else might do the same thing to me?"

With numerous temptations hitting billions of people every single day, we all need a predetermined defense or we're in big trouble. We are trying to fulfill an innate desire that few realize is even a desire. It is the desire to get something for nothing. When we give into temptation we feel as if we got away with something. "Nobody will know about my indiscretion, and it will give me immediate satisfaction, and it will relieve the stress of my current situation. I deserve to feel that way, even if it's short-lived." Sound familiar?

To yield to temptation is to escape reality for just a brief period of time. But reality will always come back, and we'll be in a reduced state of control the more we give into temptation, whatever it is. Sometimes it feels good simply to know we're giving up the control. Then we can make the excuse we weren't in control and that's why we did the act. Why do so many people drink alcohol? Because they feel they are not responsible for what they do while intoxicated. I've done some of the stupidest things while drinking socially with friends. Usually it is something I've said. But I am responsible for making the choice to drink in the first place. Many of us struggle with this because it is so prevalent in our society. Again, if we're going to be stupid we need to be smart about it. And that means nobody else gets hurt in the process. If we can also learn how to avoid hurting ourselves, then we'll be starting down the road of saying "no" to temptation.

This is not foolproof. Everyone is different, so we need to know ourselves and what temptations are the most alluring to us and the most damaging. Those are the ones to focus on. This isn't a process of trying to be perfect, just a process of trying to better ourselves. No matter how hard we try and how well we perfect the art of dodging temptation, there will still be times when we give into it. God gave us free will. He doesn't expect us to be perfect. He knows we are going to stumble. And He wants us to ask for His forgiveness when we fall and to put our honest effort into trying to fight off temptations while looking to Him for strength. When we put it back into His hands through prayer we are saying, "God, we're partners in this. I need Your help. I can't do this on my own." He will honor that if it is sincere. By asking God for help we are taking the burden off our own shoulders and letting Him carry the weight. Not all of it—we still have responsibility in our choices, but God will be our partner in seeing that the way of escape is provided.

He wants happiness for us, and He wants to see us work on our weaknesses and our temptations and to do our best to win out over them as often as we can. Let's have a plan to do that—a plan to better ourselves, even though we know we'll stumble; but to also know we can ask for forgiveness and start over again. Our goal is to become better and better at it and gain the most control our individual, God-given personalities can achieve.

Understanding why we are tempted is the start—knowing it will satisfy a perceived need, usually in secret, but is an improper method to attaining satisfaction. Recognizing our own personal nature and limitations is also key. But asking God to be our partner and doing our best to keep our commitment to Him is most important.

The opening verse says it all. "…and God is faithful, who will not allow you to be tempted beyond what you are able, but with the temptation will provide the way of escape also, so that you will be able to endure it" (1 Corinthians 10:13). He doesn't tempt us, but He allows us to be tempted through our own free will. He provides the way of escape because He is a merciful God and wants to see us make the right choice—the choice we know is right deep within our heart and soul, and the choice we know will please Him.

And when we stumble, as we will, we need to keep His rescue in sight as we ask for His forgiveness and to praise our one and only God, who always has the capacity to say, "It's okay. I forgive you, and I'm still with you."

"The Lord knows how to rescue the godly from temptation."

2 PETER 2:9

Chapter Seven

HABITS

"Do you want to know who you are? Don't ask.
Act! Action will delineate and define you."

THOMAS JEFFERSON

THIS CHAPTER COULD HAVE easily been combined with chapter sixteen about "Who's In Control?" but I felt this topic needed its own place because of its importance and because so many people ignore its power—at their own peril.

Habits are about self-control. I define habits as "the comfortable and routine gestures, acts, and imitations one does in everyday life." The problem is habits are just too comfortable. But with some practice this can be made to work in our favor.

Habits, by nature, control us. Again, this can be a good thing if it is a beneficial habit. But, for most people, if we weigh their good habits against their bad habits they come out very short on the positive side. It is like the proverbial angel on one shoulder and the devil on the other. The devil is laughing because his side, all too often, is winning.

The reason the angel's side struggles is because he has no plan. The devil is winning because his whole world is built around just that—people having no plan. The devil's way is to entice us into living by what feels good and by what offers the least resistance. Things that take very little effort seem attractive at first simply because we don't have to work as hard. Why work for something if we can get it without the work? That's how a bad habit makes us think. The reason we don't control it is because we don't really want to control it, just like the temptation we discussed in the previous chapter. If we were to take control and change, it would take away the comfort and satisfaction the habit brings. But we can temper it, and that is the key. We must be in control of it, and not the other way around. Most things of value in our lives cannot be earned or learned the easy way. They usually take great effort.

"All human actions have one or more of these seven causes:
chance, nature, compulsion, habit, reason, passion and desire."

ARISTOTLE

We all have them—our habits. Some of them are vices, some we look forward to, some we certainly don't want to be doing, and then there are the ones we don't even realize we're doing. Some habits help us to relax, reduce stress, and make it through our daily struggles. These are not bad if we remain in control. Occasionally choosing to let them be in control is all right, as long as we know we are making that choice and it's only for a short time.

I remember moving my son Paul into his dorm room at UC Berkeley his third year of college. At the end of the day we hugged, and I walked away to drive home. But then I stopped and turned around and said, "Paul, remember what your dad always says—if you're going to be stupid, be smart about it." He laughed, but he knew what that meant.

We all have some familiar habits primarily because of the comfort they give us: the way we talk, the way we sleep, whether we are punctual or late for appointments, the way we say goodbye on the phone, even our signature. They become so routine we don't realize we do them. These are the little habits—the ones that don't affect us much.

I have a habit of straightening things in front of me. Sometimes when I'm at a table talking with someone, I'm distracted by my glass not sitting in the center of its coaster or the utensils being crooked. As I'm repositioning them—not always, but usually—I catch myself and think, *What am I doing?* It's just an organizational habit, but it distracts me from where my attention ought to be—listening to the person I'm with. I also realize the reason for this habit of mine. It is because I've seen the negative impact of being disorganized in my life and business. Straightening things gives me a sense of order and, therefore, success. My problem is I need to separate my business from my pleasure activities, and I'm constantly in one mode while my mind is still in the other. I have to consciously work on this. The more I am aware of it and make the effort to change, the easier it becomes to recognize and correct.

Now on to the big habits—the ones that can ruin us. They are different for each of us. Alcohol, smoking, eating, sex, gossip, exercise, work—just to name a few. Do you have to have a drink every night to unwind? Or is it food or a drug that does the job? Maybe you relieve your anxiety through sex and possibly too much of it. If a habit controls your thoughts throughout the day, then it is a burden on you and it has control over you. If you're obsessing, "I can't wait to do this or that," it is controlling you.

You need to recognize which habits in your life control you and which ones you control. Make a list and then work on changing them, one habit at a time. It might take a month or more focusing on each bad habit until you begin to control them. Studies show it takes three weeks to form a habit, so don't get discouraged if it takes time to alter ingrained patterns. First, decide how much of the habit is good for you, if any, and then make the necessary goal to get the habit to a tolerable level or eliminate it altogether if you can't control it. There is no in-between. You control it, or it controls you. If giving in to the habit at all causes you to lose control of how much you do and how much you know is an acceptable amount for you—not for someone else, but for you—then it must be eliminated completely. If you can remain in control, then you may keep the habit (if it is not harmful to anyone) and enjoy it to its *controlled* fullest.

Let's take food. I think most of us struggle with this one. It is not my biggest struggle, but I still have to think about it constantly to stay in the driver's seat. Choosing to eat good food over junk food is my toughest problem. Fast food is just too accessible and too tempting for me, not to mention tasty—a very bad habit for me. I try to balance it with not overeating and also by trying to keep the junk out of my sight. In other words—not tempting myself. If the junk food is around, I'll eat it. If it's not, I'm not tempted.

Exercise is also essential in keeping one's diet and body in balance with the food it takes in. A goal to exercise a few times a week is important, and making a plan gives you an advantage. Let the angel gain the upper hand by having a plan. Maybe your plan is something like this: workouts on Monday, Wednesday, Friday, and a walk on Sunday. Maybe weekends are the "time out" zone where you can relax and eat liberally and enjoy that extra ice cream, hamburger, or glass of wine. But on Monday you know you are back to your routine—your new and solid routine, your new habit.

If you are a messy person, then practice a few little organizational things at first. Start with a clean room. Make your bed. Promise yourself you won't set anything down, but return it to its "home." Keep your shoes in only one place when they're not on your feet. Put your wallet, purse, phone, and keys in the same place always. Practice this, and organization will start to become the habit.

Something I do that has been a huge help in my life and that I would be totally lost without is this: I write a list at the end of my workday every day. I use a five-by-eight-inch sheet of paper—small enough to have with me throughout the day and large enough to handle it all. I've been doing this for twenty years. It is fast and simple. In the top left corner I write the date and below it the day of the week. About a third of the way down on the left side I write "Calls" and underline it. Beside it on the right, I write and underline the word "Visits." I draw a line separating the calls and visits sections.

Under "Calls" I list all the phone calls I need to make, with the person's name and phone number so I don't have to look up the number the next day. If I have to look it up and I'm busy, I might skip it. Knowing this about myself, I take the risk away by creating this good habit—writing the number down the day before when I'm not rushed. Under "Visits," I list all the places I need to go that day, just as a quick-glance area of the different stops I'll be making, and this helps me plan the most efficient order to make those stops. Under the "Calls" section, I write down the days later in the week with a dash after the day indicating a planned meeting, who I'm meeting, and what time the meeting starts. At the very bottom I leave space for any notes and reminders. The top third of the paper is where I write that day's times and places I have committed to be since those are the most important commitments, having transferred them from the previous day's page. This is my lifesaver. I'm organized with it, I don't miss meetings, I'm rarely late, and I don't forget to do the things I promise people I'm going to do.

The best part is, after I write my list for the next day, I can totally relax and forget about it for the entire night. I don't have to be thinking, *Don't forget to do this or don't forget to do that.* It is all organized for the next day and I can let it go. No stress in the evenings, no worries. I know when the morning starts I can quickly look over my list and know what I need to do—I'm good to go all day long. As things happen during the day. I write them on the back of the paper in preparation for the next day's list. The cycle continues smoothly all week long.

I now have a perfect record with phone numbers and times of everything I've done in the past, which I file for future reference. I can tell you what I did twelve years ago on the second Tuesday in February. And this comes in handy if someone questions something contractually or if I need proof something happened or didn't happen as I was building their home. It has helped make me who I am. And I have no doubt it has made my reputation what it is—reliable.

Let me correct one thing, though. I said I have no stress in the evenings, but, remember, I have three kids so that's not entirely true. However, I can reduce my work stress to a minimal level by this method of organization.

You don't have to be in the construction business to need an organized list to make life run more smoothly. Without it I don't know how anyone can function properly. Making this a habit for me has been my formula for success.

Yes, habits can be good things. And bad ones can be made into good ones— pleasurable experiences that are governed. I also think if you really are in control of your habits then you can occasionally give yourself permission to overdo it—with the self-commitment that it will be the exception and not the rule and it will be temporary.

To make bad habits into good ones and to create good ones where there are none takes a commitment to look inward and ask, "How can I improve myself? How can I take my faults and shine them up?" The alternative is to let them control you, driving your self-esteem down, and depressing your mind into a devil-controlled path of least resistance instead of an angel-controlled path of structure. The one with a plan will win.

Be still. Look inward and see your faults, and do this often. Be still, and let the solution of how to make changes in yourself happen by means of connecting with your own truths about what you control and what you don't. Be still and ask yourself, "What do I not like about myself?" and "What do I think others probably don't like about me?"

Then decide to do something about this. Make a habit out of the new plan, and practice it until you conquer it. Each little success will add up to a big success. You'll become what you want to become and you'll be in control to best of your ability. It starts with a look inward and then a true commitment to change. But before that—it starts with being still and asking God for the power and the plan and the courage to say no to the devil.

"It takes less time to do a thing right, than it does to explain why you did it wrong."

HENRY WADSWORTH LONGFELLOW

Chapter Eight

REPUTATION

"A good name is to be more desired than great wealth."

PROVERBS 22:1

MOST AMERICANS HAVE HEARD of John D. Rockefeller, the industrialist who revolutionized the petroleum industry and became the first U.S. billionaire. But did you know he founded Standard Oil with a group of partners? One partner was Henry Flagler. You probably haven't heard of him; however, if you live in Florida, then you most certainly have. His name is everywhere along Florida's eastern coast. More than any one individual, he played a major role in Florida's development in the late 1800s.

While one man is known for building his wealth, the other continued to spread it around to build up his adopted state. The meeting of the two men was primarily due to reputation. Flagler's reputation for honesty and hard work caught the eye of Rockefeller. Both were in the grain business prior to their involvement in the oil industry. Earlier, Flagler had amassed a fortune, some $50,000—a great amount of wealth in the mid-1800s. Soon, he found a new opportunity in the salt business during the Civil War. When salt prices fell severely at the end of the war, Flagler lost his investment and found himself badly in debt. After being one of the wealthiest men in the world, he was now broke. He immediately went back to what he did best, the grain business, and was able to pay off his debts and reestablish himself. It was at this time the two met. Rockefeller later said, "The idea of the Standard Oil combine was born in the mind of Henry Flagler."

To be able to achieve success, lose it, regain it, and then to catch the eye of a man like John D. Rockefeller was only possible by having a flawless reputation, as did Henry Flagler. In my opinion, Flagler was one of the single greatest contributors to commerce and to the development of a single state in our country, and certainly one of the greatest men known by too few people, considering all he accomplished. But Flagler wasn't interested in making history and being famous, he just wanted to do what he believed was right. His charities were countless. I am much more impressed with this man when compared with his towering partner, Rockefeller.

A person's reputation really is everything. I learned this early in my life. I'm grateful I was taught to place such value on it because it has paid me great dividends. My reputation has made me who I am and has provided a good living for my family. Most of my agreements to build homes for my clients have been through word of mouth and performed on handshakes alone. Almost always, within thirty days I had my client's complete trust. I made sure this trust would not be violated in any way. My reputation carried on to the point of awarding work to my company without having to bid against others. This alone was a great reward. I have been rewarded for my honesty, dependability, and trust; not only financially but in valuable and loyal friendships—something no one can put a price on.

A great reputation takes time to earn. But honesty, dependability, and trust are the building blocks. Like Flagler, a man can have nothing in the bank, and yet his reputation is his wealth. Such wealth is easy to translate into monetary wealth. Try buying a good reputation. It is impossible. But a good reputation can buy you wealth. That in itself proves its value. A good reputation is everything in business, and it should be everything in your everyday life. Your relationships with your spouse, your children, your friends, and your family also depend on your reputation. Without a good reputation trust is diminished, followed by diminished effort, followed by diminished respect, followed by diminished acts. A good reputation builds character in all that it touches, and a bad reputation tears it down slowly but surely. And "surely" is the operative word. A bad reputation will tear down the greatest successes.

The year was 1974, and I was thirteen years old in junior high school. I remember it like it was yesterday. I was sitting in my eighth grade science class, second row on the left as I faced the teacher. I was a student of good grades, but also a goof-off. I loved the attention. One day, I turned around to the boy behind me. His name was Richard. I picked up his pencil and broke it in half. Kids laughed, and I certainly got the attention I sought. I continued to do that to Richard quite often. For some reason, we were still somewhat friends. Richard let me get away with it because he had this classic funny look every time I'd perform the act. It always got great laughs, so Richard was kind of in on the stunt.

Then came the day when, after the pencil-breaking ritual, Richard looked at me differently, and it left a deep impression on me. He was hurt and he was tired of it all. I knew what I saw in his eyes that day was his true feeling inside. At that moment, my cruel little heart changed in an instant, and I made a commitment to myself that I would never break another pencil in my life. In fact, I could tell he didn't really trust me with anything and certainly not anything that came out of my mouth. In other words, my word wasn't worth anything. For some reason that day it really bothered me. I made a commitment deep inside myself to change. I was also determined to gain his trust.

It took the rest of the year and most of ninth grade, but the change I was making in myself started to show returns, not only with Richard, but in other friendships too. I had no idea about the great power in one's reputation, but it was becoming quite apparent. By tenth grade, Richard and I were very good friends. He showed me his ultimate trust by recommending to his parents I housesit their upscale home in Park Estates during Christmas break while his family went skiing in Utah for two weeks. That was the day I knew my life-changing commitment had come to fruition. I had reached my goal of turning my reputation around. And I would stay committed to keeping it golden.

Richard's family left for vacation, and I was in charge. I made sure the home was immaculate when they returned. I even lined up every item in the refrigerator perfectly so there would be no mistake this boy was on top of things. More than anything, I wanted to prove myself worthy of their trust. His parents were so impressed with me that I continued to housesit for them during their annual holiday trip to Utah for many years after that.

"Men acquire a particular quality by constantly acting a particular way…
you become just by performing just actions,
temperate by performing temperate actions,
brave by performing brave actions."

ARISTOTLE

You become dependable by consistently performing dependable actions. It was this type of trust others had in me that made me want to have a flawless reputation. Any lack of trust was just as uncomfortable on the negative side. Any doubt shown in me by anyone would be an immediate challenge to prove myself worthy. I had formed a habit in that nature of mine.

Now, what about you? If you don't have a good reputation then now is the time to start over. It is never too late. It may take a year or more to prove yourself to others, but they will see a change in you in short order and it will impress them. And then it will start paying dividends. Let people know you intend to change and you expect them to warn you if they see anything to the contrary. Be steadfast in your effort. Be solid and dependable. When you commit to someone, you must follow through to the end. Your first commitment should always be the one you keep. Never break a first commitment because the appearance of a better offer comes along afterward. Even if you know the second offer is superior, do not accept it. The breaking of the first commitment is the breaking of your reputation, and that loss is far greater then the gain from the second offer. This also goes for committing your time to someone else, even social time. The first commitment stands firm, always. Children need to be taught this lesson because it will transfer to adult life and they will reap the benefits.

Another reason your reputation is so important is because it attracts the type of person who practices the same behavior you exhibit. My mother once told me, "Bob, if you want to marry a princess then you need to act like a prince." It is true. Good attracts good. Evil attracts evil. Poor reputations attract others with poor reputations.

"Do not be deceived: 'Bad company corrupts good morals.'"

1 CORINTHIANS 15:33

By having a good reputation you attract quality people into your life. There is little doubt quality friends make a quality life. How you act will determine whom you attract.

You must know how important your reputation is, and your marriage, your friendships, your work relationships, and your relationship with God. Others are watching you. Just as you are watching them.

Always keep in mind that your actions will prove your reputation—most assuredly.

"Actions lie louder than words."

CAROLYN WELLS

Chapter Nine

FRIENDSHIPS

"Greater love has no one than this, that one lay down his life for his friends."

JOHN 15:13

ONE OF THINGS I REMEMBER fondly about my relationship with my father was how the words he said to me always left an impression. Up until now I haven't talked about my father much. I'm pausing as I write to consider why this is so. With a little thought, it becomes obvious to me. After over seventeen years without him, I'm still in denial. He was my best friend in the whole world, and I still to this day I cannot think about him without crying inside. Even before this sentence is finished I already have tears. There was no one like him. He was selfless and wanted nothing except to be with his family. He was the most humble man, and he loved to live through me and my experiences.

Everything Dad ever told me I took as law. As a young boy, I would go to school with stories from my dad. When confronted by the other kids, I would bet my life on defending what he had told me as the final truth. If he said I could jump off the roof of a three-story building and I'd be fine, I'd do it in a heartbeat without any hesitation. No father has ever had a son more loyal than I was to my father. And no father deserved it more. Don't get me wrong. I don't go around depressed or obsessed about having lost him. But it was a tragedy, and it happened at such an important time in my life. I choose not to dwell on it out of respect for Dad. I don't think he'd want me to continue to bemoan it over and over again.

As I mentioned before, my father was electrocuted while on vacation at Havasu Lake, California, in 1992, a month before he was to retire. It still hurts to think about it, and there's a reason for that. It should have been me who died on that June day. I suppose this is another reason why I have trouble talking about it, even to this day. I had been there all week with him at his trailer on the waterfront. He told me he wanted to install a hose bib at one corner of the house. Of course, I offered to do the dirty work and crawl underneath to cut the plastic pipe and glue in the new fittings. The next day, I injured my leg severely while goofing around with my brother-in-law on the ski boat. An x-ray revealed it was not broken, but it was severe enough to cause me to be on crutches and to keep me from being able to crawl under the house to do the repair.

A couple days later, I left with Susie to travel to San Francisco for her college roommate's wedding. My parents had plans to have good friends come visit that weekend. Dad told me not to worry and assured me he would take care of the plumbing with his friend Dave within a few days after my departure. Two days later, I got the call from my mother. I was sitting in a San Francisco church minutes before the bride was to walk down the aisle when someone came to me and said I had an important phone call I must take. I couldn't figure out how anyone knew where I was. *It must be some kind of mistake*, I thought.

My mother was on the other end. I could hear her crying, and I knew something terrible had happened. I knew it was going to be bad, but I had no idea how bad. She said, "Oh, Bob!" and she paused for what seamed like an eternity as she wept.

I said, "What, Mom? What happened?" And I immediately thought of our two young boys they were watching for us.

She said, "The kids are all right."

I remember saying, "Dad?"

She said, "We lost your father!"

And I said, "Oh, no, Mom...No! No!"

I've never wept so hard for so long in my life. All night I wept. And Susie could do nothing but feel my intense suffering and just hold me. The days that followed up until the funeral, I kept thinking I'd wake up from this nightmare. I didn't.

I can only imagine what my father's friend Dave went through when he pulled Dad's limp body out from under the house—his hand still fused to the metal cutters that were half imbedded into the plastic water pipe. Only the pipe didn't carry water. It carried deadly 220-volt electrical wiring, which had been installed in the wrong type of white PVC plastic piping, the kind normally used for water.

God spared me the terrible experience of having to pull Dad out. And, for some reason, God took my father in my place. It should have been my dad pulling me out. I would have switched places if I could; certainly death would have been desirable over my agony.

A few weeks after his funeral, Mom told me something I'll never forget. She was thankful that, between me and my dad, if one of us had to go, it was better it was him instead of me. She said, "I've never told anyone this, but, as much as he loved me, it didn't compare to how much he loved you. No one meant as much to your father as you did. He literally could not have gone on without you." It hurt me to think she really believed he loved me more. The point is, we had an extremely rare and special relationship—one of complete trust and loyalty and true love. It should have been me who died that day, not him.

Yes, anything my dad said to me sank in and stuck. "If you don't have friends you, don't have anything!" he told me once. As simple as that statement sounds and as good-mannered as my father was, and add to that the fact he rarely used hard language, it made it unforgettable to me because he said an expletive in place of the word "anything." I couldn't believe it when he said it. *Why did he cuss?* I thought for a moment, and then I realized why—because he wanted it to have life-lasting impact on me. And since he rarely cursed it had exactly that effect. I've never forgotten how important that concept is because for it to mean so much to my father meant it was a lesson I should cherish forever. And I have.

Friendship is more than someone to hang out with. It's more than someone to relate to about life's journey. It's about complete trust and loyalty and love. To want the very best for a friend without any form of jealousy is where it starts. And to know your friend feels the same for you makes the relationship genuine. This is the key, that both people honor the importance of putting the other's needs ahead of their own. Of course, this is also true in marriage. Marriage is certainly the highest form of friendship.

It is important people have friendships outside of their marriages. I'm referring to friendships of the same sex. We need a close bond with someone who can relate to our feelings, emotions, and experiences. Only someone of the same sex can fill that void completely. I cannot possibly relate to the pains my wife felt during childbirth. I cannot relate to the experiences of having a female body and all that it entails, and she could not for me. Therefore, we need close friends of the same sex to relate, to whom we can vent the frustrations of everyday life and console each other. Members of the opposite sex cannot and do not fill that role, and therefore they cannot fulfill the need.

Do not make the mistake of controlling your spouse to the point that he or she cannot find a close friend of the same sex. It will be detrimental to your relationship. And if you feel your spouse is closing off your ability to have that close friend, you must also insist on the genuine need to have one. It is not a putdown toward the spouse to need someone else. It is a normal, God-given condition that human beings require a relationship with someone of the same gender to be happy and have balance in life.

Having a close friendship with someone of the opposite sex when you are married is a different story. It should be the exception to the rule and should be entered into with extreme caution. The reason is simple. That close friend at some point will be your comfort at a time when your spouse and you are at odds with one another, and then an emotional bond at a deeper level will take place. This place is far too dangerous for most, if not all people, to handle properly. Once that emotional barrier is crossed, which will usually lead to the crossing of the sexual barrier, then they both experience having their needs met by an extremely close bond from a friend outside of marriage. And the worst part is the problem doesn't get solved, it just becomes more of a problem. Now, having used this other friend for an escape from reality, both are simply and temporarily covering the ugliness of the first problem with the ugliness of a second problem.

The temporary gain you feel is merely a narcotic that takes you away from your original problem with your spouse. But the problem remains, and now a secondary problem is growing right behind it. This secondary problem has the added complication of another's feelings, possibly the spouse, the issue of infidelity, the potential of marriages broken and kids and other family members involved, and the list goes on. Do not have a very close friend of the opposite sex if you are married. That is what your marriage partner is for. To play with that scenario against the greatest of odds will find you hurt and broken, and most likely other innocent family members will be harmed in your trail of destruction. I'm not speaking from personal experience, but I have seen it unfold as I've described in a close friendship of mine.

If you are single, then it is completely different. After all, a good marriage often starts as a good friendship.

Obviously, friendships come in many different flavors: your best friend, the friends you went to school with but rarely see anymore, and the good friends you stay in touch with but only a few times a year. Maybe your lives have taken you to different places or your kids are at different ages. Maybe some of your friends never had children while you did, and that has been a factor in your friendship. Many have a friend who is a generation ahead or behind them. I have such a friend. So does my wife.

I met Frank when I was in my late twenties. He was a cabinetmaker, and I hired him to work on one of my jobs. We had an immediate admiration for each other's accomplishments, and we worked together from then on. I've since moved about twenty miles away to another city, and we only talk about twice a year, but I value the input I receive from my friend's wisdom—especially because he's sixteen years my senior. But, mostly, because we are cut out of the same cloth. You know you're getting old when you say, "This new generation just doesn't get it. And I just don't understand them." Frank and I often say that.

Each of these different friendships is valuable in ways the others are not. They all have their special places in your life, and they all take on different forms, sharing your experiences while learning from theirs. Don't discount one friend over another. I often tell my friends they fulfill a need and a place in my heart no other friend can fill. This is the truth. Your closest friends will be the ones you can be yourself around. They are friends who allow you to be "all you," the real you, and that you feel totally comfortable being emotionally open with.

Realize all your different friendships have their place in your life to give you balance. Don't forsake friends you only see once in a blue moon. They have a valuable place in your heart and mind. And you for them. If it's been too long since you've talked, then look them up and make contact. It is like shining up an old heirloom and seeing its beauty all over again.

Be the best friend you can for your friends. That means when they call on you, you drop everything and go to them and help solve their problem. Whatever they need, you help them to the best of your ability. Usually it is words they need more than anything. But if they need more than words, you should be there to give it to them, unconditionally and with an open heart. They will do the same for you.

If a friend is not there for you when you really need him, then you'll find that out, and most likely you'll keep that in mind and proceed at a lower level of friendship. Friendship proves itself over time. There is no other way. Be a rock for your friends, steadfast, dependable, and loyal, and your friendships will prove to be your greatest form of wealth.

"A friend loves at all times."

PROVERBS 17:17

Chapter Ten

COMMUNICATION

*"Words—so innocent and powerless as they are, as standing in a dictionary,
how potent for good and evil they become,
in the hands of one who knows how to combine them."*

NATHANIEL HAWTHORNE

AS ORGANIZATION IS THE KEY to success in business, so communication is the key to success in relationships because it is the organizer of the mind. Good communication lets both parties know where they stand at all times. When the mind is organized in its relationships then one knows with certainty the right way to act with the right person at the right time. This is the formula for success in relationships, especially marriage.

Communication, through a myriad of actions—words, silence, facial expressions, emotions, and especially through the way we treat others—is the means by which we express our feelings. What could be more important than letting someone else know how we feel? And what could be more important than asking someone how they feel? At the end of the day, all we really care about is that someone we love understands us and cares about how we feel. We want to know someone else realizes what we are going through. This is why friendship with someone of the same sex is so important—it brings an understanding based on that aspect alone.

By far, my most relevant relationship problems in my past have always been connected to bad communication. Since it takes at least two for communication to exist, then you could say I am always at fault, at least to some degree. Even if someone else is failing to communicate to me properly, my perception of the situation is my responsibility. I need to ask questions like, "Is something bothering you? Is it something I said? Is it something I've done?" Maybe another relationship is the problem. Maybe it is a problem entirely unrelated to me. What matters is that I talk about it. What matters is that you talk about it. Communicate! You have to make your feelings known, and you have to discover the feelings of the one with whom you are communicating.

When I think about the times I've argued with my wife or my kids or a good friend, I can almost always recall one moment that, if I could return and rephrase my words or respond differently to their words, I am certain the whole argument would have been avoided. In fact, I could make a point of not letting the conflict start in the first place. If this is true, why not stop and think when you feel the contentious moment arise, and reword your initial response before you say it in the first place? Or, at least, why not say, "I'm sorry, I didn't put that the way I meant for it to come out. This is what I'm really trying to communicate to you." Or, in response to someone else's apparent attack, you could say, "I want to understand what you are telling me because I want to make things better." Usually such a sentence will catch your opponent off guard. It takes the fight out of them. Why would they go after someone who has just declared he is on their side? The desire for a mutually beneficial outcome for both is now a team working together toward a common goal—to understand each other's needs and to communicate back and forth how to satisfy those needs. This is essential to successful communication and to successful outcomes.

This all sounds easy, but it is not. The problem, which will work against this method of communication, is that more often than not we are in a moment of heated emotion. Or we are in a moment of need for instant gratification; we want someone to say, "You're right; I'm wrong." Instead of discussing the conflict or the goal with a calm voice, we are in a hurry to get it done our way. No discussion necessary. "Why should I have to explain everything to everyone? After all, I'm right!" Isn't that the attitude we take when we're impatient and want quick results? The problem is most of the time we *need* others in order to have harmony in our lives and to accomplish our goals. Knowing this, we must communicate calmly and effectively to them in order to achieve those goals. Also, we need to listen calmly and effectively. One without the other is a one-sided communication, which is not a meeting of the minds but a declaration of only one mind.

A most helpful tool in communicating is to repeat the intention or the goal, acknowledging an understanding back to the one who stated it. "You mean the reason you're usually late is because I'm usually late? Let me understand this. Normally you would be on time? But because you think I'm always running late and I keep you waiting, you tend to be late when you're meeting me because you don't want to stand and waste time waiting on me?" It would appear in this scenario that both people are contributing to the problem. It is a self-fulfilling prophecy one person started and the other person fed on, which then caused the first person to feed even more, and so on. They are communicating all sorts of things to each other by being late all the time, and it is being communicated through a lack of words, only by their actions. Not a good situation. I know this scenario to be true in many of our lives with people who, for whatever reason, can't be on time. And this scenario takes on many other forms. Maybe we're helping to drive the problem to the next level by not using words to communicate how the situation could be improved. It takes two to improve it. But usually we just put up with it or they put up with us, and nothing is ever said to each other. It becomes a never-ending cycle of actions that try but never really accomplish communicating true feelings.

Here's another one. You say to yourself, "That person is bothering me. Don't they know it bothers me when they do that?" Most times the person has no idea the little thing they do bothers you. They don't realize they're being noisy when you're trying to concentrate. They don't know you're used to the toilet paper coming off the top of the roll or the toothpaste tube squeezed from the bottom. Recently, I was sitting in a McDonald's reading my newspaper during lunch. I had ordered a coffee, which I rarely drink because I get too wired. I was involved in my own little world, thinking about the article I was reading, when the voice behind me pulled me back to reality. "Sir, you're shaking the whole booth!"

I was embarrassed. I had been shaking my leg up and down rapidly on the pad of my foot like a nervous person, and I didn't even realize it. He thought we were having an earthquake, and I was completely unaware of my actions. I quickly responded, "I'm so sorry—I think I've had too much coffee." We both laughed. But I had no idea I'd been bugging someone else.

It wasn't long after that when I was sitting in another fast-food booth reading my paper, and this time someone else was doing the nervous shake. It started to bother me, and then I caught myself thinking, *That was me just a few weeks ago bugging someone else. Let it go and just laugh about it.* So it did. I didn't even tell the guy he was bothering me because once I realized how trivial it was, not to mention the fact I was recently guilty of the same thing, all of a sudden it didn't bother me anymore. In fact, I got a kick out of it. This certainly ties into our perspective on things.

Conflicts usually start when one person thinks another person doesn't have his best interest at heart. It is hard for someone to communicate good feelings to another person when concerned only about his own well being. Most people aren't stupid. At least, they're not stupid when it comes to sizing up if they are in danger. And being in danger includes sensing that someone else doesn't have your best interest in mind. In other words, people who are only looking after their own interests are much more likely to hurt those around them, either emotionally or physically. And most people are aware of that type of person because they've been hurt by someone like that. Getting hurt in life is one of the best ways for one's mind to memorize a situation and its outcome. God made us this way. Our memories are quite remarkable when it comes to protecting ourselves. How many times do you need to be reminded fire is hot? Or that a self-absorbed person will leave you in their path of destruction.

Now, how does this tie into communication? Simply that one has to care about another's best interest in order for his actions and words to genuinely communicate to the other person. The receiver of the words will not be listening properly if he suspects the sender is not sincere. By properly, I mean he will not listen with the intention of communicating back with honesty and openness. He is, in effect, protecting himself. And this feeds back and forth between both parties.

The opposite is also true, and obviously much more desirable, because now the element of trust starts to strengthen as the conversations and actions between the parties continue—to the point of reaching mutually beneficial agreements. Partnerships and marriages can both be properly formed. This doesn't mean they will all be successful, but it drives home the fact that the trust developed over time is built on proper communication—a communication with each other's best interest at heart.

This is crucial. Again, we're focusing on others. We're talking about treating other people like we want to be treated. And we're looking at effective communication, where we're always thinking about how the other person will benefit from our intentions. If both parties conduct their communication in this manner then the outcome will be successful. Sometimes that outcome can be the mutual agreement to terminate part of the relationship—a part that is damaging the whole relationship. This can be the right decision for both parties, and it is only realized through honest communication. Ending part of a relationship may be necessary to preserve the overall relationship. If one party is not comfortable with even a small thing, then that should be communicated in a positive manner. Otherwise the small thing will grow into a large one.

Here's an example: You could say, "I value our relationship so much that I feel if I don't tell you about this one thing that bothers me it will keep our friendship from being what I want it to be. I think I should stop coming to our weekly social meeting because all we do is gossip. Half the time we're gossiping about friends who are important to me, and I don't want to continue talking behind their backs. It's not right, and it makes me very uncomfortable. I hope you understand." By cutting off the bad element, you can maintain the good with this friend. How could your friend not be receptive when you put it like that? Then expand on it and solve the problem with them. Maybe the solution will be the termination, but it will be done with an honest and open and loving intention, and a joint decision.

Remember, good communication has the goal of a mutual benefit to both parties. Even if you're the only one who sees it this way, it is almost always successful communication because you can usually control the direction. When both parties see communication in this way, it will definitely be successful communication.

Remember, sometimes silence is necessary in communication because it means you're listening. T.S. Eliot puts it perfectly:

> *"Where shall the word be found, where will the word*
> *Resound? Not here, there is not enough silence."*

PART II

ABOUT GOD

Chapter Eleven

BE STILL—
REGARDING GOD'S NATURE

"For where two or three have gathered together in My name,
I am there in their midst."

MATTHEW 18:20

DOES GOD HAVE TO "BE STILL" to get in touch with you? Yes, He does. What I mean is that when you're communicating with Him, He's all yours. And you should be all His—like there's no one else in the world. Of course, this is not easy for you and I to do, and we'll get to that in a minute. But for God, there is no distraction. I know this seems impossible, but God is capable of multi-tasking His entire creation simultaneously. Humans can't understand it. When you are "still" with Him, He is "still" with you. He's not too busy for you. He doesn't say, "I'm occupied with more important things." He can handle an infinite amount of things at the same time and give each His full attention as if it were the only one. When you're one-on-one with God, there isn't anything more important to Him than you. His whole plan is integrated into every atom of the universe being at the right place at the right time to accomplish His will. And yet there is "free will" in the equation. He simply knows what is going to happen.

You may say, "If God knows what will happen then how can we have free will?" Here's how. God exists in Heaven, in a different environment than we do. It doesn't have the same restrictions we have here on earth. He is living in the past, present, and future at the same time. Why should this seem odd when He created all of them in the first place? Does this mean that God can't be surprised because He knows the future? No, He loves surprises, especially when we make the right choices because we have the free will not to. But if He exists in all time frames then He knows what is going to happen, right? He can know if He wants, and He can separate Himself from His own power, just as He did on the cross.

To be able to let man know He can relate to us, He had to separate Himself from Himself and become just like us. And He cried out to Himself saying,

"My God, why have You forsaken me?" right before He let Himself die. We have to stop putting restrictions on what God can and can't do. He can do anything with any of it, at any time. Let's stop trying to figure out things we cannot possibly ever know or understand and let Him rule. Yes, it's fun to think about it and summarize our own little theories, but let's not get sidetracked debating theory. Allow God to be God. Do you want to know about the God who created you? The Bible has some pretty clear descriptions of our God and His nature.

First, what does He look like? Genesis clearly says we were made in His image so He must look somewhat like man does, or, I should say, we look like Him. But God is spirit also. He obviously doesn't need eyes to see and hands to get His tasks done. But, in the physical sense, when He wants to take it on, He looks somewhat like we do, otherwise Genesis would not have said so. But His spirit and His will for the universe and for man is what God's essence is all about, not His appearance. This is clear because countless times in the Bible God talks about the heart of man being what gets His attention, not looks or accomplishments. And He also clearly tells us we cannot get to heaven by our works, but only through faith.

> *"For by grace you have been saved through faith;*
> *and that not of yourselves, it is the gift of God;*
> *not as a result of works, so that no one may boast."*

EPHESIANS 2:8–9

I don't believe God is impressed with His own looks or accomplishments either. The sun and the stars and the planets and all that is in the universe are impressive, but not nearly as much as the choices of His creatures, to whom He has given free will. Why should this be difficult to believe? Look at us—we admire our homes and our cars and our bank accounts, but rarely does a man or woman get as much joy out of those things as they do when they raise a good child and see that child spread goodness to others. Watching one's child grow up happy is much higher on the satisfaction scale because it depends on that child's choices and not only ours. It is the same for God.

Let's discuss the nature of the one and only God, who created you and me and everything in the universe. What does He want? What's on His divine mind? What does He expect from you and from me? And how can we have confidence in knowing it is the truth?

First, we must know God responds to how sincere we are in relating to Him and how willing we are to give all of ourselves over to Him when we're talking to Him. If we merely say, "God bless this and God bless that" and quickly move on, I think He gives equal weight in listening and answering. If we stop and be still and clear our minds only for Him, then He will give us that much more attention. It is not that He doesn't want to give us more, but He won't because our relationship with Him depends on our effort not His.

As I write this, I am forty-seven years old, and I recently realized something about myself. I always seem to get nervous when I say a prayer before dinner in front of a large group on holidays or big events. For so long I couldn't figure out why I would go into this zone where something had control over me. My voice would quiver and I would be very uncomfortable. It occurred again two weeks ago at Thanksgiving dinner. I finally realized what was happening and how to solve the problem. I feel stupid it took so long to figure out, but I'm so relieved by the solution. Now that I know how to solve the problem I've realized I don't want to solve it. I realize I become very emotional when I'm talking to God. I can't help it. I'm just not capable of going through the motions with Him without it coming from my heart. If I'm talking to Him, I mean it. When others are in the room, I still mean it. There is no falseness with me and Him. I don't talk to Him seriously when I'm alone and then fake it to sound good when I'm not. So, my solution for being able to sound smooth during my holiday blessings is to fake it, to go through the motions and say the right words but not to feel them, lest I become emotionally involved. Guess what? I'm not going to do that! Now, at least I can be proud of my nervousness. Who knows? Maybe I won't be nervous anymore since I understand it and choose to accept it.

All too often we talk to God, but we don't really *feel* it. We mean it with our minds, but we don't feel it in our hearts at the moment. How would you like it if a loved one, when expressing love for you, meant it but didn't really *feel* it? I'm guilty of this. I frequently tell my wife I love her, but rarely do I stop and feel it first and then say it. What a difference. Pause and experience the love first. Then express it. This makes a difference to God also.

The quote at the beginning of this chapter is significant: "For where two or three have gathered together in My name, there I am in their midst." It doesn't say if only one is gathered in His name He is not there. And we know that is not true. Many of the great biblical figures have had their most heartfelt and divine interventions when they spent time one-on-one with God. But what He is saying is that He wants to have a relationship with us. If we get together to honor Him, to worship Him, and to learn more about Him and, most importantly, to talk to Him, then He is right there in our midst, listening, answering, and honoring us.

We need to communicate to God with meaning—from our hearts and not just our minds. We do mundane tasks every day that we don't have to think about. We brush our teeth, we drive to work, we eat while we read our papers, or while we talk to friends, and we go through the motions of everyday life. God does not want us to go through the motions with Him. That is not His nature. His nature is that He wants to have all of us when we are spending time with Him. Let's not insult Him by multitasking while spending time with Him.

Did you know God wants only one thing? That's right. He wants to have a relationship with you. He's not concerned with all the earthly things that are going to pass away. You want to know His nature? Here it is. His relationship with you is all that matters to Him. He doesn't care about how good or bad you look or what car you drive or how rich or poor you become. Material things are just molecules in pleasant forms to our eyes, but they all look exactly the same to Him. God sees beauty in living things, especially people. We are the ones who try to make beauty out of mixing elements and creating compounds that we call jewelry and glass and steel, and even in natural things such as gemstones. They are merely molecules of different mixes.

God created all the atoms that make up all these molecules and elements. A beautiful bronze statue is just the two elements of copper and tin molded together into a pleasant-looking shape. Gold and lead are only three steps from each other on the periodic table. Do you think God sees one being more impressive then the other? We certainly do. I haven't seen a lead wedding ring yet. And mercury is right next to gold on the periodic table. One makes you look good, and the other will kill you. God doesn't see value in stuff. It's all the same to Him. The truth is, people are just the opposite. They see what's on the outside and say, "Wow that's impressive. I want to be with that person. He looks good. He dresses well. He drives a nice car and lives in a nice-looking home." We miss what's on the inside of people because we're looking at the outside.

Why do you think "sex" sells so well to men? Because they were created to feel with their eyes. If something looks good, men want it, now. Our society is half-built on this concept—how to get us to buy on impulse. It works. God made man that way. He also gave us enough brains to know it won't make us happy. And many women take advantage of that weakness in men. Many men also take advantage of how women are made by falsely appealing to women's emotions. He can attract her merely by mixing the right words in the right way. But this also is external when it is not genuine. Where is the substance when either sex takes advantage of the other's nature? God doesn't view the exterior as we do. He cares about what's inside. The heart is what God looks at. And, yes, most of man's choices about how he shows his "outside" reveal the true nature about what's inside. I'm talking about women too.

God also understands we are driven to better ourselves and our comfort levels in life because that is how He designed us. In fact, He made us this way on purpose so we would be distracted. If that sounds odd, it shouldn't. Free will only has meaning if it has sacrifice attached to it. By being creatures who want more and more of the beautiful molecules surrounding us and by knowing God doesn't see value in these things, it becomes clear the only things He does value are those whom He has given the freedom to choose. Everything else in the universe is secondary to the beings God gifted with free will. This is quite an eye-opening revelation.

More importantly, what ultimately pleases God is when we embrace the wisdom and understanding that our comforts and ambition need to be properly balanced with a meaningful relationship with Him, along with our commitment to keep that relationship our top priority. God wants to be at the head of everything in life. Ahead of our ambitions, ahead of our stuff, and even ahead of our loved ones. When we use our free will to make a decision for Him, while sacrificing something of value to us, then we are not letting the distractions around us become our main focus—and nothing pleases Him more. It wouldn't have the same value to Him if we didn't have the distractions. Look at it this way, how special would you feel about your spouse's decision to marry you and have you as a lifelong companion if there were no other choices? No other distractions or opportunities adding costs to the decision? Not as appealing, right? The fact that you were chosen over many others gives the value to it.

Such was God's test for Abraham in Genesis 22, when He asked him to offer his son as a sacrifice. This would show where God stood in Abraham's sight. God was, in essence, saying, "Who holds first place, Abraham—Me or the son you love more than anything else?" Oh, that God would find so much favor in us that He would put us to the test. Yet, it's good we haven't been, at least not to that level. Would we pass?

This is the nature of our incredible God. Why would anyone create anything without the intention of spending time with his creations? No one would. And God didn't.

God desires, above all else, to have a relationship with us and for us to be obedient to Him. The way we show our obedience is through our faith. The last biblical quote in this book, Hebrews 11:1, defines faith as "the assurance of things hoped for, the conviction of things not seen." The key words are "hoped for" and "not seen." God knows the value of our relationship with Him lies in our faith, in what we cannot see or touch. That is its great value. To show Himself to us is to take away our faith, and with it, the value of believing and hoping for what we cannot see. I've heard many people who are not believers say, "You are hoping for an awful lot based on something you'll never be able to know for sure." That is the point. That is the way He designed it. That is the only way it has great value. Parents don't give a child something they know is bad for him. And they don't take away something they know is good. Neither will God. He's not going to take away from the value of our faith by showing Himself in full form. But He does show Himself in other ways.

I must include a few things that are the most important to God regarding our nature. First, let's talk about the things God hates most about His creations. I'll save the worst for last, but one thing God abhors is fear. The word fear is found 366 times in the Bible, and for a good reason—because He hates it when we act out of fear. Fear is a lack of faith. It proves we are relying on ourselves, and we already know how often we fail. When we have true faith in God, we are not living in fear but in confidence, and that's how He wants us to live every minute of our lives.

Worse than fear is hypocrisy. When we say one thing and do another, we are liars and cheaters. We are taking His precious code and throwing it out the window. We expect people to act a certain way, and yet we do not live up to our own standard. If you think God hates this sin, then brace yourself because rebellion is even higher on His list. He is not angered by sin as much as by rebellion because He expects sin. He knows He cannot have a relationship with someone who doesn't need Him. Rebellious people don't need God, or don't think they do. They believe they aren't doing anything wrong when, in fact, they are.

God cannot have a relationship with someone who doesn't see himself as he really is, someone who thinks he can handle life on his own. What does God do then? He lets the individual handle it on his own—sometimes for a little while, sometimes forever. Another form of rebellion is the person who does believe in God and who does have a relationship with Him but keeps putting Him off. I'm ashamed to admit this was me for many years. I kept saying, "I'll get to You, God, but I need to make a lot of money first. I need to be successful first. I need to have the big home and the nice cars first. Then I'll get around to doing good things for You." I'll tell you what God thinks of this. He says, "I may have other things to tend to when you finally get around to giving Me your time. I'll probably be giving My attention to those who put Me first instead of last on their list." Our choice not to choose God first causes Him to treat us in like manner.

Lastly, the thing God hates most, which is usually the root cause of all the other problems, is pride. The Bible is clear on this. Pride is the number one trait God despises in His creatures. Here is why: Most of the sins of man are known by man to be wrong. But when we act from pride and speak with hypocrisy, we often don't think we're doing anything wrong.

"Pride goes before destruction,
And a haughty spirit before stumbling."

PROVERBS 16:18

We can all remember being put in our places when we were full of pride. God does not let us get away with it. Don't test Him on it. You'll lose big time. When we think too highly of ourselves He will surely allow us to be knocked down, and deservedly so.

Now on to the brighter side—the things that God loves in His creations. The most important are these four: obedience, justice, mercy, and faith. He wants us all to show our obedience to Him by our relationship with Him and our trust in Him. He wants us to show justice in our dealings with others, treating each other as we want to be treated. He wants us to show mercy and to listen to that inner voice of His telling us when to give a helping hand to someone in need. And, most important, He wants us to show our faith in Him and set aside our pride in doing so. These are not easy things to practice, but they are shining virtues that will make Him smile on us. But all the great virtues are proven through the last one—faith. Faith is proven with more than just words. It is proven in our actions when we replace our fears with the peace of God's Word. Also when we replace our stress with the comfort of God's Word. And when we replace our worry with the assurance of God's Word.

Faith is so powerful because it is on the opposite side of pride. Pride is all about us. Faith is all about God. Pride is all about how great we are. Faith is all about how great God is. And faith is essential in pleasing God, so much so it is impossible to please Him without it.

> *"And without faith it is impossible to please Him,*
> *for he who comes to God must believe that He is*
> *and that He is a rewarder of those who seek Him."*

HEBREWS 11:6

Chapter Twelve

RELIGIONS AND THEIR DIFFERENCES

"Everything has its beauty but not everyone sees it."

CONFUCIUS

THE GREATEST OF CONCEPTS and philosophies known to man are greatly diminished if they cannot be communicated properly and effectively to the rest of the world. This is especially true in our present time. Technology has made our world much smaller. Countries are now much closer to each other's pulses. We are able to communicate instantly, swiftly exchanging commerce with each other, assuming certain governments allow it. We know immediately when things happen around the world. We can come to each other's aid much quicker. We can also quickly learn of another country's transgressions. When we decide to act, the world sees our decisions and motives, and they make their judgments, solidifying our reputation. We do the same thing to others, sometimes without fully understanding them.

Understanding the various philosophies of life others embrace is essential. At the time of this writing, America is at war in Iraq. Our understandings and misunderstandings of each other's cultures and religions influence the fate of our future and well-being.

Therefore, it is the purpose of this chapter to summarize the most common religions, that is, those that include the highest percentage of the human population. Did you know there are over 4,000 religions in the world? Most likely, there are many unknown ones also. If an in-depth understanding is desired, I suggest the reader research a particular religion. This overview is intended to show the "big picture"—what the majority of people are thinking and acting on in regard to their beliefs, customs, and eternal expectations. In an effort to remain unbiased, these are presented in alphabetical order.

Buddhism: One of the three most prominent religions of China, its followers today number between 350 million and 500 million people. Buddhism was founded in India around 500 B.C. by Siddhartha Gautama, who was called Buddha, meaning "enlightened one." Buddhists believe there have been many Buddhas in the past, Jesus Christ included, and there will be more in the future. The goal of Buddhism is to achieve Nirvana (the absolute truth—the universal soul) by means of being released from karma (cause and effect, the positive and negative in the world's past and future). Buddhists live trying to avoid self-indulgence while focusing on moderation.

Buddha, living five centuries before Christ, was said to have spoken words very similar to the Golden Rule as a way to treat others while seeking Nirvana. He taught Four Noble Truths that describe their philosophy:

1. Suffering is everywhere.
2. Suffering is caused by craving.
3. Nirvana is the end of suffering.
4. The right conduct can lead you out of suffering.

> "The gift of truth excels all other gifts."
>
> BUDDHA

Christianity: Since I am Christian and this chapter is intended to be objectively informative, I will keep the summary brief in hopes the remainder of the book has already sufficed in a further understanding of Christianity.

Christianity is based on the life of Jesus Christ and His teachings. It has over two billion adherents in the world, with Roman Catholicism comprising about 1.1 billion. Protestants total about 350 million and Eastern Orthodoxy a little over 200 million. The remaining 350 million included in this diverse group are divided among such denominations as Anglican (80 million), Mormon (10 million), Baptist, Methodist, Lutheran, Presbyterian, Mennonite, Amish, Adventist, Deists, Jehovah's Witnesses, and more. Some of these denounce others as not being biblical or not interpreting the Bible properly. Some of them also have their own books written by their founders.

The name Christian began as a mocking term for followers of Jesus, the Messiah, who was crucified by Roman authorities early in the first century. You could say that the first Christians were actually Jews who believed in Jesus; whereas Judaism does not rely on Jesus as a means to get to heaven, Christianity does. The majority of Christians believe that God's Son, Jesus Christ, is the only way to eternal life. Jesus was God incarnate and came to earth in the form of a man. At age thirty, He began His public ministry, teaching and healing and working miracles. The four Gospels in the New Testament of the Bible tell His life story. Christians believe the death of Jesus was the payment for all of mankind's sins. His rising from the dead three days later represents His living presence, and He is now seated at the right hand of the Father in heaven. Most Christians believe in God the Father, Jesus the Son, and the Holy Spirit as three Persons in one God, called the Trinity; that heaven cannot be earned; and that God gives the free gift of eternal life only through faith in Jesus.

Since Roman Catholics outnumber all other Christian groups combined, a brief outline of Catholicism seems appropriate. Catholicism is built upon a church hierarchy, where Jesus is the invisible head giving authority to the pope, who acts as the visible head of the church. Under the pope are cardinals, bishops, and priests. There are over one hundred cardinals, chosen by the pope to govern over the bishops, each of whom presides over a group of parishes in a particular region called a diocese. Dioceses have numerous churches, each having at least one assigned priest. The priests conduct the church service, called Mass, and administer sacraments such as baptism, confession, communion, and matrimony. Catholics also reverence Jesus' mother, the Blessed Virgin Mary, and honor the saints, those recognized for their godly lives.

"I am the way, and the truth, and the life;
no one comes to the Father but through Me"

JOHN 14:6

Confucianism Confucius was born in China in 551 B.C. during a time of political violence. He married at nineteen and had two children. He developed ideas about education, society, and government, and worked to better the human condition through his teachings. His philosophies were well received as a means of social restoration. Confucius considered himself to be a transmitter, drawing from the wisdom of the past. Poetry, history, and literature were at the core of his teachings, and his most valued principle was the importance of a child's devotion and obedience toward his or her parents. He believed the purpose of sex was only to conceive children, with boys being the primary goal of conception. His sayings are widely known and intended to provide wisdom for human conduct. This moral code is based primarily on five things: courtesy, good faith, diligence, tolerance, and kindness. Confucianism, pervasive in Asia, influences the beliefs of about 1.5 billion people.

"Men's natures are alike, it is their habits that carry them far apart."

Confucius

Hinduism: With more than 900 million adherents (some estimate the world's third largest religion has over one billion) and eighty to ninety percent of them living in the country of India, Hindus worship neither a single prophet nor one God. The religion has no known founder, lacks an authority, and has no formal organization. Hinduism regards other forms of religion as merely inadequate but not wrong. Therefore, it could be said that Hinduism is an acceptance of all forms of belief and worship. Hindus do believe in higher beings and their ability to act out scenarios in human bodily form in order to teach humans. Well-known names such as Krishna and Rama are higher beings known as Avatars. Hindus believe all actions produce an effect in the future. They also believe in reincarnation, that people are reborn over and over again into suffering, and previous acts are factors in determining one's condition in the cycle. Sometimes Hindus use the Buddhist term Nirvana to describe their place of eternal peace, which comes only through the breaking of the reincarnation cycle. It is believed by Hindus that the desire for worldly possessions is a key factor in preventing the soul's migration into eternal peace. When a Hindu becomes one with "being," the cycle of reincarnation is broken and eternal peace is found. It is their belief that any human attempt to define Hinduism will prove unsatisfactory.

"May good thoughts come to us from all sides."

Hindu prayer

Islam: With close to 1.5 billion adherents, mainly in the Middle East, Islam was founded by Muhammad, who was born in Mecca in A.D. 570. A monotheistic religion, based on one God (Allah), its basic foundation was said to have been revealed by the angel Gabriel, who appeared to Muhammad when he was forty. Muhammad began preaching and founded a state and a religion. By 634, the entire Arabian peninsula was under Muslim control. In the twentieth century, the separation of religion and government began.

Muslims practice the five pillars of Islam:

1. Profession of faith—"There is no God but Allah, and Muhammad is his prophet."
2. Prayer—Muslims are to pray five times a day facing the city of Mecca.
3. The *Zakat*—each Muslim must pay this obligatory tax once a year.
4. Fasting—practiced the ninth month of the year (called Ramadan) starting each day at sunrise and lasting until sunset—no eating, drinking, smoking, or sexual relations.
5. Hajj—the commitment to make a journey during one's lifetime to the city of Mecca.

The Muslim's overall purpose is to worship the one and only God and to live a moral lifestyle. Their sacred text is the Quran (Koran).

"O God, grant me to love Thee and to love those who love Thee,
And whatsoever brings me nearer to Thy love,
And make Thy love more precious to me than cold water to the thirsty."

MOHAMMAD

Jainism: Although there are other religions with more adherents, Jainism dates back over 2,500 years. Its estimated 4.5 million followers live by the creed of nonviolence. A religion of India, founded by Mahavira, it closely resembles Hinduism and Buddhism—where karma and successive lives help to determine future lives. Jainists describe karma as a substance that binds the soul to the physical world. One gets freedom or salvation from burning the karma accumulated in past lives. Mahavira's five ways to accomplish this are:

1. Nonviolence—to cause no harm to living beings.
2. Truth—to always speak the truth in a harmless manner.
3. Non-stealing—to not take anything that is not willingly given.
4. Celibacy—to not indulge in sensual pleasures.
5. Non-possession—to detach from people, places, and material things.

Jainism gets its teaching from twenty-four historical persona and sixty-four gods, or "great souls" as they are called. Jainists believe the "universe of being" is made up of two everlasting, coexisting, and independent realities—*jiva* and *ajiva*. One is the enjoyer, and the other enjoyed. Jiva has consciousness and ajiva does not, although ajiva can be seen, tasted, smelled, and touched. The animate beings are composed of soul and body, the soul being eternal. Around A.D. 300 Jainism split off into a group that declared complete nudity was necessary to detach oneself from material temptations. Although its numbers don't reflect the interest of Buddhism or Hinduism, the Jains have had a major influence on the arts, astrology, philosophy, mathematics, and even architecture. Again, the Golden Rule seems to apply here, especially since the main theme of the religion is nonviolence.

> *"There is nothing to help the Soul but the Soul itself."*
>
> MAHAVIRA

Juche: With about 19 million adherents, this religion was modeled after Christianity by North Korea's dictator Kim Il-sung. He took Christianity, removed God the Father, Jesus the Son, and the Holy Spirit, and replaced them with himself, his wife, and his son as the new trinity. Juche teaches "man is the master of everything and decides everything," and is the official ideology of North Korea.

> *"The oppressed peoples can liberate themselves only through struggle. This is a simple and clear truth confirmed by history."*
>
> KIM IL-SUNG

Judaism: With about 14 million adherents, Judaism was one of the first recorded monotheistic faiths and the basis for other religions that would follow, primarily Christianity and Islam. Abraham is considered the father of the Jewish people. His children were to inherit the land of Israel. They eventually became enslaved in Egypt and were led to freedom by Moses, who gave the people God's teachings in writings known as the Torah, the first five books of the Bible. Hebrew writings also include the *Nevi'im*, comprised of thirty-four books. Twenty-two of these books are about the former prophets, with the remaining twelve books about the latter prophets.

The Jewish community centers around the synagogue, where services are held each Sabbath, which starts at dusk on Friday and ends at dusk on Saturday. Food is not allowed to be cooked on the Sabbath, so any food preparation must be done before Friday evening. A ceremony called *Havdalah* marks the ending of the Sabbath. The purpose of the synagogue is threefold: a place for worship, assembly, and study. The rabbi, a teacher educated in *halakhah* (Jewish law), is the local leader. Each synagogue has an ark, a type of alcove that faces Jerusalem, which contains the scrolls of the Torah (Jewish Bible). Every adult male is expected, at some time, to take a turn at reading aloud from the Torah. A ceremony called a Bar Mitzvah celebrates the male becoming an adult in religious terms, at age thirteen, thus taking responsibility for himself to be obedient to the law. Jewish men often wear yarmulkes, small round caps on their heads, as symbols of their submission to God.

There are five major Jewish celebrations during the year.

1. Rosh Hashanah—the day of judgment, also known as the Jewish New Year, lasts ten days and is a period of self examination and penitence.
2. Yom Kippur—the Day of Atonement that concludes Rosh Hashanah, where Jews seek forgiveness while repenting from their sins. They abstain from sexual relations, food, and drink from sunup to sundown.
3. Pesach or Passover is a week-long festival celebrating the deliverance of the Israelites from Egypt.
4. Shavuot, celebrated seven weeks after Passover, represents God's giving His laws to Moses on Mount Sinai.
5. Sukkot celebrates the end of harvest season and lasts one week, primarily focusing on meditation.

"I will insist the Hebrews have contributed more to civilize men than any other nation. If I was an atheist and believed in blind eternal fate, I should still believe that fate had ordained the Jews to be the most essential instrument for civilizing the nations. They are the most glorious nation that ever inhabited this earth. The Romans and their empire were but a bubble in comparison to the Jews. They have given religion to three quarters of the globe and have influenced the affairs of mankind more and more happily than any other nation, ancient or modern."

PRESIDENT JOHN ADAMS
(FROM A LETTER TO F.A. VAN DER KEMP, FEBRUARY 16, 1808)

Scientology: Scientology came about from a best-selling book called *Dianetics: The Modern Science of Mental Health*. Its creator and author, L. Ron Hubbard, received formal establishment of the religion in 1954 against much resistance from government, which, at the time, thought it merely a means to escape taxes for Hubbard.

According to its official Web site, Scientology means "the Study of Truth." It deals with handling the spirit in relationship to itself, others, and all of life. Scientology comprises a body of knowledge extending from its fundamental truths. Prime among these are: Man is an immortal, spiritual being. His experience extends well beyond a single lifetime. His capabilities are unlimited, even if not presently realized—and those capabilities can be realized. He is able to not only solve his own problems, accomplish his goals, and gain lasting happiness, but also achieve new, higher states of awareness and ability.

In Scientology no one is asked to accept anything as belief or on faith. That which is true for you is what you have observed to be true. An individual discovers for himself that Scientology works by personally applying its principles and observing or experiencing results. Scientologists believe man is basically good, and his experiences, not his nature, have led him to commit evil deeds. Often, he mistakenly seeks to solve his problems by considering only his own interests, causing trouble for both himself and others.

"If things were a little better known and understood, we would all live happier lives."

L. RON HUBBARD

Sikhism: Ranked as the fifth largest organized religion in the world, Sikhism rests its faith in a universal god known as Waheguru. Most of the 23 million adherents live in Punjab in the country of India. In the fifteenth century, Guru Nanak Dev, the first of ten Sikh gurus, said that God must be seen from "the inward eye" or the heart of a human being. Sikhs must carry out three duties: Pray, Work, and Give. Nanak taught that there was not a final destination of heaven or hell, but rather a spiritual union with God that leads to salvation. The religion practices the avoidance of what they call the five vices: pride, anger, attachment, lust, and greed.

"There is but One God, His name is Truth, He is the Creator,
He fears none, He is without hate, He never dies,

He is beyond the cycle of births and death, He is self-illuminated,
He is realized by the kindness of the True Guru.
He was True in the beginning,
He was True when the ages commenced and has ever been True,
He is also True now."

GURU NANAK DEV

Taoism: Taoism (or Daoism) is the last of the three most prominent Chinese religions. It was founded in 550 B.C. by Lao-Tze and regarded as the state religion in 440 B.C. Taoists' ultimate reality is called the "Way" or "Path." To be in harmony and at peace with nature is Tao. That all things are combined to be "One" through a connecting force of life is Tao. Tao is the description of an interconnected universe, a harmony of everything in existence, and an acceptance of its believers, and that it remain beyond human comprehension and description. The opposing yet complementary forces of *yin* and *yang* are central to Taoism.

"There is a thing. Formless yet complete. Before heaven and earth it existed.
Without sound, without substance, it stands alone and unchanging.
It is all-pervading and unfailing. We do not know its name, but we call it Tao.
Being one with the universe the sage is in accord with the Tao."

LAO-TZE

Atheism: In all fairness, even though atheism is not generally considered a religion, it is the belief and practice of a philosophy based on non-religion. Many people who claim to be atheists started out, like so many religious people, as agnostic—doubting the existence of a higher being.

Atheists believe people should be "freethinkers." A freethinker is one who is prepared to consider any possibility and who determines which ideas are right or wrong by bringing reason to bear, according to a consistent set of rules such as the scientific method. Some atheists adhere to the philosophy of secular humanism (described in the next section).

Many atheists go beyond a mere absence of belief in God; they actively believe that particular gods, or all gods, do not exist. Lacking belief in a God is often referred to as the "weak atheist" position; whereas believing that gods do not (or cannot) exist is known as "strong atheism."

Most atheists think the idea of God as presented by the major religions is essentially self-contradictory and that it is logically impossible such a God could exist. Others are atheists through skepticism, because they see no evidence that God exists. For some, it is simply the most comfortable, common-sense position to take. Here's how one atheist puts it:

> *"I contend we are both atheists, I just believe in one fewer god than you do.*
> *When you understand why you dismiss all the other possible gods,*
> *you will understand why I dismiss yours."*

STEPHEN ROBERTS

Secular Humanism: Humanists feel their philosophy is a joyous alternative to religions that believe in a supernatural god and life in a hereafter. Humanists believe this is the only life of which we have certain knowledge and we owe it to ourselves and others to make it the best life possible for ourselves and all with whom we share this fragile planet. They claim when people are free to think for themselves, using reason and knowledge as their tools, they are best able to solve this world's problems. Humanism holds an appreciation for art, literature, music, and crafts, which are our heritage from the past, and of the creativity that, if nourished, can continuously enrich our lives. Humanism is, in sum, a philosophy of those in love with life. Humanists take responsibility for their own lives and relish the adventure of being part of new discoveries, seeking new knowledge, exploring new options. Instead of finding solace in prefabricated answers to the great questions of life, humanists enjoy the open-ended quest and freedom of discovery this entails.

Humanists affirm that humans have the freedom to give meaning, value, and purpose to their lives by their own independent thought, free inquiry, and responsible creative activity. Humanists affirm this natural world as being wondrous and precious while offering limitless opportunities for exploration, fascination, creativity, companionship, and joy.

Someone I know who considers himself a humanist has listed the five major personal philosophies that influence how he behaves and thinks. In order, they are:

1.   Do onto others as you would have them do onto you.
2.   A huge sense of fairness.
3.   Sustainability in systems and processes.

4. A strong desire to minimize waste.
5. Maximization of happiness.

He said, "Although the above principles are not specific to humanism, one or more of them influence my decisions every day of my life."

When I became convinced that the universe is natural—that all the ghosts and gods are myths, there entered into my brain, into my soul, into every drop of my blood the sense, the feeling, the joy of freedom. The walls of my prison crumbled and fell. The dungeon was flooded with light and all the bolts and bars and manacles became dust. I was no longer a servant, a serf, or a slave. There was for me no master in all the world—not even infinite space. I was free—free to think, to express my thoughts—free to live my own ideal—free to live for myself and those I loved—free to use all my faculties, all my senses, free to spread imagination's wings—free to investigate, to guess and dream and hope—free to judge and determine for myself…I was free. I stood erect and fearlessly, joyously faced all worlds.

ROBERT INGERSOLL

Chapter Thirteen

EXPERIMENT #1—
A VIEW FROM THE OTHER SIDE

"You shall not put the Lord your God to the test."

DEUTERONOMY 6:16

THE DAY IS JANUARY 4, 2004. I would like to conduct an experiment between a declared Christian and a declared atheist. I want both people to keep open minds and to learn from the experience. I really only have one friend whom I know to be a true atheist. Dave and I met when I was ten years old. He is definitely the smartest guy I know, and I know some really smart people. Dave graduated from high school with a 4.0. He currently works in the defense industry for the Navy with classified weapons. He was a math/computer science major, and his IQ is off the charts. I've seen Dave solve incredibly hard problems using computers for which he himself wrote the programs. The guy's a genius. I will be the declared Christian, and Dave will be the declared atheist.

Susie and I had eighteen beautiful bridesmaids and groomsmen supporting us at the altar when we were married on Valentine's Day in 1987. Dave was one of my nine groomsmen. I was honored to give the toast at Dave's wedding. We have always had the utmost respect for one another, even though we have had opposing viewpoints in most areas of our lives involving politics and religion. He works for the government. I'm self-employed. He's atheist; I'm Christian. He's a Democrat; I'm a Republican. The list goes on. He cannot understand why I believe in God, and I cannot understand why he hasn't given God a chance.

You might wonder why we are such good friends. I think it is because we challenge each other and really make the other person think about his position. We can agree to disagree. I also think both of us expect the other will someday have an epiphany and come over to the other side. However, the truth is both of us have become more solidified in our own beliefs as the years have passed. But we still respect each other and can admire the other's strengths.

Dave has wonderful organizational skills. He goes about problem solving in such a way that he always finds the solution. And he's rarely wrong. It fascinates me to watch his methodology and logic, which is usually hard to deny. We can get together and, if we don't discuss politics and religion, everything is fine. But when we decide to, I think he sees me as his project and I see him as mine. He thinks I need to lose God, and I think he needs to find God. Anyway, our mutual respect for so many years has kept us together as very good friends.

I have asked Dave if he would be interested in sharing this experiment with me because he's the perfect person for it. He's smart, responsible, organized, and honest. And I trust him. If he tells me something it will be the truth about what he is thinking or feeling, and that's the most important thing in this experiment—honesty.

Dave has agreed to my experiment where we will switch places. Not physically, but mentally. I will tell him how I look at the world as a Christian, and Dave will try his best to see the world through my eyes, using my philosophy on life and Christian point of view. That is, seeing everything around him is a gift from God and that God is present in his life; that he should talk with God and ask God for direction and attempt to have a relationship with God.

I will do the opposite. I will try my very best to accept Dave's philosophy of life and see the world through his eyes—the eyes of an atheist and secular humanist. I will view the world as a random happening, a world that simply followed the laws of physics, chemistry, and probability. I will live as if maximizing one's happiness is central, but I will also follow certain laws that give my life the best chance of being a happy one. The humanist philosophy also believes in treating others fairly and in sustaining systems and processes while minimizing waste. Logic is also central to this philosophy, as is one's reason, experience, and reliable knowledge.

I will have Dave's perspective on life, and he will have mine, and we will compare notes and our experiences at the end. The goal is to spend one month in each other's place. I will take notes and record the findings and feelings of both Dave and me.

BOB'S NOTES

June 5, 2004—This is so strange for me. It is not easy. I cannot simply switch off my feelings for my God. He is around me and I am aware of it, but I have a terrible feeling of betrayal. I must have a last conversation with God before I begin. I know He knows my every thought, but I must tell Him this is only an experiment, that I will come back to Him at the end of the thirty days. I am asking for His permission to be away from Him. This really hurts even though I know He understands my goal is to become even closer to Him from my experiences.

But then I'm thinking, *Can I really do this experiment fairly if I have already agreed to 'come back' to my God?* Maybe the agreement needs to be that I don't agree to come back, and then we'll see what happens. After all, this is what I'm expecting from Dave—that he opens his mind enough to let God in and ultimately that he changes—to what I believe to be a great benefit for him. He will expect the same of me, and I know he also thinks that if I convert to atheism it will be a great benefit to my life. So I can't agree to anything with God other than to let me go and see what happens. Otherwise, this isn't a true learning experience and it will not be a true experiment.

I must trust that God knows my heart and will let me conduct this experiment openly and honestly. But I am afraid He might punish me for taking on such a daring and God-testing endeavor. I will have my last prayer now and trust He'll honor my heart. After all, a choice for God must be a free-will choice, so I will allow myself to risk it all—to be changed if change makes sense to me. Maybe this is my way of tricking myself into making all of this somehow acceptable.

I have finished my prayer. I am alone now. This is foreign to me. I must put God out of my mind. Every time I think of Him or see something around me that reminds me of Him, I must immediately put it out of my mind and believe only chance and probability have made my surroundings what they are. This will certainly take more effort than I originally thought.

June 7, 2004—I am having a real feeling of guilt over this whole thing. I want to quit. I can't help but feel there is some selfish reason I have initiated this experiment—that I will enjoy the freedom of not having to worry about any repercussions to my actions. Do I really go "all out" here? Do I attempt to do things I know are wrong? Do I experiment with sex? Do I experiment with corruption? Do I experiment with money, that is, an irresponsible spending or even the earning of money? Do I lie to others for personal gain? If so, how do I try these things without hurting someone else or ruining a lifetime of reputation or violating my commitments to my wife and kids? And here's the worst part—no one but Dave knows of this experiment. Can I do some of these things at a scaled back, controlled level—small enough for the experience but large enough that I can know what the other side is all about, and again small enough so no one will find out? Will I even be able to write about it if I violate too much? Probably not.

This is very dangerous territory, and I know it. I will take risks here and I will learn. The worst part is I can't even pray for any help in knowing where the line should be. I'm on my own here. I've already decided after two days that I may not record all of my doings. Just saying that feels dirty. I'm prepared to go all out and make this the true experiment it is meant to be. But now I'm thinking, *Why am I inferring that adopting an atheist viewpoint has to mean doing something immoral? Why aren't these mutually exclusive events in my mind?* I believe Dave will think something is terribly wrong with my perception of this. And, yet, it is how I'm feeling.

To be away from God is to go the way of man on his own, and I know man's weaknesses will lead him to immoral acts if he doesn't have checks and balances in his life. At least, that's the way I see my own life. But Dave has often told me that secular humanism is superior because of that very reason—because humanists want to do good without any ulterior motive of thinking there will be some reward from a God. They just want to do the right thing because it's the right thing. This is a good point of his. I want to do the right thing also. I just know God is watching, and, yes, I do feel He has the authority and the power and oftentimes the desire to change the course of man for the better when man pleases Him. And I want to please Him because I feel He's given me so much for free, with no strings attached. I just feel it in my soul that He's around me all the time and He has a perfect plan for all of this.

Left to my own devices, I know I will start to let the world creep into my soul to the point that it will corrupt me. I guess that's just me. If Dave doesn't need to think of God as being in control and can feel like he doesn't need anything but his own will to always do the right thing, then he is one up on me. My new sense of freedom by being disconnected to God makes me feel like sin has no repercussion. I guess that's what I'm feeling. Like I have a pass for thirty days. Something isn't adding up entirely.

June 8, 2004—I really have feelings of guilt. Many thoughts go through my mind of what I can do and that I have a free pass to do them. Is this just a way to trick myself into having an unfounded freedom of violation? I hope not, but must find out. I still have thoughts of God that pop into my mind during the day, but I dismiss them as quickly as I can. I am feeling a disconnect with God now because of this. I'm realizing it only takes a very short time to let corruption enter one's thoughts and ultimately his life. It starts with a thought, then more thought, and eventually action. The same way I'm putting God out of my mind now is the same way one must constantly put corruption out of mind if one is to walk a moral life. It is hard enough for me when I tried to practice this with God in my life. How does someone stay away from corruption when they don't have God? I'm not judging anyone else at this moment. I just can't believe how weak I am when I'm on my own.

June 11, 2004—I checked in with Dave and confessed that I am really putting his philosophy to the test. I am disappointed to find out he isn't as open-minded to talking with God. I tell him he must do it. He must, at least, tell God he is giving God a chance to enter his life and just see what happens. Have I picked the wrong person for this experiment? Is any atheist capable of this? I'm having my doubts. If Dave doesn't give this the "all-out" try and I do, I'm going to feel even worse about my all-out experiences, especially since, honestly, a part of me is enjoying the perceived absence of accountability in this lifestyle. Guilt is ever present but easier to dismiss now.

June 15, 2004—I'm starting to get better at this, and that worries me. Is it so easy to change oneself? Is my religion that corruptible in such a short amount of time? Better to say, "Am I that corruptible in such a short amount of time?" Is this the true nature of man—that left alone to his own devices for very long (or short in this case) the world quickly takes over? I think it is true, and I am disappointed in myself.

June 20, 2004—I didn't want to write for a while. I just didn't want to say anything. There seems to be no purpose. My attitude is terrible. I am mentally separated. I can do what I want, when I want. I am actually quite good at hiding my feelings and doings—starting to feel like I could get away with anything. After all, who's watching? I wonder if Susie suspects a change in me. How could she not? But so far she has shown no sign or inclination to think anything is not the norm. I will continue. I am worried that if she asks about me I will not be able to respond properly or truthfully or maybe she'll read right through me, forcing me to come clean about this experiment. But, if I lie, who's going to find out? I will rehearse my lines in case I am confronted. This really does feel terrible. I am lying already before I lie. I haven't really done anything *super* wrong but wrong enough for me. I still have half the time left. Will I do something I regret by the end of this thing? My freedom still imparts guilt. What if it eventually does not? What am I capable of once the line gets crossed?

June 21, 2004—I talked with Dave again. Still some resistance from him to totally open himself up to God. I tell him I've been Godless but don't quite see as much point in life. "What is the meaning at the end of it all?" I ask. He lets me know the end is irrelevant. I should be living only for the now and for the near future, that is, "the probable future." He asks how I like my freedom and how my "acts of good" feel because the act is solely from me without any expectation of getting rewarded from a god. Any act of mine is even more impressive, he claims, because it is all from me. I'm thinking I really haven't done as many good acts since I started this experiment. But what he says makes sense. Maybe there is virtue in a good act that has no expectations. This has opened my eyes to the good in Dave. He does good things also, at least in his eyes, and he has no ulterior motive. Do I have one when I treat others as I want to be treated?

I tell Dave he must let himself go completely. Talk with God and let God come in. It is hard to talk to each other because it is a reminder of who we really are. It is as if we have to leave our new selves for the conversation and then quickly revert back. I say the word God for the first time in ten days while talking with him, and that feels strange, and then a feeling of guilt again especially because I'm so easily able to throw God out of my mind. Surely I'm going to be struck down for this. Back to being the "forced atheist" again. How strange. I really have allowed myself to change. But deep inside I can't wait to be with my God again. Is this thought unfair? I must put it out of my mind again.

June 23, 2004—I have had opportunities to do things normally I would not. Enough said. I'm wondering if the devil has me in his sights—knowing I'm prime for His suggestions. But I can't think about that either because the atheist doesn't believe in the devil. That feels comforting. I wonder if this new thought about not having to worry about the devil is part of the allure of atheism. It really is a comfort to think that even though there is no glory in the end at least there is no worry either. Just nothingness. How bad can that be? Seems very sad to me though.

July 4, 2004—I haven't written for almost two weeks now. I went into sort of a numb stage of living. My life started to become void of the things that make life exciting to me. I've discovered I need to have meaning and purpose in my life to be happy. To just have fun and to be selfish about my day-to-day living brings me a feeling of guilt and disrespect. It's as if someone is watching over me and I'm certain that they're disappointed in my behavior. I guess it is fitting that today is the Fourth of July—a day celebrated as a new start for a nation that wanted to live under its own laws, a nation that wanted to be free. God has given all of us free gifts—the free gift of life and the gift of free will to choose or reject Him. I just know what I know deep within my soul—that He is watching over me. And He does not want me to live a life of self-absorbed thoughts and ambitions, but to think of my fellow man and help others along my journey in life. I know this life on earth will be short-lived and it is a preparation for my eternity in heaven with God. I also know I don't deserve that eternity in heaven, but it is a free gift from Him to me because I have faith in Him.

This simple truth is what makes His gift so incredible—the fact that it is so easy to obtain for some and yet nearly impossible for others. Not because He doesn't want them in His heaven, but because their hearts are so hardened against letting God have a chance to show them how great He is and how much He loves them. This is tragic to me. As this experiment comes to an end now, I pray for my friend and ask God to open his heart at some point before he dies. I pray God will grant my wish to have a last chance with Dave, to be used by God to save him, so I'll have eternity with my very good friend, whom I admire and love. I pray God will show the same mercy on Dave that He has shown me. Hope is one of the great ingredients of happiness, and I'll continue to have hope, not only for my friend, but for all humanity and for God's gracious heart to give all humanity a chance to make the choice for Him.

I know Dave will be disappointed with my perception that the humanist philosophy is selfish. I truly believe he is able to live a life that does consider others and wants what is best for mankind. But I'm not capable of living this philosophy without becoming selfish. Maybe it takes a special and unique person to live decently as a humanist. I guess the same can be said for Christians also.

Dave's Summary of the Experiment

(Dave's thoughts on the experiment are in his own words. "You" refers to me, Bob.)

In talking with you about our impending experiment of switching belief systems, you wanted me to open my mind to possible signs from God. However, your examples struck me as more coincidence than anything, and I had a significant amount of trouble getting past this. Every time I hear the word persimmon, I still think about how you perceived the rapid succession of hearing and seeing the word persimmon as a sign from God. Until God parts the waters to Catalina, I don't think I'll ever be able to make this kind of leap. One-in-a-million events happen every day (lotto winners, for example). You see God, and I see probability at work.

For our experiment, I also want to say it was harder for me to temporarily believe in a God than it was for you to temporarily suspend belief of a higher power. I really found it difficult to attribute a beautiful sunset to God rather than the rotation of the earth and the sunlight refracting off particles in the air (nonetheless, I still find the sunset beautiful).

I also found it interesting that, during the experiment, you were having trouble with the idea God wasn't going to hold you accountable for your behavior. You were essentially free to cheat and steal with no eternal consequences. I'm not saying you took advantage of this situation, but you were wrestling with the moral issues it presented. I always thought nonbelievers were getting a bum rap when many believers assume nonbelievers possess low moral values (voting preference polls have atheists ranking at the bottom). I could make a case that nonbelievers have higher moral values than believers do. I don't cheat and steal because it's just not right on a basic human level. I hold *myself* accountable for my behavior. I suspect that a significant reason why believers don't cheat and steal is because their religion says it's a sin and their God will hold them accountable and banish them to an eternity in hell. Which person has higher moral values?

I believe I recall you indicating that some event that occurred in your life firmly pushed you into a becoming a believer, but it was something you were not comfortable sharing with me. I believe most believers fall into two categories: the ones who were raised from a young age in a religious environment and ones in which some significant life event occurred that caused them to believe. I think the first group wasn't given the opportunity to make a mature decision and the second group is giving God credit for what would have happened anyway. I suspect you fall into both camps, at least to some degree.

Lastly, I was quite surprised at the degree of your religiousness. I had thought (or maybe had hoped) you were only mildly religious, but that was not the case.

My Response

This is taken directly from my e-mail to Dave:

> Dave,
>
> Thanks for your input about your experience. I think you're probably right, that it was easier for me to adopt your philosophy than for you to give God a chance. I do remember feeling like I had less accountability and could be much more selfish.
>
> As far as my testimonial about my faith. I'd love to share it with you. No, there was no big moment of change for me, and my parents were Methodist church attendees but not Bible-based believers, so they were not my religious influence. My sister was the one God used in bringing me to Christ. She just showed up at Wilson High one day when I was a junior. I had just left my second-period physics class. It was May 22, 1978. She said she had a dream the night before and I died in her dream, and she woke up crying about me, thinking I wouldn't be in heaven with her someday. She took me aside, told me about her dream and shared what the Bible said about God's Word regarding eternal life and heaven. She had studied the Bible in her first year of college and I knew she was educated on what it had to say.
>
> Just like I asked you when we switched places, she asked me if I would have faith in God and give Him a chance and accept Christ that day as my Savior. I had always felt like God was a part of my life before that, but I did not know that accepting Christ and the gospel (the story and meaning of His life) as truth was essential in getting to heaven. This was not a hard decision for me, but I did not take it lightly either. Why not trust the God I had always believed in anyway? So I did, and I have always felt it was the best thing I ever did. I'm even more thankful He chose to give me an open heart about it. I have trusted in Him

by faith alone, and I've become stronger in my faith over the years from my own experiences and my relationship with God. No big moment. But there are plenty of big moments in the little things if you look around with an open heart. I still love the persimmons story because I don't think it was probability that day. I think it was Him getting my attention.

As you said, you see it as probability. I see it as probability too, but with God always in the driver's seat, changing the outcome whenever He chooses. I believe He is a God of surprises. If you're waiting for the waters to part, that's not the way He operates. He doesn't want your heart because something has been proven to you beyond a shadow of a doubt. He wants it when you have plenty of reason to do just that— to doubt—but then you choose to have faith instead. That's where the real value is to Him. Otherwise, He could have created drones without free will.

I realize you and I will probably never change our beliefs. I think it's a tribute to our friendship that we can still respect each other's walk in life while continuing to enjoy what each of us bring to our friendship.

Dave, I really appreciate you giving this a little more time so I could get closure in my writings. Sorry if I started pontificating, but I didn't know I had never shared my testimony with you. Thanks again
Your friend,
Bob

In closing this chapter I thought the reader might want to know what the "persimmons" story was all about, as both Dave and I alluded to it. One day, while driving, I saw a sign at the side of the road that said "Free Persimmons" above a little basket on a table. At the exact moment my eyes saw the word persimmons, I heard someone on the radio say the word persimmons precisely as I read it. I immediately thought of God as I often do when something happens that is against all probability. The word orange or apple might not have brought it into such a category in my mind. But persimmons? I've never even tasted one, and most people don't even know what one is. I've never heard of anyone offering them for free. They don't really grow them in our area. The oddity of the whole thing came up in a conversation with Dave shortly after that, and he had a very difficult time with my referring to it as a means for God to get my attention, which is where my mind went.

> *"Let no one say when he is tempted, 'I am being tempted by God';*
> *for God cannot be tempted by evil, and He Himself does not tempt anyone."*

JAMES 1:13

Chapter Fourteen

AN EXISTENCE WITHOUT GOD— THE UNBALANCED STATE OF DISORDER

"When I was an atheist I had to try to persuade myself that most of the human race have always been wrong ..."

C. S. LEWIS

I HAVE ALWAYS LIKED MATHEMATICS. Numbers and I just seem to get along. In my experience very few people have a good mind for both numbers and words. They seem to be one or the other—a numbers person or a words person—but rarely both. Numbers are my strong suit; words are not. And here I am writing, so go figure. It's not that I can't use words well to get my thoughts across, it's that I don't remember them as well as I remember numbers. You could say numbers have more exactness to them, they are more objective; whereas words have more need for interpretation and feeling and are more subjective in nature. But both play equally important parts in our lives.

In high school I took a psychology class. On the very first day, the teacher asked the students to write down as many phone numbers by memory as they could. He went around the class one by one. The usual response was between six and twelve phone numbers. A couple students made it into the high teens, but not one person had more than twenty written down. When it came to me I told him I had counted forty-six numbers I had written. Everyone looked at me like I was nuts. In fact, the teacher didn't believe me and asked to see the list of phone numbers. Then, in a blatant attempt to discredit me in front of the whole class, he read off a number and said, "Whose number is 598–5095?"

I said, "That's my friend Erik's number."

"Whose number is 595–5705?"

"That's my dad's work number."

This went on and on, and then I said, "If you want to call any or all of the numbers, I'll stake my grade and my reputation that every one of them is accurate." I must have said it with the kind of conviction and confidence that is undeniable because he looked right at me and knew it was the truth. And so did everyone else in the class. I learned two things that day: First, the truth is the truth and standing up for the truth becomes evident and eventually wins out; and, second, I was better than the average person with numbers.

Words, however, are a quite another matter. Letters don't seem to stay in my mind the way numbers do. Someone will ask me how I enjoyed dining out last weekend, and I'll struggle to remember the name of the restaurant, or to recall the movie I had seen. I have to make an extra effort to remember the name of someone I just met. No, words are not my bag. The older I get, the more I find myself in a dictionary checking my spelling and looking up meanings I used to know. Thank God for spell check on the computer.

What is the significance of whether someone is a numbers person or a words person? How one's mind works determines how one sees things. One's philosophy is shaped by the method in which he or she processes information and experiences, which is just one of many explanations as to why people are so different in their analysis of life. It is just one part of a very large equation of why people perceive things the way they do. If someone wants to convince another a certain viewpoint is the truth, knowing whether that person is a numbers person or a words person is an effective tool. The numbers person is going to want things to add up. The words person is going to want things to feel right.

All people are a complex combination of both, among other things, in a percentage unique unto themselves. Finally, we get to a point—which is a discussion between unique people with distinctively unique minds and experiences. Both are trying to discover common ground or truths about their existence in order to live in harmony and achieve greater personal happiness. This interaction obviously increases the probability of success for society to live in harmony, the result being the greater good for all civilization. Too idealistic? Maybe, but no good comes without the intention to do good. And if nothing else is agreed on except mutual respect for each other's different philosophies of life, then that in itself is a worthy goal.

This is the root of our problem in trying to sustain peace with other countries. We cannot come to an agreement about what is good and evil, what is proper and not proper, what is the truth and what is a lie, especially in regards to religion. Some religions want death to those who don't agree with them.

Surely this cannot be the solution, but it is what we face today in the world. But for now, let's stay on track.

For most people to be convinced something is true it must satisfy both conditions—it must add up, satisfying the brain's left-side analytical thinking, while being balanced with the brain's right-side feelings, either innate or through past experiences. Think about your own decision-making process when buying a car or a home or choosing a life partner or making the decision to have children or even investing your hard-earned money. First, you weigh all the mathematical processes in your mind or on paper. Can I afford it? Is the interest rate too high? Is it a good investment? Crunching the numbers must take place in order to make a wise decision. But then the feelings side enters the equation. Does it seem right? Do I love this person? How will I feel if I lose this money? The list goes on and on. But what is happening is a battle, a checks-and-balances system, between numbers and words actually trying to protect each other in order to achieve the best decision.

Since this is the normal process by which most of us make decisions, simplified as I may have made it sound, then it makes sense to use the same approach in our analysis of whether God exists and how this affects our philosophies and the way we live. Not only do we, as individuals, use this process of numbers (calculations) with words (feelings), but the progress of mankind is where it is today because of it. Every great invention and every great accomplishment has been the combination of a dream or goal—the words followed by the formulas, methods, and equations (the numbers) as to how to get there. You want to put a man on the moon? That's the passion. And that's great, but if you really want to make it happen then bring in the engineers. They are the number crunchers. If you want to write a symphony or build a skyscraper or start a foundation to feed and house the homeless, it begins with a passion and is carried out with calculation and action. Otherwise, it doesn't happen at all. The whole cannot happen without its parts, and, therefore, it makes sense that a whole and proper analysis of our philosophies cannot be accomplished without separating and understanding both parts—the words and the numbers, or the passion and the technical analysis.

Let us begin by examining the claim, "There is no God." We'll start with the numbers. Actually, the theory of evolution has done much of the scientific numbers for us already, and, for the sake of argument, especially since we are assuming there is no Creator, I will proceed on the assumption the scientist's numbers are accurate. The Big Bang Theory—an explosion—sent out debris, also known as planets, which caught in gravitational pull by a star. The third planet from the star has the right atmosphere and elements to sustain life that over billions of years evolves—living cells, amoeba, plants, kingdom, phylum, class, order, family, genus, species, you get the picture—ape to man—evolution of the fittest and strongest and smartest. Let's not argue about whether or not the universe could have been formed in such a manner. Let's let the numbers add up as scientists claim.

Now, let's consider the other side of the brain. Does this conclusion feel right? With most experiments in which man tries to reconstruct events that were not witnessed, assumptions have to be made. Every non-witnessed event will have theories plugged with guesses filling the holes of uncertainty. There's no way around it. But let's say it all adds up and it almost feels right. Why doesn't it feel perfectly right? Let us ask the question, "Does it have a purpose?" Better yet, "Does man have purpose?" If the answer is no, then do the numbers add up? Evolution's answer is clearly yes. Why not? What does purpose have to do with random atoms following the laws of physics? And again, evolution-wise, the strong continue and the weak disappear. The universe is simply on a path following the laws of physics until the elements and chemicals that make up the entire system possibly morph into a phase that would make it possible to start the process all over again, maybe in a few trillion years, or maybe not. It's all random. Anything can happen. No purpose, no glory, no real end. Just a continuation of probability and atoms playing their complex games of chance.

But if that is true, then why not adopt the philosophy of getting away with whatever one thinks he or she can get away with? Why should I care about my fellow human being? If I am stronger and smarter, then he deserves to fall and I deserve to conquer. This is true evolution. If I am the weaker, then I deserve to fall. And why worry about the earth and nature and global warming and recycling for the future? After all, I won't have to deal with the fallout. In a few short years I'll be gone. What about my kids? Well, if I pass along the same philosophy to them, they shouldn't worry about it either. The goal should be to maximize one's happiness during the short stay on earth. After that it's all dust anyway. The only rule is, "My rule rules!" If I can get away with it and at the same time gain from it, then it will be my new philosophy of life.

But you may ask, "What if the immediate gain causes pain in the future?" Then my answer is, "Don't make that decision for immediate gain unless it outweighs the future price to pay." If you're going to have this philosophy, you have to be smart about it, otherwise you might not be the one who survives. If the overall self-good outweighs the overall self-bad, then do it. And remember, I said *self*-bad, not someone else's bad. Is this a selfish philosophy? Of course, it is. But does that make it bad? When an animal in the wild attacks and kills another animal, is that bad? It is only doing what its instinct tells it—to survive—to do what it thinks is in its own best interest.

Now, it becomes clear that if my rules are no better or worse than your rules, no more or less moral (after all, morality in this philosophy is entirely subjective), then it is up to the individual to decide the proper way to conduct himself and how to treat others. Without a higher governing power, a supreme being above man, God, then man is the ultimate authority. I take that back— some people believe animals should have just as much right, power, and status as man does. I won't go there. Wait, maybe I will—because in this philosophy the strongest will prevail, and if animals are stronger than man then they will prevail. But they haven't yet, so in this philosophy it would seem already proven by history that animals and man are not equal.

The point is that animals are acting on instinct and playing by their own rules. As long as one man sees his own rules as being superior to another man's rules, there can be no agreement in governing and no agreement on morality and the best and proper way of life. It is, therefore, the survival of the fittest— the strong and the intelligent will prevail. If we are honest, we will admit this is the way things are today on earth. If evil is strongest, then evil will prevail, and if good is strongest, then good prevails. I believe that, as a country, the United States has good intentions for all mankind to have freedom and peace. Of course, there's some greed thrown in because of the objective of capitalism and the nature of man, and whether the United States goes about it the right way is a topic for another book. But what is the definition of good?

In a godless society there is no real definition of good. At least not one that can be agreed upon, because there is no agreement about an ultimate authority who has defined good for us. And this works, because if there is no definition of good then there is no definition of evil. If everything is good, then nothing is really good. There has to be something that differentiates. This is the problem in the world today. We cannot agree on a supreme authority all man should obey. And we cannot agree on the difference between good and evil. What one authority or person is going to decide this for all of us?

Without God there is a feeling of no purpose. Dust, even after being refined into temporary useable products, will return to dust. And man will wake up and eat and sleep over and over again and wander meaninglessly back into dust again. How long this process lasts doesn't really matter. It all has the same point-less end. What difference does it make if it is next year or in a thousand years? If there is no God, then maximizing one's happiness, however that can be accomplished, would be man's main goal. In this philosophy there is no after-life, no consequences after you are gone. The only price is the one you pay while you are alive. After that, there isn't anything. Get the picture? Order can-not possibly come from this philosophy of life.

Even if you can make the numbers add up to this being the truth, the feelings sure don't add up. What a meaningless world without an ultimate Creator—without God. What a lose/lose situation. If losing is the only solution and the only end to it all, then certainly it cannot be right. Certainly it does not feel right and certainly it cannot be the truth. How can the cosmos of billions of years of evolution not end up refining itself into something better than lose/lose, where there is no order other than that of what the probability of all the atoms make of it? After billions of years of the natural progression of the uni-verse, you'd think it would start getting it right—that it would evolve into some kind of order that makes sense and can continue on bettering itself. Isn't that what evolution supposes—the bettering of itself? Proof enough to me evolution is not the ultimate answer because it is still failing after so much time. The fact that so many people have cancer is proof enough. Billions of years of evolution can't create beings who can keep their own cells from mutating. What losers! Things made from molecules are losers! Evolution is a loser! It can't get it right. How much more proof do you need? And since this philosophy is not better-ing itself, but continuing to have conflict with something as simple as what is good and bad, then it cannot be true. This makes perfect sense.

Therefore I submit that man is not the ultimate authority and that any designer, with the ultimate goal of success, would have designed the end result to be win/win and have meaning and purpose in its design, and that this must be the truth. If so, let's see if the numbers and the words add up. Let's see if the science and the heart agree. Thankfully there's another chapter. One that was written a very long time ago.

I opened this chapter with a quote from the great atheist-turned-Christian writer, C. S. Lewis. It seems appropriate to also close with his words:

"As in arithmetic—there is only one right answer to a sum,
and all other answers are wrong,
but some of the wrong answers are much nearer being right than others."

C. S. LEWIS

Chapter Fifteen

AN EXISTENCE WITH GOD— ORDER IN PERFECT BALANCE

"Let all your things have their places; let each part of your business have its time."

BENJAMIN FRANKLIN

I HAVE ALWAYS ADMIRED Benjamin Franklin. He was born the fifteenth child and the lastborn son of seventeen children. My father was also the fifteenth child and the lastborn of his family. Is it this uncanny coincidence that makes me a Franklin lover? No, I think it is much more about how impressive the man was. Benjamin Franklin, in my opinion and in the opinion of many scholars, was the most influential person in convincing France to back the United States in the Revolutionary War. Without the support of the French, America probably would have lost its battle for independence from Britain. Our nation would have developed quite differently, possibly not at all—at least not in the way we know it. I love to read about Benjamin Franklin. To list all his incredible inventions and how they have helped mankind would take a book in itself. But even more impressive than his contributions to society in improving the quality of life was his methodology of how to conduct oneself in order to be successful. He was a man of intense self-discipline and order.

Order was one of Franklin's "Thirteen Virtues." He kept a quarterly log. Each week he would concentrate on one virtue, practicing it every day and rating himself. The next week he would practice another virtue, and so on, until he had completed all thirteen. He would repeat the process four times a year, making a neat fifty-two-week year of practicing what he felt were the most important personality traits to better himself.

I tried this for a full year, and I couldn't believe how much I was able to start looking inward at my own faults and how it enabled me to make improvements in myself. It requires effort, but it is definitely worth it. I would leave my virtues chart on my desk. At the end of every day I would rate myself from one to ten on how well I felt I handled that particular virtue. At the end of the week I would see how I had improved. If I didn't, I would usually repeat it for a second week or until I saw some improvement. Some virtues were natural to me and took very little work, while I struggled with others since they grated against my nature. That is where I had to focus the most. I can't emphasize enough how much this has helped me. It is a practice everyone can benefit from.

Franklin's virtues are widely known:

1. Temperance—Eat not to dullness; drink not to elevation.
2. Silence—Speak not but what may benefit others or yourself; avoid trifling conversation.
3. Order—Let all your things have their places; let each part of your business have its time.
4. Resolution—Resolve to perform what you ought; perform without fail what you resolve.
5. Frugality—Make no expense but to do good to others or yourself. Waste nothing.
6. Industry—Lose no time; be always employed in something useful; cut off all unnecessary actions.
7. Sincerity—Use no hurtful deceit; think innocently and justly, and if you speak, speak accordingly.
8. Justice—Wrong none by doing injuries or omitting the benefits that are your duty.
9. Moderation—Avoid extremes; forbear resenting injuries so much as you think they deserve.
10. Cleanliness—Tolerate nothing unclean in body, clothes, or habitation.
11. Tranquility—Be not disturbed at trifles, or at accidents common or unavoidable.
12. Chastity—Rarely use venery but for health or offspring, never to dullness, weakness, or the injury of your own or another's peace or reputation.
13. Humility—Imitate Jesus and Socrates.

In his autobiography Franklin claimed the virtues were written in order of their importance to him. He also admits that order was his weakest virtue and he had to constantly work on it. I think order was in his top three for a reason.

Without order things seem to fall apart quickly. Even the best plan without an order of execution usually lands by the wayside in short time. I have told my children countless times that "organization is the key to success." This has been my experience as a self-employed businessman for twenty-five years. Why is order so important? It's not that something can't be successful without order; in fact, some things are better when they are spontaneous—the art of creation being performed on the fly—it comes across as more natural and honest, especially in the arts. But what great, complex, and sophisticated plan has ever been successful without great planning and order? Franklin was not a regular church attendee and did not publicly reveal himself to be a highly religious man, but here is a quote from his autobiography in his own words. Upon reading it, you can only come to one conclusion about Franklin's true heart regarding God:

> *Revolving this project in my mind, as to be undertaken hereafter, when my circumstances should afford me the necessary leisure, I put down from time to time, on pieces of paper such thoughts as occurred to me respecting it. Most of these are lost; but I find one purporting to be the substance of an intended creed, containing, as I thought, the essentials of every known religion, and being free of everything that might shock the professors of any religion. It is expressed in these words…:*
> *"That there is one God, who made all things.*
> *"That He governs the world by his Providence.*
> *"That He ought to be worshipped by adoration, prayer, and thanksgiving.*
> *"But that the most acceptable Service of God is doing good to man.*
> *"That the soul is immortal,*
> *"And that God will certainly reward virtue and punish vice, either here or hereafter."*
>
> BENJAMIN FRANKLIN

That's why I love Benjamin Franklin so much, because he puts my feelings into words very poetically.

With his thoughts about God freshly in mind let us again make the claim that there is a God. And again, let's start with the numbers. If there is a supreme Creator who can do anything at any time any way He wants, then He would have designed a win/win plan for success. No God with unlimited power would have a plan to lose. And His plan would have to make sense, at least to Him. It would need to have order and a beginning and an end. Or maybe a plan for no end—after all, it's His plan. But, at least, a plan. If you were an omnipotent being, you certainly would have a plan that was perfect and right in your eyes and that ended in success. So, our claim now will be that there is a God and He can do anything and He has a perfect plan with a perfect and successful ending.

With this claim we have Creation—that God created man and the earth and the universe we live in. Maybe the Big Bang Theory is true. God could have put things into motion in that way—so the numbers would still add up just as without God. The difference is that we have a Creator and a reason for the creation—success. And this plan is built upon order as its foundation. Such a world could be made to follow the directions of its Creator and still have purpose, but it would have no meaning. In order to have meaning, God's creations must have free will so that a free choice for good truly would be good and a free choice for evil truly would be evil. God would have to allow both good and evil in order for there to be a clear choice. I believe this to be the truth. God did create the universe, and He did allow for good and evil, and He set both upon the earth and gave man the free will to choose.

"However things may seem, no evil thing is success and no good thing is failure."

HENRY WADSWORTH LONGFELLOW

Do the numbers add up? Does the probability of a Creator setting up order outweigh the probability of something coming from nothing, or order coming out of disorder? Only one of these choices can be true. Either someone or something created it all or it didn't. I love the quote by the great astronomer Copernicus in the early 1500s during the time when his theory that the earth actually revolved around the sun was finally being noticed:

"I began to be annoyed that philosophers had discovered no sure scheme
for the movements of the machinery of the world,
created for our sake by the best and most systematic Artist of all."

COPERNICUS

For the average person to really trust in the numbers concerning proof as to whether or not God exists, I believe the most powerful tool must be the same one we use in today's world. Numbers are how we prove or disprove things in modern society. It's called a jury. And the representatives who sway the jury toward proving or disproving whether or not something happened or didn't happen are called witnesses. When someone says he saw a certain thing happen, it carries a lot of weight. When numerous persons (more numbers) say they saw the same thing, it carries more weight. The number of witnesses who can corroborate the experience offers proof whether or not something actually occurred.

It can be easily proved I went to work last Monday because my client met with me, and I saw his children, and I also met with subcontractors that day. They could all stand as witnesses and say I worked that particular day. This provides proof for someone who didn't witness it. I also signed for some materials that were delivered. That's more proof. Of course, someone could have forged my signature. You see, there can always be doubt thrown in by someone who wants to deny the numbers. But these numbers (actual people) confirm I was at a certain place at a specific time and performed noted tasks. This is certainly the best form of proof by numbers, and it is the same form we use in today's society. So, why not rely on it for the numbers about whether or not Christ existed and whether or not He really was God in the form of man?

Some of the best books written on this subject have been published by author Josh McDowell, such as *More than a Carpenter* and *Evidence that Demands a Verdict*. He takes the numbers and easily shows how the proof is undeniable when some 20,000-plus manuscripts of the New Testament dwarf the number of manuscripts written about other famous figures in our past. There are numerous writings from people who lived with Jesus, who witnessed His walk, His miracles, and His rising from the dead. There were too many people, over 500 witnesses who saw Him after He rose from the dead. Some of them wrote about it. Those are the best numbers proof can demand. Josh McDowell talks about Julius Caesar and the fact that only about ten manuscripts were written about him, and those that remain date 1,000 years after his death, and yet we don't doubt he existed and ruled as the historians claim.

With so many more witnesses and written claims about Jesus, why do we doubt the authenticity of such numbers? It's because Jesus performed miracles only God could perform and Caesar didn't. So, just because we haven't witnessed the same kind of supernatural miracles in our lives, are we to deny all these claims from people who did? There you have it. That's the difference. But it doesn't change the numbers. The numbers are undeniable when so many people write the exact same things about the same person. And the stories don't contradict each other. These witnesses are too great in number, and thus they are undeniable, unless one has a reason to deny them. And there are many reasons people do not want to believe the biblical writings about Jesus are true. One, for instance, is the fact that if we do have a just God, some day when we die and face God, we will be held accountable for all the personal injustices we inflicted on others. Not a pretty thought, is it? If there is no God, then there is no accountability. That seems to solve the problem for so many. But then there would be no chance for an eternal heaven with our Creator.

Now for the feelings. If you are the type who goes strictly by the numbers, then you can easily make up your mind. But most of us are not robots in our thinking. Feelings are usually a big part in making up our minds. Proverbs 3:5 says, "Trust in the LORD with all your heart and do not lean on your own understanding." It is saying to us that we should not rely solely on the calculations in our heads (the numbers) but to also trust the feelings in our hearts (the words).

It is worth repeating that an omnipotent being would have the power to have a plan that wins—the definition of "win" being there is a purpose and a meaning and all things add up to that purpose and meaning in the end. If you believe in God and yet don't have enough faith that all things will add up in the end with God's plan, then you are doing Him a great injustice and paying Him a great insult.

I ended chapter four with a rather strong quote from C. S. Lewis, that there is only one right answer—a very provocative quote. Please don't think all Christians believe it is "my way or the highway." I would be doing Christianity a disservice if I didn't clarify that it is true Christians do believe Christ is the only way to eternal life with our Creator. But self-righteousness has no place in the Christian heart or any heart. Christians are getting a bad wrap, and in many cases deservedly so, being stereotyped this way. The true Christian mind should be firmly planted in the belief that God sees the heart. Whether you call yourself Christian, Jewish, Muslim, Hindu, or whatever, anyone can be saved and can have a true heart for God and can have God's assurance of eternal life. It is what is in our hearts, our faith, that determines how God finds favor in us. And that is solely up to God. Many self-proclaimed Christians may not find the path to heaven, and many who consider themselves non-Christian may find it. What we call ourselves is irrelevant. What we believe in our hearts, which is what God sees, is what counts. And it is everything!

The numbers add up even better when there can be no wrong during something that is perfectly planned. When I was in high school, my buddies and I drove to one of our favorite local spots during our school lunch break. I had a self-proclaimed reputation—only from talk, of course—that I was pretty good at understanding and fixing car engines because I was always helping my dad fix one of our broken-down cars. The guys started kidding me about it, and one day I got the semi-brilliant idea I would show them. I opened the hood of my buddy's car while they were eating and loosened the center distributor cap lead wire from the coil, knowing the slightest movement would render the car helpless at some point. We were on our way back to school when, right in the middle of an intersection waiting to turn left, the car went into perfect theatrics, sputtering, and then stalling. I quickly said, "Open the hood." I ran out, and knowing how to remedy the situation in an instant, said, "Try it now," whereupon it started perfectly, and we were on our way, myself the hero of the hour. I only have two worries now, one that you'll have just lost all respect for me, and, two, that my buddies are going to read this and I'm going to have some explaining to do. I guess it's time I come clean anyway. But there is a point here—I stacked the deck—I created a situation that was a win/win for myself, as conniving as it may have been. How much more can a Creator, with unlimited power, stack the deck in His favor if He wants to? And why wouldn't He? And why wouldn't His perfect plan make perfect sense? Just because we can't see the stacking doesn't mean it isn't already stacked up to work out perfectly.

Since I'm in this deep already—on another occasion, and keep in mind these things happened many years ago, and I'm pretty sure I'm beyond this kind of behavior now—I was with family and friends on a small boat in a little cove on the Colorado River by Havasu, Arizona. One of the guests, Dan, was a work associate of my father-in-law's, about five years my junior and a member of the Neptunes, a world-class free-diving club known for its world records in holding their breaths and setting all sorts of spear-fishing records. Free-diving means no tanks; you have to hold your breath. I had practiced holding my breath as a kid with my father and had some diving experience because of my father's association with the Sea Scouts. Dan had brought his own specially designed skin-diving fins with him. For fun, we challenged each other as to how far out from the boat we could swim before having to come up for air.

Dan went first, and his distance was quite impressive. Then it was my turn. I actually thought I could beat him without resorting to any trickery. But the wheels had been turning while he was attempting his swim, and I surmised I could probably swim far enough under water that I could actually exit the cove on the left side, come up for air hidden behind the rocks, breathe for about thirty seconds, and then swim back out into the cove at a steep angle away from the boat and surface a couple minutes later at a far greater distance than anything I could do in a fair bet. Since it was just for bragging rights, I decided to go with this dastardly (and I'd like to think harmless) plan. When I came up, I was so far away from the boat and so far past his mark that I thought to myself, *I think I overdid it.* I would have had to have been half-fish to pull that off, and he was shaking his head in disbelief, and maybe a little skeptical, to say the least. Soon after that we became good friends, bought a diving boat together, and dove for many years. I never did tell Dan the truth about that day.

Obviously, I don't recommend deceiving people, even if just for bragging rights. No good comes from it, and you're left with a lifetime of having to keep up a reputation only a good magician can pull off. That can be tiring. But if we can't learn from our past behavior and mistakes and share this with others, then what good can come from them? By the way, previously I mentioned "order" as being Franklin's weakness. But he considered "pride" the most dangerous. Don't I know it! Pride is certainly what made me act the way I did.

Back to the point of my story—having the knowledge or the power to already have won before you even start makes the numbers add up very nicely. You can't lose. That day in the cove I couldn't lose—certainly not with the help of my secret scheme. I believe God has already crossed the finish line victoriously. He has already planned it all, and His perfect plan already won long before you and I came along.

As I have said before, the fact that evolution has had so much time to get things right and has failed in so many areas should convince us. How many people have to have some sort of life-altering ailment to prove the evolution of man's body is not improving but deteriorating? After all these generations, the body can't pass along to the next generation an ability to fight off disease? What's wrong with evolution that it is so powerless? It's because evolution is false. God made us, and it is not God's will for us to have ironclad bodies. He wants us to remain frail to the extent that we will not see ourselves as gods but as creatures in need of a higher authority and protector. It is His plan we are the way we are; otherwise, if evolution were true it would have figured it out by now. It would have corrected so many wrongs after all this time. But it hasn't. It's had supposedly billions of years to figure it out. How much more time must we give this false conclusion to realize it's false? The fact that it hasn't made a perfect universe by now is proof to me it is not the truth. God's plan is the truth. Here are three points to help us grasp this:

1. We don't have to understand something for it to be the truth.
2. God doesn't intend for us to fully understand everything while we are on earth.
3. In regard to man, God's perfect plan is designed to work through faith. If He were to remove all doubt, our free will would be undermined.

An existence with God is the only logical conclusion since it works for both the numbers and the words. This has it all—the numbers together with our feelings through faith—in a perfect plan with purpose for our lives. And over all is our God, the universal authority, who distinguishes between good and evil, right and wrong, and nothingness or eternity in heaven.

"It is expressed in these words...
That there is one God, who made all things."

BENJAMIN FRANKLIN

Chapter Sixteen

WHO'S IN CONTROL?

"The mind of a man plans his way,
But the Lord directs his steps."

PROVERBS 16:9

ARE YOU IN CONTROL of your life? I like to think I am. Isn't one of the primary goals of all men and women to be in control? How can one make daily decisions without feeling there is a direction, a purpose, or a goal he or she is trying to obtain? Without direction we would all be like wandering ships without rudders. To be in control, shouldn't we be pushing our goals and our directions onto ourselves constantly? Or should we have the opposite mindset—to realize we are not in control, and let life take us in the direction it would naturally go on its own? Of course, I'm not about to suggest we all just go along our merry ways without a purpose and a direction. Maybe a combination of the two is the answer. With these thoughts in mind, I am about to suggest something that may not be along the lines of your usual thinking. If by being in control we are saying we are the sole power in determining our fate, then the ultimate prize should be in reaching certain goals you and I have. Since I have experienced living on both sides of this equation, here is my suggestion, mainly because it worked for me, but more so because it is biblically based:

"Delight yourself in the LORD,
And He will give you the desires of your heart."

PSALM 37:4

For the first thirty-six years of my life I always said, "God, give me wealth and then watch what I do for you." Then, in the thirty-seventh year, I said this, "God, watch what I do for you, and then I'll leave it up to You." Why did I change? Because what I had been doing wasn't working. Therefore, I concluded a new way of thinking and a new action was needed. If I were really smart, I would have figured that out before thirty-seven years of age. God is obviously incredibly patient because He must have been thinking, "I'm still waiting for you, Bob—you make the first move." And for thirty-six years I was an idiot. Why He didn't give up on me I don't know. But I'm grateful for finally seeing the truth about how He operates. Let me tell you why I think I was blind for so long.

When one is focused on something so intently, he or she can become blind to reality even when reality is very obvious. My deep focus was one of my biggest enemies. But let me say this reality is not one obvious to the common man because most people do not believe Psalm 37:4 is true. But I believe it is. And my life's experiences have proven it to be true for me. My biggest problem was, and still sometimes is, I think happiness will be achieved by becoming financially independent. That is, being able to afford what I want when I want it and being able to do what I want when I want would provide complete control and, thus, complete happiness.

What I found out about myself is something it hurts to admit: I can't handle complete control and happiness. I get bored when things are seemingly perfect, and then I get myself into trouble. The saying "Idle hands are the devil's workshop" is certainly true with me. That's a shame. I mean, that's sad! But there can be a bright side to it. Realizing this personal weakness and admitting it makes it possible for me to be careful about getting too content with things. I need challenges, and I need a goal to be working toward constantly. The trick for me is to find goals worthy of my time and effort.

But, enough about me. What about you? What are your goals? Are they worthy of your great efforts and time? Are you going after them alone? Are you a partner with someone? Are you in control of how to get where you want to be? These are all good and honest questions, with no right or wrong answers. The correct answers to these questions, or let me rephrase that, the best answer in order for it to be able to help you and improve your situation depends on what type of person you are. Understanding yourself first is key. Most of us don't stop and spend the time to figure ourselves out. We don't analyze and understand ourselves. If you go to a therapist, he is going to want to know what type of person you are and how you think before he can help you. It is no different when you are trying to help yourself. You must understand yourself first. Susie's father, Howard, would always say, "A problem well-defined is half-solved." If so, then a person well-defined is already half-understood.

Human beings can only control so much in life, but we should strive to be the best we can at controlling the simple things God has given us to control. Each of us needs to take personal inventory, beginning with our personalities and emotions, and eventually our habits and our tendencies. Ask yourself: "Am I organized?" If so, maybe you can go it alone or maybe you would make a good partner for someone. Obviously, a poorly organized person would be a bad partner for you if you are organized. "Am I tenacious?" If so, maybe you don't need the help or hindrance of another as you blaze your own trail. If you are a procrastinator or have trouble motivating yourself, then reevaluate whether your goal fits you. Self-employment will probably not be your best choice. Maybe being a musician or an artist might be. There is usually not the demand for instant results with the latter occupations.

If it seems I am on a tangent, it is merely to get you to think about what type of person you are. How you describe yourself will help determine how well you believe you are in control and, more importantly, how well you really are in control of your life. The first depends on your own perspective of yourself and your life, and the second depends on two things: how well you adapt your perspective into becoming reality and how willing you are to admit one of the truths of life—you are not in total control.

Now, I have done it. I either lose your trust that what I have said is true, in which case you may as well leave the rest for someone else to read since you do not have the ability to let your guard down long enough to even consider this to be so, or I earn your consideration that maybe there is some truth to this statement.

God gives each and every one of us things to control and to be in charge of. For one—our bodies. We all have some forms of personal property He graces us with. Some of us have children over whom we have charge. Most likely, some-day our children will probably have charge over us as we lose our memories and need physical help from them. Yes, God does grace us with responsibilities, property, and bodies that He gives to us for our betterment and enjoyment. But, beyond these personal things, how much control do we really have? Our sim-plest expectations can easily be dashed by anther person's actions, an unexpected turn in our health, even the weather—all of which are out of our control.

Personally, I think it is a relief to know I am only capable of doing my best. And that's as good as it gets. Consider this: If we ask our heavenly Father above to take control, then we are not directing our steps, even though we are tak-ing the steps. I'm not making this up. I'm just restating this chapter's opening biblical quote, Proverbs 16:9, in plain English. "The mind of a man plans his way, but the LORD directs his steps."

It is up to God to let me know if I need to alter my course when I ask Him to take over. What we do when we ask this of our heavenly Father is to simply place the responsibility of our pleasing Him on Him. What a relief! That doesn't mean I sit and wait for divine intervention and do nothing until I get it. It means I am asking God to interject into my life by whatever means He wishes to let me know if I am going in the direction He wants me to go. Or better yet, to give me signs of the direction in which not only will I be happier and more content but that will satisfy His utmost desire and perfect plan for my life. The truth is we are only in control as long as He gives us the control and only to the extent He gives it to us. And no more.

To think we are always in control is to be naive. It is the wise man who considers changing his course when he sees his current direction may be wrong or simply not working. For most, it is normal to be so involved in their own lives, just getting through the day, that they feel they must be in control of everything. If not, they fear all will come crashing down on them. This is not much different than what most highly successful and goal-oriented people are blinded by—the lack of ability to stop hustling and bustling, to stop being fixated on their inner drive or inner self for long enough, or better said, for a short enough time to realize there may be a better way. Or a way that is more right—that is, more in line with the truth about their lives and thus more likely to succeed because now they are learning to balance the control God has given them with His ultimate control. This is what took me so long to learn. Reaching goals does not bring happiness if balance and perspective are missing. Self-absorbed people (myself included, at times) have their perspective mixed up most of the time.

Stop. Be still. Cease striving. Let our incredible Creator have a chance to enter your thoughts. Feel Him in your soul. Ask Him for wisdom and for a calmness to come over you. Be still and feel. He will connect with you in some way if you stop and give yourself over to Him. It only takes a few moments, and yet we seldom do this. This practice can connect you with the truth.

Truth is reality. Here is a truth: We are eventually going to die, and we are either going to heaven or we are not. There is either something after physical death on this earth, or there is nothingness afterwards. One of those is the truth and the reality, and the other is false and will not be the reality. Pick one or don't. No one can change the truth about which one is right or wrong and which one will eventually happen to you. But one of those will happen to you and to me and to every living person. There is no denying one of those must happen. There is no in-between. We are not going to kind of go there or kind of pass away into nothingness. I'm not even trying to ask you to choose at this point. Just admit one of those must be the truth because there is no middle ground or partial answer.

If you believe as the atheist, then it really doesn't matter to you, does it? If I am wrong and the atheist is right, then we will all pass away into nothingness. But if what I believe turns out to be the truth, then the atheists will have a huge price to pay and they will be paying it for eternity. That seems like an awful risk to take. If I am wrong, we go to the same place—nothingness. If I am right, we don't go to the same place. Here are my ever-so-presumptuous thoughts about heaven: Think of your most passionate desires and your most cherished needs. Think of having a perfect body, never sick, never feeling pain in any way. Think of even the simple pleasures of life here on earth, such as the warmth of the sun or the beauty of a perfect sunset or the sound of your favorite song or the taste of your favorite food. And then know that these are nothing. These things are all merely mortal pleasures of the common man in a fragile body existing on a finite substance known as planet earth in a finite universe—which all have an ending. They will cease to exist someday. But heaven will not.

Heaven is unlike any of these petty pleasures you or I can conjure up in our little minds. Heaven is something you and I cannot comprehend. It will be that incredible. It will be that beautiful. To use your senses to enjoy pleasure is one thing. To understand pleasure through one's soul is quite another. That will be the difference. One that I cannot explain but certainly one that is beyond our wildest dreams. If you want all the riches and power of the universe, I can only laugh because heaven's treasures will dwarf that. It won't be riches and power. It will be eternal bliss, never-ending love and joy, and you will never become tired of it, you will never want for anything, and it will last forever. Know that God wants this for you, and He gives you the free will to choose.

In this, He gives you the control. What value would your choice be if He made it for you? Again, if He wanted that He would have created puppets on strings without free will. He would have commanded His creations to love Him and to obey Him and to be perfect and do good always. But there would be no value in such creations. If one is programmed only to know good, then there is no good. Unless one has the free will to choose good over evil then a choice for good is not really a choice for good.

Knowing what is right and wrong is instilled in man from God. How many times have you done something knowing it was wrong before you did it? I would chance a guess most of the time when we made morally wrong decisions we knew it before we did it. That sure makes mankind sound awful. The word sin comes to mind. I'm not preaching here because I am very aware of my own record book of sins—a novel in itself. But I am trying to make the point I was aware of almost every single one of them before I committed them. That is hard to admit. But it feels good to admit it and to understand myself. I am not perfect, and you are not perfect. We never will be, and to say the truth about it feels good. But did you know you can be perfect in God's eyes? And did you know He wants to see you that way? "Therefore you are to be perfect, as your heavenly Father is perfect" (Matthew 5:48). But how is this possible?

There is only one way to achieve this. It is the same way one receives heaven from the only One who is capable of giving it—the One who created it—your heavenly Father. The way to start is this: Be still and know He is God. And then talk to Him. Ask Him to take control. By doing this you will gain His control.

If you are a parent, you will be able to relate in this way. When one of your children brings new friends home they are welcome in your home because your son or daughter has invited them. When you are holding the hand of Christ, God doesn't see your sin anymore. He says, "You're welcome into my home because you are with my Son." This is how God is able to finally see you as perfect and allow you into His heaven. It is the only way. Christ took your book of sins to the cross with Him. It's gone now, and God does not see it anymore. If you're holding Christ's hand, you're perfect in God's eyes. That seems unbelievable, but it is the truth.

God knows you are not perfect, and He does not expect you to be. But when you and I stumble and then get up and confess and ask Him for forgiveness through His Son, He washes away the sin and sees us as perfect again.

"Knowing that the testing of your faith produces endurance.
And let endurance have its perfect result, so that you may be perfect
and complete, lacking in nothing."

JAMES 1:3–4

Chapter Seventeen

ABOUT JUSTICE

*"And we know that God causes all things to work together for good
to those who love God, to those who are called according to His purpose."*

ROMANS 8:28

YESTERDAY I HAD IT OUT WITH GOD. At least I'm honest about it. And at least I'm not afraid to tell Him how I feel. If He truly wants a relationship with me, and I know He does, then it is comforting to know I can be mad at Him and tell Him I'm mad at Him. You see, this year I made a commitment to myself to be the very best I could be, to honor my God, and to support my struggling church financially in their time of need. My church asked me to be one of four members on the financial committee, so I was able to see firsthand how they were not making ends meet. I figured out how much each member would have to give in order for the church to break even every month, and I decided to divide that amount by the number of members and give that amount so I was doing my part. When someone came to me needing more, I gave it. That was my promise, and I've kept it.

All I asked God for was direction in my life. I prayed and asked Him to shut the doors where He did not want me to go, primarily with my construction career, and to open the door where He did want me to go. I looked to Him for signs of His direction. After much prayer, I made peace with the fact that it seemed clear He wanted me to accept work offered to me in the construction industry again. A place I did not want to go. But all the doors opened up in that direction. I agonized over the decision for a solid month, making sure I was right in doing what I felt God wanted me to do—jumping back into a job I hated.

With two of my children entering college at the same time, I had a renewed sense of financial responsibility added to the table. But every day has been a challenge. The construction income is helpful, and it is making my extra giving possible, but I cannot see the answer as to why God wants me back here again. Why would He want me to be miserable? And yet I know I've followed His direction. Of that I am certain. I can't help but think He doesn't have great plans for me. Just to work in a business in which I'm certainly burned out? I can't see the good in it, and I can't understand why He's allowing me to be tortured. Sound harsh? Well, I'm feeling harsh. I'm trying to keep my faith, and I continually tell Him I'm not giving up on Him, but I'm being tested constantly, and I'm fed up with it.

So, yesterday I let Him know everything I was feeling, and I said to God, "Use me or let me go." I had tears over it. "God, use me or let me go, but don't keep me with a desire to do great things for You and then never give me the power to do them. It's not fair. Either get something going or take me out of it. And I don't care if taking me out means all the way out. Take my life if You want, I don't care. Don't use me if I'm not right for You. But just tell me. Don't leave me wondering and wandering around anymore. I'm impatient and I'm tired, but I'm still there for You and I'm not leaving You. I'm not quitting, but I'm asking You to quit on me if You're not going to get the show on the road. I'm getting too old and tired to keep going. You make the choice now on whether You're leaving me or not. And, then, please do it." I added, "I can live with Your answer, but I need one, and I need one now. If You love me, don't leave me hanging any longer."

Lately, this is exactly how I feel: "If I called and He answered me, I could not believe that He was listening to my voice. For He bruises me with a tempest, and multiplies my wounds without cause. He will not allow me to get my breath, but saturates me with bitterness. If it is a matter of power, behold He is the strong one! And if it is a matter of justice, who can summon Him?" The only thing is—those aren't my words. They're Job's words, recorded in Job 9:16–19. "Justice? Who can summon Him?" Job expresses the depths of my heart.

> *"Though He slay me, I will hope in Him.*
> *Nevertheless I will argue my ways before Him."*
>
> JOB 13:15

Now, maybe my prayer to God is harsh. But it is honest, and just like Job I'm arguing my ways before Him. For certain, He will do what He wants in His own way in His own time. I have a hard time accepting this, and yet I must. One of my biggest problems with God is that I don't see justice the same way He does. I know His justice is the true justice, but I can't see it clearly and I can't understand it. It frustrates me to think that no matter how good I try to be and how much I desire something, even something noble and worthy and selfless, God may not grant my desires. Maybe never. He might have something entirely different in mind. But I want to go where my passion tells me to go. Why would He give me passion for something and then tell me to concentrate on something else? I don't understand that. It is even more frustrating to think I may never know and He expects me to continue on in faith every day. Faith that His plan is the best and my passions are a very distant second. To trust Him even if He doesn't give me a sign. And to keep saying, "I'm staying with You, God. I'm not leaving. I'm waiting for You to tell me where to go and what to do. And I'm excited about Your plan, not mine." Well, I'm sorry; that's very difficult for us mortals to do day after day after day. At least it is for me. And so I got mad, and I'm still mad. I need to settle down again and learn from it and trust Him, even though it's frustrated trust. This is very hard to do when I'm feeling down. And right now I'm down!

Here's the answer, and I've given this serious consideration. You and I have to accept that His justice isn't our justice. What happens on earth will not be a perfect story with a happy ending. Only what happens in heaven will be. And for mortal beings to accept that their justice will not come until they have left their mortal bodies is a plan that is hard to accept. I know I will never be happy here if I cannot accept God's plan to be the best plan, even if He doesn't want to let me in on the plan. I have to accept it even though it is difficult to accept. But I can count on this—however hard it is on this earth, it will be rewarded that much more in heaven. If I can see it through down here, He'll see it through with full understanding in my mind up there. I know this, even though I don't like it. I want results right now, down here, or else what is my purpose here? Is it just to exist and raise kids so they can exist? Or is it to discover the truth about our great God and to find happiness at a greater level—because of greater understanding? That has to be the answer because there isn't anything else.

Why has He built a world that isn't just? Why have some been born into a life of misery and not others? Why not give people the power to change it when they have a heart to change it? Why give power to some who have no heart for God? Why, more often then not, is justice like a four-letter word on this earth?

If you try to make sense out of this world by how well things work out for you then you're in for a big disappointment. If you make sense out of it by knowing you're walking right with God and trusting His plan is a perfect plan and He'll make it work out right in the end, then you've got it right. But that end might not be down here. And, yes, this takes a lot of faith. Do you have faith? Will it last? Do I have faith? Can I keep it in the face of so much injustice? That's the question. And every day I have to say, "I'm not giving up. I have faith in You. I trust You. And I accept what You have in store for me because I know it is part of Your perfect plan." This next biblical quote is so important to remember:

"Without faith it is impossible to please Him ..."

HEBREWS 11:6

Do you understand this? Faith is everything to God! Now, even though I understand it, I have to repeat it over and over again so I fully get it. It is everything! Everything!

I continue to have moments of frustration with my impatience, and God's timing more often than not is not my timing. And I keep asking, "When?"

Another man, a great man, often asked the same question: "When?" Martin Luther King Jr., at the funeral of four girls who died in the bombing of Birmingham's 16th Street Church in 1963, had this to say:

"In spite of the darkness of this hour, we must not despair.
We must not become bitter, nor must we harbor the desire to retaliate with violence.
No, we must not lose faith in our white brothers.
Somehow we must believe that the most misguided among them
can learn to respect the dignity and worth of all human personality."

I'm sure just about every day of his life he asked, "When? When is there going to finally be justice?" But he had the right perspective. These were also his words:

"I said to myself over and over again, 'Keep Martin Luther King in the background
and God in the foreground, and everything will be all right.
Remember you are a channel of the gospel and not the source.'"

Then I hear that inner voice asking me the same thing: "When? When, Bob, are you going to stop and be still and let Me be God?" And when I sense His inner voice, I have peace with it all. It just doesn't happen often enough, and that's a problem I have to work on. Be still Bob, be still. And let God be God. I need to have peace with His form of justice through faith—not through understanding, but through faith. So that I can sow the right seeds, and sow them on faith alone.

"Do not be deceived, God is not mocked;
for whatever a man sows, this he will also reap."

PAUL, GALATIANS 6:7

Chapter Eighteen

WHAT IS FAITH?

"Who made heaven and earth,
The sea and all that is in them;
Who keeps faith forever."

PSALM 146:6

IT REALLY IS AMAZING how God works. This chapter ended up being the last one I wrote. I can't believe I almost left it out. I was literally about to hit the send button on my completed manuscript to my editor when my sister, Lori, called from North Carolina. She said, "How would you like to start a Bible study through e-mail with me?"

This morning I woke up thinking about what topic would be good to begin our study, and I thought about how faith is really the most essential ingredient in our relationship with God. Upon going to my own past writings about it, I realized that, although I had touched on its absolute importance, I had not dedicated the proper attention it deserved. There definitely would be a hole in a book about discovering God without a full chapter dedicated to the most important attribute man must fully wrap his arms around—faith. I'm going to take the e-mail I sent to my sister, the same one-and-only sister who brought me to the Lord and was my inspiration to start writing, and let you read it. I want to share our correspondence with you because it left me seeing things differently than when I started.

Lori,

I was praying this morning, and it popped into my mind about how important faith is and that we should make faith the focus of our study. Do you mind if I take the initiative? I immediately thought of you and our commitment to start a Bible study and thought, *What a perfect place to start.* If that sounds good to you, then…let's start with what the Bible says in Hebrews 11:1, "Now faith is the assurance of things hoped for, the conviction of things not seen."

It seems to me an assurance needs to come from someone outside of yourself, whereas conviction is inside one's self. I know I'm being analytical here, but I want to understand the verse as it is written. So, it appears there are two people (or things) needed in order for one to have faith in the other. I guess you could technically have faith in a chair that it will hold you up and not collapse. Which takes me to my second thought—having faith in the chair not to collapse is only half of the equation. There is the act of sitting in the chair to express your faith, so there is a difference in having faith and expressing faith.

Now, back to God, which is a relationship where both of us can show and express faith in each other. I've never thought about it that way. Does God sometimes say to me, "Bob, I have faith in you, that you can make the right choice and do the right thing in order for us to have a better relationship. But I'm giving you free will to choose while putting My faith in you. And I'm hoping you don't let Me down." Wow, that's powerful. Why not? Why can't God have faith in us also? I think He definitely puts His faith in us at times, and those are times I pray I can come through for Him. So, now I'm getting tears in my eyes just thinking about this concept, which I believe is true.

According to the verse, there is an assurance of the thing hoped for. How can one give an assurance to himself? He can't. But God can. And that's why a relationship with God must first be in place in order for faith to have a foundation to work. Otherwise you have faith in something you don't really believe in, and no one sits in a chair they think will collapse. Without a way to express one's faith, it proves itself to be worthless.

So, we have two people in a relationship (in this case, God is one of them), both with two parts to their faith. For you "numbers people" out there, let's do this mathematically. After all, God made His universe very precisely, and I believe it all adds up to His perfect plan.

GOD	BOB
1. Faith	3. Faith
2. Act	4. Act

Let both God and myself have both the possibility of having two qualities, faith and the act (showing) of that faith.

You can see that there are four ways to have only one thing, that is, where only one party has one of the qualities.

You can see that there are six ways to have only two qualities: One and three—God and I can have faith, but no one acts; two and four—God and I can both act, but not based on any faith; one and two—God has faith and acts on it, but I have neither; three and four—I have faith and act, but God has neither; one and four—God has faith but doesn't act on it at the same time that I have no faith but am showing some kind of act; and, lastly, two and three—I have faith but don't act on it, and God does not have faith but shows some sort of act anyway.

So, now we have ten different scenarios that could occur. But we're not done yet. There can also be four combinations where exactly three of the qualities above are in play, and then one final possibility of having all four in play. Now, we have a total of fifteen possible scenarios. Sounds overwhelming, doesn't it? But let's eliminate some of the obvious and simplify things.

God wouldn't be God if He couldn't create His own faith and be able to act on it in a perfect manner. We humans are the ones who can do the unholy with our free will. If numbers one and two above are fixed it simplifies things, but not that much because even though God has faith in us, we must act first for Him to be able to respond. The parent reacts to the child's learning and knows when the child is ready for the next step. God does not impatiently act out toward us until we have proven our faith by acting out toward Him first. The parent also would not give the child his inheritance before he has been proven worthy of it.

We have number one fixed—God's faith in us—if we can show our faith first. And number four as the closer, God's reaction to our act of living out our faith. Now, we can understand that most of the fifteen possibilities can never exist, and for the few possibilities that remain, they must happen in an order. A child learns to walk before learning to run. And the child who has a parent who loves him and wants to teach him has a much better chance of success. We have that in our God. He's waiting for all of us to take the first baby steps in our faith.

So, what's left of our mathematical summary? Number three must happen first—our baby step of faith, no matter how small. Look at the sinner on the cross. It only took one sentence, one little baby step at the very last moment, to gain eternity in heaven.

Given that we can make that baby step, God can open wider His faith in us. So, one and two alone, with nothing else, is a possibility—like having plans to build your home, but never building it. If we make the choice to act on our faith then numbers one, three, and four are a possibility—the plans with the building of the house. And God promises He will do His part if we do ours. He'll make sure number four gets added in the end—the completion of the home, which is not something physical, but a promise we can live there forever.

We could go through all the other combinations, but you can see that taking combinations like one, two, and four are not possible because the act cannot come before the commitment. It is also important to notice that having just number three is not possible. Number one always follows and immediately takes its hand. Once the child takes its very first step, something must happen; he either takes another or he falls. But the parent is right there making sure he won't fall. Eventually, he is given the chance to fall on his own. So are we.

All the fifteen possibilities boil down to Bob having or not having faith, acting or not acting on it, and then God doing what He always does and has promised to do. "And without faith it is impossible to please Him, for he who comes to God must believe that He is and that He is a rewarder of those who seek Him." Hebrews 11:6.

Once I profess my faith, act on it, and prove myself worthy to God, then God is open to profess His faith in me and react. All the other possibilities die on the vine before they can ever start to ripen. It must happen in the order of three, one, four, and then two.

Lori, I don't know what you think about all of this, but I have a clarity I didn't have before. I hope this was a good start for our study. I love you.

Bob

This was my sister Lori's response to my e-mail and her input about faith as we continued our study together. Upon reading it, you'll understand I have a great sister, an incredible woman of God who is a very talented teacher.

Dear Bob,

I've been enjoying thinking through your topic of faith; and while I haven't finished thinking through this inexhaustible subject, I have a few thoughts to share. First, I like your analogy about having faith in the chair requiring both belief and action. Hebrews 11:1 makes that implication fairly clear. If we have assurance and conviction (belief and trust that something is so), we will follow through with action.

This is also clearly indicated in James 2:14–18, "What use is it, my brethren, if someone says he has faith but he has no works? Can that faith save him? If a brother or sister is without clothing and in need of daily food, and one of you says to them, 'Go in peace, be warmed and filled,' and yet you do not give them what is necessary for their body, what use is that? Even so faith, if it has no works, is dead, being by itself. But someone may well say, 'You have faith and I have works; show me your faith without the works, and I will show you my faith by my works.'" [John Piper, in *A Godward Life*, said:] "You see that faith was active along with [Abraham's] works, and faith was completed by his works." This passage is *not* saying we are saved by our works, but that our faith is expressed *through* our works (our actions).

You have an interesting perspective here that I hadn't considered. However, I think I would reword your statement as follows: God's faith is not in us but in Himself; therefore, His confidence in our ability to do something—anything—for Him is rooted in His own omnipotent ability to accomplish whatever He wills. He is "the author and perfecter of faith" (Hebrews 12:2). Ephesians 2:8–9 says, "For by grace you have been saved through faith; and that not of yourselves, it is the gift of God; not as a result of works, so that no one may boast." Philippians 2:12–13 gives us the command to "work out" our salvation—not work *for* our salvation—but to demonstrate our faith through our actions. "For it is God who is at work in you, both to will and to work for his good pleasure."

Obviously, the rest of your mathematical equation rests on your premise about God's faith in us; and I have changed the focus of that premise. Feel free to disagree with me—that's what makes this Bible study productive and meaningful (and, I might add, enjoyable). I need to see supporting Scripture for that premise though.

Let me share something I read by John Piper [in his book *A Godward Life*] just last week that helped clarify my earlier thoughts. It is an essay called "Gift and Grit—Thoughts on Human Effort and Divine Enabling."

"*Question:* If God is the one who gives our varied measures of faith, should we pursue greater faith? *Answer:* Yes! With all our might! Through prayer, word, fellowship, and obedience.

"Faith is a gift of God. Romans 12:3 says to think with 'sound judgment, as God has allotted to each a measure of faith.' God measures to each believer a measure of faith. Ephesians 2:8 says, 'For by grace you have been saved through faith; and that not of yourselves, it is the gift of God.' The word 'that' refers to the whole act of God, including the accomplishment of salvation on the cross and the application of salvation through faith. Philippians 1:29 says, 'For to you it has been granted for Christ's sake, not only to believe on Him, but also to suffer for His sake.' Believing and suffering are both gifts from God. Similarly, repentance (the flip side of faith) is called a gift of God (2 Timothy 2:25; Acts 11:18). The revelation of Christ to the heart that makes faith possible is also a gift (Matthew 16:17; 2 Corinthians 4:4, 6).

"This does not mean faith is static or that we should not pursue it more and more. In 2 Thessalonians 1:3 Paul says, '… your faith is greatly enlarged, and the love of each one of you toward one another grows ever greater.' In 2 Corinthians 10:15, Paul says he hopes their faith will increase.

"Therefore, it is clear that faith should grow and not remain static. The fact that God gave you yesterday's level of faith does not mean His will for you today is the same amount of faith. His purpose for you today may be far greater faith. His command is to 'trust in Him at all times' (Psalm 62:8) and to 'grow in the grace and knowledge of our Lord and Savior Jesus Christ' (2 Peter 3:18).

"God commands what He wills, and grants in measure what He commands, but we should always pursue what He commands. He says, 'Work out your salvation…for it is God who is at work in you, both to will and to work for His good pleasure' (Philippians 2:12–13). God does not say, 'Since I work, you shouldn't.' He says, 'Because I do, you can.' God's gift does not replace our effort; it enables and carries it.

"We say with Paul, '[God's] grace toward me did not prove vain' (1 Corinthians 15:10). The gift of grace produced the grit of hard work. It is not the other way around. He goes on, 'but I labored even more than all of them, yet not I, but the grace of God with me.' Even Paul's working is a gift of grace. Yes, it feels like our effort. It is an effort! But that is not all it is. That is not what it is at root. If it is virtuous, 'it is God working in you, both to will and to work for His good pleasure' (Philippians 2:13). God 'fulfill[s] every desire for goodness and the work of faith with power' (2 Thessalonians 1:11). He equips us with 'every good thing to do His will, working in us that which is pleasing in His sight…' (Hebrews 13:21).

"Therefore let us press on to the greatest faith possible with all the means of grace God has given. Let us be like Paul and strive "according to His power, which mightily works within [us]" (Colossians 1:29). And when we have labored, let us not think more highly of ourselves than is necessary, but say with Paul, "I will not presume to speak of anything except what Christ has accomplished through me…in the power of the Spirit" (Romans 15:18–19). There is a place for grit in the Christian life ('I worked hard'), but it is preceded by and enabled by gift ('It was the grace of God'). Therefore, all grit is living by faith in future grace."

In closing, I'll echo the words of Jesus, 'Apart from [Him], [I] can do nothing' (John 15:5). If I keep it in proper perspective, there is no disappointment in that statement; rather, there is hope, joy, and confidence because everything is coming from a loving, grace-giving, all-powerful God.

I look forward to hearing your response to these thoughts.
I love you so much,
Lori

Do you get the feeling my sister should be writing this book and not me? It is very apparent to me when reviewing my own e-mail that I was in the left side of my brain, the numbers side, as opposed to the right side, the artistic side, during my analysis of Hebrews 11:1 on faith. But that is where God took me that morning. If we cannot understand that our relationship with our God is based on faith and it comes through a progression that must be in proper order, then we cannot move as easily. Anyone can move, but those who are moving in a direction with understanding and purpose can move with confidence and assurance.

Faith can and should be analyzed by man, but it is much more a necessity that it also be felt by man. And that comes from our brain's right side, the creative side, rather than the analytical side.

Leonardo da Vinci once said, "A good painter has two chief objects to paint, man and the intention of his soul." Wow, that might say it all right there. Is your faith in the chair that may fail you, or in our great God who cannot fail you? You can only fail Him. What is the intention of your soul?

My pastor describes faith like this:

"Faith is the supernatural ability to trust God to pull off the impossible. Faith sees the invisible, believes the incredible, and receives the impossible."

RICK RZESZEWSKI
PASTOR OF ORANGE COAST COMMUNITY CHURCH

How do know when you're really walking in faith? You'll know because you will have no worry, no stress, and no fear in your life. But there's even a better reason to walk by faith in God throughout your life. Because "without faith it is impossible to please Him" Hebrews 11:6. Shouldn't that be enough for us? Do we need to know any more? If we want to please Him, He tells us right there it cannot be done without our faith. So we must have faith. Let's not only have it, but also act on it, so God can act on it. Stop looking around for it, but look up and close your eyes because it is not something to be seen, but lived, as the intention of your soul.

"For we walk by faith, not by sight."

PAUL, 2 CORINTHIANS 5:7

Chapter Nineteen

LETTING GOD BE GOD

"I AM WHO I AM."

GOD, EXODUS 3:14

WHAT IS WRONG WITH US? Why do we always feel like we need proof God exists? I think we need to understand what we are really asking for when we demand proof. To accomplish this I'm going to ask myself some questions. Do I have proof my wife loves me? Would I even want that? At first glance, it seems I would certainly want to know if she truly loves me. But then, upon further consideration, I don't think proof is what I'm really after. There's no excitement in proof. And I'm pretty sure love needs excitement to be at its best. Part of the wonderful mystery of love is that it reveals itself in all sorts of unexpected ways. If we were to have absolute proof about it at all times, it would take away from its beauty and the spontaneity that makes it so incredible. When love is given unexpectedly and without any motive, that's its ultimate beauty. Why would God create His love for us any differently? And why do we seem to need proof in order to believe? What are we really asking for when we say things like, "How can I believe in a God when there's no way to prove He exists?" Or, "I'd have total faith in Him if He'd just give me a sign He exists." Or, as my friend Dave said in chapter thirteen, "Until God parts the waters to Catalina, I don't think I'll ever be able to make this kind of leap."

What do we truly seek? Here's the answer: These kinds of questions, and we've all had them, are asking for something you and I don't really want. We just think we do. God's love would be diminished if He gave us absolute proof. That's why we shouldn't desire it. And even if He proved His love beyond a shadow of a doubt, wouldn't many of us still question it? If He came riding on the clouds and proclaimed He is God, wouldn't many of us say, "How do we know You're not just some other supernatural powerful being that could be posing as God and trying to trick us? How do we know you are really God? If God exists, maybe He's testing us with the likes of you?" You see, there is no real proof for human beings. Nothing would ever be perfectly satisfying as proof in the eyes of predisposed doubtful human beings. So, we're asking for something that would actually make it worse for us—pretty good proof we'll still find some level of doubt. Then, when we finally discover the truth, we can really be ashamed of our doubt.

My point is: God already gives us proof at a level that will not diminish us but still has the benefit of victory through faith—the bridging of the gap we call doubt. Our faith is where all the glory and victory and power is held. That is also where God sees our strength and our worthiness of redemption for all our shortcomings. He delights in rewarding us for being satisfied with our faith alone and for seeing the signs of His existence in our daily lives, without the need for absolute proof, which we would most certainly doubt anyway.

Why can't we just let God be God? I interpret the following verse as God's way of asking us to do that.

"Cease Striving and know that I am God."

PSALM 46:10

He is asking us to let Him be who He is. What's wrong with us that we can't seem to do this simple thing? What is so hard about acknowledging we are fortunate to be alive on this beautiful planet, with a life given to us for free? Even if you don't believe in God, you should be able to acknowledge that your life was given to you from someone else. Why aren't we more thankful for this?

The answer is that society teaches us to obtain our success through strength. Strength comes from power. Power comes from influence. Influence comes from having something others want. Now, what comes to mind? Money, status, position, fame, talent, and even knowledge, to name a few.

Here is the diabolical dichotomy: Man works through life obtaining success through strength, but God works through man from man's place of weakness. Now, you've answered your next question—how is it possible to have both at the same time? And the answer is simple—it is not possible. Or more accurately, I should say, those two alone are not possible.

Almost all my writings have come at times when I am down, not up. God speaks to me much more clearly when my heart is open to Him. Not when I'm so up on my own accomplishments and goals that I don't have time for Him. When I'm down, I'm listening. When I'm up, I'm usually not listening as well and I'm much more likely to let my pride rule the day. I do try to realize this and then stop and say, "Okay, don't lose sight of who's in control," especially when I'm feeling most in control. And that helps, but the natural tendency is for me to feel like I've got a grip on the world and nothing's stopping me. That's when all hell is about to break loose. That's when I need to stop, be still, and say, "God, I'm going to let You be God!" When I get carried away in my own little successes, that's when I need to hand them over to God and say, "Okay, what's next? How is this benefitting You? How is this action honoring Your will?" Then I'm back on track and able to smile about it. Otherwise, I feel myself slipping. I feel myself "selling out." It's like saying, "I know You've done a lot for me, and I'm thankful, but I don't need You right now. I'm doing just fine on my own." Heaven help me when I start to think like this.

I want to be in a place of strength and yet remain close to God. God wants me to be in a place of strength too, but, more often than not, finds me much more approachable when I'm in a place of weakness. So, how can this dichotomy be reconciled to make sense? How can I become a winner in my own goals and successes and, at the same time, be pleasing God by being moldable, especially since this is what both of us want? The answer is not to change the two ingredients of strength and weakness, which are both needed, but to add another ingredient to the mix. Like a good cooking recipe, it's not that something needs to be taken away but rather something needs to be added to bring balance to the two things in conflict. This is true in music also. Adding a third note can often take away the dissonance of two single notes in conflict. I am going to get back to the answer in just a second, but first ...

Like I said before, it is not likely you can operate at full personal strength and be closest to God at the same time. The reason is because we are human. This is why monks practice self-sacrifice and Catholic priests don't marry and some religions practice fasting or sacrificing during certain holidays. I'm not agreeing or disagreeing with every religion's practices. I'm simply saying the reason for such acts is because they know they are less likely to be close to God when they are not sacrificing something. It makes them focus on God because of the conditions they have placed themselves in. When you're hungry for something, whether it be food or anything else, and you hunger for it from your own self-appointed sacrifice, as a means of forcing yourself to draw closer to God, then you're really in the act of being still and letting God be God. You're in essence saying, "God, I want to sacrifice so I'll feel the need, and then be forced to remember why I'm feeling the need—to get closer to You, to have You talk to me in any way that gets my attention—so I can build my faith stronger in You."

This doesn't mean you have to sacrifice something in order to be close to God. It simply means you need to know what state of mind is necessary in order to be close to God. And for some, having a reminder is necessary in order to act a certain way, just as an alarm clock is a reminder you've made a commitment to get up at a certain time. Again, when things are going so well for you that you don't need anyone else, you're not in a good mindset to be open to God. This is the hardest time to realize it, but it is also the most essential time to realize it and the time when you must set your own spiritual alarm clocks. They need to ring and say, "Okay, everything is going my way. I know it probably won't stay that way for long because life doesn't work that way. So I'm going to appreciate where I'm at right now and be thankful to God for all these free gifts He's giving me. And now I'm going to look to You, God, and say, 'How can I put it all out there for Your glory? How can I let You be God and not get carried away in myself? How can I make You proud with these free blessings?'"

Now, back to answering the question I threw out there—How can I become a winner in my own goals and successes and, at the same time, be pleasing God by being moldable, especially since this is what both of us want? In other words, how can I remain strong in my mind and achievements and also be the most pliable for God? Here's the missing third ingredient that needs to be added: Be strong in your achievements, but remain humble in your mind. God hates pride, but He loves the opposite, which is a humble heart. He wants you to be powerful and strong; He wants you to keep Him at the forefront of it all and not get wrapped up in your own admiration and pride. By practicing this concept, you're letting Him be God, and you are the servant. And you'll be a servant He'll take very good care of. This is the win/win formula. But that doesn't make it easy. In fact, it is very difficult to succeed in life while remaining humble because it is against our very nature and society has groomed us against it. But, as we all know, society doesn't always have the best methods for us to live our lives by. Power and success with a humble heart equals victory in both man's and God's eyes. That's the answer.

Here is another significant question we must ask ourselves, and then be honest in how we answer: Will we trust God to come through for us in His own way and in His own time? I love what John Piper has to say about this in his book, *A Godward Life.* "Human promises are broken because people do not trust God. In fact they don't even think of God. He is not in the equation. Money is in the equation. Shrewdness is in the equation. Human probabilities are in the equation. But God is forgotten. He is just not as real as the money we might lose." That really hits home, doesn't it? "He is just not as real as the money we might lose." Wow! Or the sickness we feel. Or the broken relationship we're going through. Or the job we just lost. He is not as real as the things you can see or touch. Well, He is as real, even more so. He's in control of it all. He made it all. Are we idiots?

Piper then challenges us, "I call you to reckon with Him. Take seriously the powerful, relevant, present, promising reality of God. Be holy. Be faithful. Keep your promises. Fulfill your commitments. Swear to your own hurt and do not change. God will be there for you. His smile is worth more than any gain from broken promises." That is the truth—His smile is worth more than anything. What most people don't understand is that His smile can also reward with anything. One thing that surely makes God smile is when we talk about our love for Him.

How do we go about revealing our own love for God in the presence of others? This is an important topic that needs to be discussed. Is it right to say, "I'm expressing my love for God in whatever way I feel compelled, and it must be right since I'm inspired to do so?" Of course not. We need to treat others as we want to be treated, and that goes for how we share God or talk about our faith. When I feel moved to share God's beauty in the presence of others, I always ask myself, "Who am I with? What is the setting and the situation, and how is it likely to be received?" The last thing I want to do is disgrace God by being forceful or self-righteous. Is a man justified who yells on the street corner telling everyone they are sinners and they need to repent? Is this the proper form in which to go to bat for our God? I sincerely doubt it. It is undeniable that the best way to gain the trust of others is to let them know you have their best interest at heart. Yelling at them does not usually accomplish this.

It is with the people I am closest to that I have the most difficulty and the most cautious mindset. I don't know if this is good or bad, only that it is the truth about me. It may be because I have the most to lose with them. Or it may be because I know them so well that I know where they already stand and what they believe. My daily walk is probably the most influential thing I can offer my friends and family. I'm not going to positively influence anyone by being a religious nut in their presence. If you walk godly in front of others they'll notice, as you do them. Your love for God can be revealed in all sorts of subtle ways that will be perceived, just as God reveals Himself daily to you and me in all sorts of subtle ways. Your job and my job is to pitch. It's not our job whether the pitch gets swung at or not. Throw out your love for God in whatever ways are comfortable for you—not too much, not too little, but just enough to let others know you're letting someone else drive, you're letting God be God.

People love people who show confidence in the unknown. They appreciate people who say, "I don't know what tomorrow's going to bring, but I'm looking forward to it." By letting God be God you're showing you have confidence and faith in the unknown and are excited about it. Even if they don't believe in God, they'll want to have that same confidence. I rarely have to say the word God in my daily talk with others. It's easy to love God and to talk about Him without overdoing it. While looking at a great sunset with someone else, it's easy to say, "Wow, Someone knew what He was doing." And if you get a good reception from that, you can follow with, "I wonder what He has in store for us tomorrow?" Or just let the first comment go and move on. You threw out a nice fastball for your Creator, and you can smile.

I have some wonderful, close Jewish friends. I love hearing about their faith in God and also learning about their religious traditions. Everyone who believes in God will have a different way of loving God and showing that love to others. There is no right or wrong if you have other's best interest at heart. Just standing on the mound and winding up occasionally. I love when my friends find ways of talking about their love for God in their own classy and subtle ways.

We need to do more of this. We need to show others we're letting God run the show. We need to let God be God by telling Him and others we're not ultimately in control, using whatever words or actions can communicate this with grace. There is a time to stand up for God with a firm voice, and you'll know if the time is right, but most often the message can be much better delivered with a gentle and graceful touch. I can remember only three times when I was not concerned about how strong I was about showing my faith, and yet I was never noisy about it. First, when I received Christ. Second, when I spoke at my father's funeral. And third, when I spoke in front of my church offering to teach a class on sharing the Christian faith. Only three times in thirty years. The reason I know God prefers a soft and gentle touch when sharing about Him is because that's how He Himself most often acts. He doesn't force Himself on others. He patiently and gracefully offers the opportunities in our lives. He makes Himself known to each and every one of us repeatedly in His own ways along our journey in life. Every now and then, He does allow a heavy hand in getting His message across, but it is the exception and not the rule.

It's not hard to figure out how God wants us to act. All we have to do is ask ourselves, "How does He act?" He acts out of love and patience and with grace and humbleness. That's how we need to let God be God. And we need to do it regularly and acknowledge there is a Holy One constantly in our midst.

"For I am God and not man, the Holy One in your midst."

GOD, HOSEA 11:9

PART III

ABOUT CHOICES

Chapter Twenty

BE STILL—
A PERSONAL CHOICE

"…that inward eye
Which is the bliss of solitude…"

WILLIAM WORDSWORTH

SOMETIMES IT IS FRUSTRATING to know something is true, while, at the same time, feeling I cannot do it justice with my words. This is the case with what I am about to discuss. I want to be able to transfer its worth to you. I know what I am about to tell you works for me and it will work for anyone willing to open themselves up to its powerful possibilities.

I'm no expert at it. In fact, I often wonder who am I to write about this? Like everyone else, I have my moments of weakness, doubts, and shames. For that reason, and many more, this practice offers great benefit. On a personal level, it has great impact on my life. With this method, I have learned to feel in touch with God at a deeper level than any other way I've tried in the past. Being still with God is a practiced method of meditation I hope will benefit your life as much as it has mine.

There are different levels in the art of being still. When God said, "Be still and know that I am God," He had a specific reason. It was to let mankind know He is in complete control and has a perfect plan. We are constantly striving to reach our own personal goals day after day. God doesn't want us to be so involved in our own little worlds that we forget to keep Him in the forefront of our lives. Sometimes He allows us to get knocked down so that we stop and say, "Wait a second, what am I doing? Why isn't this working out for me? Why do I have this goal? Am I thinking about how God has a purpose and a plan for what I'm doing? What are my motivations, and where is my heart?" These are the questions God wants us to "be still" about. He knows we're human and we're going to get sidetracked. In Psalm 46:10 He is telling us, (my paraphrase) "Stop going after your goals for a moment and connect with Me long enough to see if we both have the same purpose." This is the true meaning behind His words and the true form of being still. But before we get to that, let's look at a couple of levels of being still that are simpler but quite helpful in our daily lives. They will also help us achieve an even higher degree of being still biblically, as God really intends for us to be with Him.

At its simplest level, being still is the act of stopping briefly before we speak, act, or react to a situation or another person. This is not a spiritual level of being still, although it has great benefits. Following this one basic rule can improve your life. It has stopped me from making commitments I didn't want to make but would have if I had reacted first without thinking it through. It has prevented me from saying the wrong thing to the wrong person at the wrong time. It has kept me on track to make better decisions simply because it gives me time to evaluate without feeling pressure. I'm speaking from the experience of having made many mistakes. Not that I'm done making mistakes, but I know they will be fewer than they would have been had I not learned to be still. When someone asks me for a commitment, I usually say, "Let me check my calendar and also check with Susie's schedule to see if I'm available, and I'll get right back to you." I buy myself a little time. Even if I suspect I'm not interested in accepting the offer, I have time to think about how to reject it in a positive and polite manner. I don't have to lie either. The alternative is to answer immediately without much thought. This always seems to get me in trouble. I might end up accepting when I really didn't want to. Or I may end up insulting the person by rejecting in a not so nice manner.

Being still long enough to gather your thoughts before responding to someone is invaluable. This is especially true when working through relationship issues, and even more so with close friendships and marriages. Answering a child's request can be equally as powerful in making a good choice for them and for yourself. The list of benefits goes on and on. This is the first level of being still.

The second level is spiritual in nature and could be considered simply as an acknowledgement to God. You are revealing your frame of mind to Him. You are establishing your desire to be in sync with His plans. Each day, I try to say: "God, this day is all about You and Your plan and me just being a little part of it. I'm setting out to accomplish certain goals I have for my day, but I want You to know they are goals I believe are part of Your plan for me. If they are not, please show me in some way and I'll change my goals. But this is all for You. I trust You'll make me productive in my endeavors. I have faith in You and accept whatever outcome You have in store for me because I know it is all part of Your perfect plan." By saying something similar to this, you are expressing your heart to God and acknowledging He's in control and you're excited to see where He's going to take you. You've just been 'still' in order to get focus and direction with healthy and proper motives. God honors this type of being still with Him even if it's only for a few moments.

Now, if you've set aside the time to really be still and take it to a higher plane, then this last level of spiritually connecting with our great God is certainly the most fulfilling and rewarding.

Artists tell us the more lines there are in a drawing, the less important each line is. This makes total sense—sometimes less is more. We all know this to be true. It is also true the mind can do miraculous things when we get rid of the clutter. I call it "the zone." I guess it depends on your mood and how much clutter you carry whether or not you will be in "the zone." I hate to compare it with anything earthly, but what else can I do other then to use earthly terms. In other words, to be still is to be outside earthly feelings. You must get rid of the earthly clutter.

My piano teacher, Michael, when he goes into his own type of zone, becomes something more then himself. He plays the most beautiful expressions with his music. There's no written music in front of him. In fact, his eyes are usually closed. He knows where every key is—not as a key, but as an extension of what he is trying to say. His music becomes a story, a dialogue of his feelings. And for some reason, even though I'm not capable of playing this language, I can understand it when I hear it—and understand it so well it can bring tears to my eyes. He can communicate so much more effectively with sound than with words.

That is the essence of being still. Don't think it. Feel it. If a wave of contentment from the surrounding of the one and only great God doesn't come over you then, wait and be still until it does. If it takes a minute, great! If it takes an hour, trust me, it's still worth it. But like me, you'll probably get impatient very quickly. That's when you have to remind yourself, "Stay focused; God wants me to make the connection with Him. He'll bring me in if I am patient and keep my thoughts on Him." Don't give up. To give up is to tell God you don't trust Him to connect with you.

The problem is you and I can't connect with Him on our own. By ourselves we can't disconnect with the world long enough to fully concentrate on Him. Remember, He gives us free will. He's not going to force anything on us. But He will answer us if we're patient and give ourselves entirely to Him. This can take some time at first, but when it happens it is like a wave that comes over you. And it's worth the wait. If you've ever experienced looking at one of those Magic Eye pieces of art where you stare at the image for a while until it finally shows its hidden picture, it is like that. All of a sudden, after staring for minutes, it suddenly appears in a split second and you "get it." That is what happens when you enter "the zone." It happens in a split second, and you feel the wave come over you. Sometimes I can't make it happen at all. Usually it's because I'm trying too hard. Remember, this is a mutual thing. It's not all about you. Other times it happens much more easily and much quicker.

One way that seems to work best for me is to comfortably lie down, remaining motionless the entire time. I close my eyes and take a few really deep breaths of air. I think only of God, while giving myself over to Him, putting all my trust in Him. I tell Him I want to connect with Him more than anything—to tap into His spiritual realm—and that I know it is also His greatest desire to share it with me.

You must concentrate on remaining connected to God with your every thought. What I mean is that, as your mind starts to wander, and believe me it will, you have to bring God into the wandering thought. For example, you imagine sitting on the beach with God watching His beautiful sunset. Then you notice the ocean waves and immediately think of your last fishing trip, and suddenly you're in the boat with a rod and reel in your hand. You must bring God into the scenario with you. It is all right for your mind wander because that is natural and you want the connection to be natural, not forced. But since your mind is prone to wander, you must take God, or invite God, to go on the journey of your wandering thoughts. Now, you're on the ocean in the boat, and you can envision God hovering above all His magnificent ocean, watching over his creatures, including your fishing boat and everyone in it. Maybe God is even sitting in the boat with you. Then you remember hooking a fish, but the line broke and it got away. You are still in your conversation with God the whole time: "I remember the line broke and I was disappointed, but that was Your plan, wasn't it, God?"

Talk with God. Try to sense His answers. Open yourself up to answers that may be the opposite of what you would normally think. Usually this is the right direction of thought because His plan is so complex it most likely isn't the thing you had in mind. As your thoughts wander, bring God along with your imagination and its constant wandering and don't let Him slip away for more than a second or two from every step of your journey. If you keep Him as the focus of the whole journey, you will get closer and closer to Him until you're in "the zone." Keep asking Him into your every thought.

This is my best description of how to be still with God. Don't give up easily if it doesn't happen right away. Practice, and it will become easier, more natural, and most definitely fulfilling. For me, there is nothing like it. Just trust Him and have faith. That is all He asks of you. That is all it takes to make it work.

Some people might think what I have just explained is meditation or yoga. There are many other terms to describe the connecting of the mind and body to spiritual things beyond our earthly world of vision, sound, taste, smell, and touch. The difference is I'm not talking about anything spiritual that counts as an outside connection. I'm talking about your relationship with the only outside connection, the only power, the One who created it all, controls it all and planned it all.

God knows when we place our faith in Him and when we do not. Usually, I know when I am not placing my faith in Him. When I practice being still with God, I am not asking for anything except to be close to Him.

I had long ago finished writing this chapter when I came across the perfect saying. It has been pinned to my filing cabinet next to my desk for over seven years, and somehow got covered up. It was written in Unity's *Daily Word*® devotional, published on May 19, 2002. This is what it said:

"When I am looking for the answer to a problem, I may do research, ask questions, study, plan, or experiment with various options. I may busy myself by attending lectures on the subject, reading books or collecting information in discussions with others.

"But the answer comes most easily when I am quiet—when I am willing to cease all activity and all the thoughts in my mind and just listen in the silence of my soul. God is always there waiting for my willingness to be still and hear the answer I seek. So I stop trying and start listening in meditation with God. I ask for the solution to be revealed to me. The answer comes to me as a feeling, as an insight, or as a deep

peace that tells me that my problem is being solved even as I rest qui-
etly in the silence with God."

Wow! That's what I've been trying to say. It's what being still is all about.
Now, that's divine intervention when, by chance, I come across the perfect words
for what needed to be communicated.

Faith can and will replace fear when one is "still" with God. I hope you find
this peace and calmness, this serenity only God can offer you and that He wants
you to have. Trust in God and be still long enough to make the connection.

You may be asking why being still is so important to me, to the point I've
made it the centerpiece of this book. The answer is because it has truly changed
my life. Psalm 46:10 is such a powerful statement from God. When you think
about it, God doesn't make that many declarative statements in the Bible. It is
only at such times, like the handing down of the commandments, when God
tells us how to be. Usually His Word is more about how things work and how
things are planned. This verse is in the special class of God speaking directly, as
a commandment in how to conduct ourselves. The reason it is my centerpiece
is because, when I am still with Him, I know deep down in my soul He is there
and everything I've expressed in these writings is the truth, without any doubt.
When we're connected to the world, we'll always have doubt. When we become
still and get in touch with God, there is no doubt.

"But he must ask in faith without doubting,
for the one who doubts is like the surf of the sea,
driven and tossed by the wind."

James 1:6

Chapter Twenty-one

EXPERIMENT #2—
LOOKING INWARD

"Leadership is a combination of strategy and character.
If you must be without one, be without the strategy."

GENERAL NORMAN SCHWARZKOPF

VERY OFTEN, STRATEGY IS MISSING in experiments. People experiment with something unknown and untested in order to discover something new in a way that cannot be discovered by any other means. Reading about something or hearing about something can have impact, but there is no substitute for hands-on experience. It goes into the mind like no other method of learning. My goal in this experiment isn't to have strategy in order to win, but to gain character. And, hopefully, to become a better leader and teacher through better understanding and wisdom. To understand pain one must experience pain. To understand the needy and the less fortunate, one must become needy and less fortunate, if only for a short time. Just like pain, it doesn't have to last long to get the meaning firmly planted into one's mind. And there is no substitute for experience.

The date is September 5, 2008. I have another idea, one that's been on my mind for a long time. I have wanted to do this for years, but have never mustered the courage nor has the opportunity been so right. It is time. This seems even more intense than my first experiment in June 2004, when I switched places with my good friend Dave, the atheist. Since the third part of this book is about personal choices, I have to wonder about so many people who are not given opportunity in life. I'm referring to those people who are born into a life with few choices, either by means of their upbringing or their location. It is of no doubt that someone born to a married couple in the United States has a better chance of success than someone born to a single mother or born in a third-world country. Although they have freedom of choice, they most likely do not have the fortune of being raised in a family with education and opportunity, and therefore free choice to them is very limited.

What is it like to live among those who have nothing? I feel I do not appreciate my lot in life as much as I should. I am constantly complaining about my work. And yet I have chosen to continue in the construction industry. I have good clients, who pay me to build homes most people in the world only dream of owning. Just this morning I had a conversation with a client, and I asked him if he really wanted to spend a thousand dollars on one master-bathroom showerhead. I tried to talk him into a less expensive, easier to install, and less ostentatious showerhead. He said, "Nope, let's go with the expensive one." Yes, I have a good job. Sometimes it makes me sick, though. I see a lot of waste and a lot of spoiled people. I feel burned out with the way I make my living, and yet I know I'm fortunate. But deep down inside I can't stop complaining, and this bothers me to no end.

So, I need this experiment. I need it for me, although I realize it borders on craziness. My wife thinks I've lost my mind even suggesting it again, but I must go through with this now. A couple months ago, I mentioned to her I had been thinking about doing this, and, of course, she gave me the look. Like I'm crazy, but she's not too worried about me going through with it because I've been talking about it for so long and have never acted on it. I am compelled to experience this, but having the courage is another matter. Next weekend is the perfect time. My wife will be taking my daughter, Bree, to a Bar Mitzvah in the San Francisco area. Our son Paul is at Berkeley, and Sean is at USC. I'll be alone for the weekend. No one has to know where I am or what I'll be doing.

This is what I feel compelled to do: I will dress in blue jeans—stained and ripped, a torn shirt, and dirty shoes, and I will be dropped off in the worst area of a nearby city, skid row, with no money, no identification, no credit card, no jacket; nothing but a small notebook and pen in my back pocket to record my thoughts and experiences. I will live for two days and two nights with no place to sleep and no means of food or shelter. First, let me say I am ashamed to think this will be a true representation of the reality, especially since so many in the world face this every day of their lives. I'll spend only forty-eight hours—to them that would be a dream come true. To me it will most likely be agony, and yet life fulfilling in what I hope to gain in wisdom. I will live with those who are in the same situation as I will face.

For the first full day I will not try to accomplish anything but to observe others and to share their feelings. I am not to tell anyone I am anything but a vagrant, down on my luck—a bum with only the clothes on my back. I will see what it takes from a person's soul to have nothing. I will learn what it takes from a person's soul to see others look down on me. Maybe I'll experience compassion from others. I hope so. Maybe I'll become more compassionate after my experiences. I hope so. I want to learn about the homeless—those whom I only see occasionally and do have compassion for. But more often than not I think, *I can't solve everyone's problems*, and I move on.

The second day, I assume, will be more of survival. I'll most likely be hungry, cold, and tired, and in need of basic survival. To make things more realistic, I will not eat or drink anything for the twenty-four-hour period before the day I start the experiment. I will attempt to offer my services in exchange for food or shelter and see how I am received, since my appearance will not be pleasant to those fortunate enough to be able to help me. In no way will I be allowed to say I am anything but what I appear to be. I cannot reveal any truths about my real life, my education, or qualifications. I must resort to offering only skills my newfound peers will have. I'll offer to wash windows, clean up trash, or anything else that gets me a meal. I hope to see how difficult or easy it is to survive in these circumstances.

The main purpose of this experiment is to be able to appreciate my life more and to see if I can be of help, in some way, to those in need. I want to appreciate how fortunate I am having been raised by two loving parents, having been educated and set into a competitive group as a child, and among adults who have ambition and drive as I've progressed through life. My thinking is that these things were instilled in me from early on. I suspect I am who I am primarily because of my parents and all the opportunity and good fortune bestowed upon me. I think life will look very different to me after this, and I know no other way to get the education and wisdom that hopefully will come from this except to do it.

It is Friday, September 12, and I left work early, at midday, to start my experiment. I'm writing quickly before I go. It really started yesterday in my mind, when I knew in my heart I would go through with this. All week long I was pretty sure I would, yet I kept that little "out" in my mind. Yesterday, I knew without a doubt I would do it. So, it has been constantly on my mind the last twenty-four hours. I saw a vacant lot and wondered, *Will I be sleeping somewhere like that tomorrow night?* Thoughts are entering my mind about how awful the next couple of days will be. For some reason, I can't wait to start, though, maybe just to get it over with. I'm already hungry and thirsty, and I haven't even officially started. But if all goes right, I will be sitting in church on Sunday, showered, and shaved, and a very new man in more ways than one. Lastly, I'm writing a note and leaving it on my desk in case something does happen to me. It says, "Susie, I've gone to live with the homeless. If something happens to me—I love you! And, by the way, if something does happen to me, I want these to be my last words…"

> *"If a man doesn't put his life on the line for something he believes in,*
> *then his life isn't worth living."*
>
> MARTIN LUTHER KING JR.

My next entry is after I return…

What a life-changing experience. Oh, my God, I don't know where to start. First off, I didn't stay the entire second night. I know what you're thinking. I couldn't hang. Quite the contrary. I learned not only how to hang, but also that I have no fear at all of hanging. What I feared the most before the experience, I have no fear of now. The second night, tonight, would certainly be much easier. After all, I know what to expect now. But I don't see the point in doing more damage to my already hurting body. I've learned plenty enough in the last thirty hours, and my goal has been accomplished. Sleeping on the concrete behind three tires in a service station parking lot with my left shoe as my pillow again tonight will not teach me anything new that I didn't get from yesterday's very long, hard night. I had not eaten in forty hours, and a short sip of water was all I had to drink in that same period.

I recorded sixty-three pages of notes on my three-by-five-inch notepad. That and a pen were all I had. I had the clothes on my back—a torn shirt with holes the size of baseballs at the armpits, the collar separated by a four-inch tear, a hole the size of a golf-ball in the chest; no jacket; and ripped blue jeans with stains and frayed at the pockets and knees. I wore old, dirty tennis shoes and a straw hat that was ripped so badly at its front brim it drooped down along the sides of my eyes and I could see only through the ripped slots. I hadn't shaved for two days going into the weekend, and I didn't shower the day before. Anyway, I looked the part, and not one person questioned, even for a second, that I wasn't one of them.

Here was my first lesson: Before I did this, I thought I'd be an outsider looking in, but in reality I quickly became an insider looking out. I really was one of them, and they became my friends. I didn't have anyone else, and I had to learn the ropes very quickly. I soon found out the "fortunates" (that's what I began calling normal people with jobs and homes) were not going to help me. In fact, I couldn't get a job for even two dollars an hour. I asked a lot of shop owners if I could do anything for them and said I didn't want a handout, that I would do any work they had for just three dollars per hour. Then I dropped my price to two, then one. Still no takers.

Where do I start? I'm anxious to jump to the end and tell about what I learned. I am so excited about how I feel right now and what insights I gained and how I see things differently. The experiences seem unimportant to me now. The knowledge I gained is the only important thing, and that's what I want share. But a solution without a clearly defined problem probably won't be understood, so I will start from the beginning. The italicized words are my exact written words that I jotted down at the time. Often, I had to write quickly and abbreviate because others were close or it was something I didn't want to forget but couldn't stop to write in length at the time. Most of my notes were written right after the experiences, when I could find a place alone to write. Again, there are sixty-three pages of notes I will attempt to condense for you.

Sometimes I'm in present tense and sometimes in past, depending on whether I'm writing just afterwards like I'm still in the moment or I'm writing after a length of time and it seems past tense to me at that point. My intention is to transfer the experience, not worry about the tense, especially since it travels in and out of the timeframe so often. Lastly, it is fitting to note the day before the experiment was September 11, 2008, the seventh year anniversary of the terrible attack on our great country. I watched a 9/11 special on TV that night, and it made me think seriously about tragedy, definitely setting the mood for what I knew would be my next forty-eight hours (only thirty in reality).

I had originally planned on Susie dropping me off in skid row on Friday and picking me up at an assigned place on Sunday, but it turned out I did this experiment by myself without anyone knowing. Here's how it went:

I just drove to a very bad place in downtown, two cities south from where I live. I parked where I thought my truck would be safe, and I'm pretty sure I can find it again in two days. There are no street sweeping signs to get a ticket, and I've removed anything of value from the inside, hoping no one will break in looking for valuables. Before I left, I emptied out the back of my truck, and hopefully it will blend in to the surrounding area. I'm in a bad area already, but I drove by a really bad area that I'm going to walk to now. I think my truck will be safer here though.

I just walked about a mile and a half. It appears I'm in the city hall area, where the jails and courts are. I see my first place that I will go—now it starts—

I'm sitting under a tree. I found a spot between two roots protruding out of the ground, and the spot is sloped nicely for a seat. There are eight of us here. All homeless. I have nothing with me except my pen and notebook. I sat for the first fifteen minutes and just observed my new peers, trying not to look at them very often, just blending in. I have nothing with me. I'm noticing my peers at least have backpacks, blankets, and jackets; one push cart is here. A middle-aged black man just asked a white woman, maybe thirty-five years old, for a cigarette. They were so polite to each other. He said, "Please." She said, "Sure, no problem." He said, "Thank you very much." She said, "You're welcome." I rarely see such manners in the well off. Another man just rode up on a bike. He's middle-aged, black, with a beard.

(Please note: Although I describe people's races, there is no prejudice. I merely want to communicate the descriptions of those I'm observing, and, later on during my experiences, I notice something that is eye-opening and it has to do with the mix of races among my new peers. For that reason I am glad I often noted the races and their interactions. It is interesting it will have significance later, even though I am not aware of it at the time of this writing.)

The black man rode up on his bike. *He obviously knows the other homeless person he is next to. He has only what's with him, as does everyone here. From what I can tell, most of them know each other, even though they have their separate spaces—about fifteen feet from each other. I am obviously the newcomer to this area, but no one really cares. I glance out the side of my head to the right through the ripped slit in the brim of my straw hat.*

A policeman rides a motorcycle through on a narrow thirty-inch-wide path of broken asphalt. I think, Are we in trouble? I've only been here a short time into my journey. Am I going to jail already? He ignores us. After all, we have nothing and we're not causing any problems—just sitting, lying around, or sleeping. One person leaves. There are now four men and two women, plus myself. I think someone else may have left while I was writing. Two fortunate women walk through as they talk, on their way to work I presume. The city buildings are only a few hundred feet away—probably their places of work. They look at us as they walk by, not breaking from their conversation. They look more curiously at the two homeless women. Not a word from any of us.

The cop rides through again in the direction from where he came five minutes ago. I just notice the first bite of cold on my arms and I'm thinking about what it will be like when the sun sets and night falls. I fear for the night for some reason. I'm not afraid of hunger, but the night has me in fear of the unknown. It is most on my mind. I have nothing. No jacket, no keys (I locked them hidden in my truck with my license, thinking I'll use the hidden key under the back tailgate when I return in two days), *no money, no ID, nothing. What is my purpose out here as a homeless person? What are my new peers' purposes? I guess we're just surviving. This is depressing. My sciatic nerve on my left side is acting up already and is giving me pain. I must get up and move.*

Note: As I chime in now (Saturday evening) in normal print, I am coming from the point of view of having had all the experiences. Little do I know this last comment I made yesterday about my back hurting is nothing compared to the soreness I will feel later on. The homeless are tough. They sleep on flat surfaces, around germs and filth all day and night. And I don't really remember any of my new friends being sick. I started feeling sick in my throat after the first five hours. They have obviously built up an immunity to the germs and conditions. I never thought about that before my experience. But now, after living it— there is no doubt it is true. My sore back, shoulders, and neck are proof. I'll bet tomorrow I'll feel even worse. Returning to yesterday—

I get up and move to hopefully relieve my sciatic pain. I ask another thin, black man, also bearded, where I can get a drink of water. He says, "The library, right over there." As I'm walking away he says, "And it's really cold too," as if this is an exciting secret he's sharing with me.

Note: I wrote the above notes after leaving the man's presence but before entering the library. This is often the case. I will be telling you about something after I have left the area, in order to record it right after it occurred. This was my first survival discovery—where I could get water and go to the bathroom.

This is a great place to use a bathroom. I walk in with my head down because I know they think I'm just another homeless person walking in to use the bathroom. Plus, I'm somewhat ashamed of how I look. It feels demeaning. It seems to be accepted easily though. I'm sure it is an occurrence that happens many times a day here. This is good. I have a place to drink and relieve my bodily functions.

I walk another block or so and stop now. I just counted the homeless. I count twenty-six homeless people here, and there are more along the sides of the building. Twenty two of them are men. Every race and color is here. Mostly Hispanic and black and a half-dozen whites. There's a younger woman, early twenties—seems odd to me that she's homeless. She's Hispanic and appears to have a boyfriend, as they seem like a pair here. He's older by ten years or so.

(Later, I will come to find out these two are part of a group I call the alpha group. They are in the younger crowd, and, at night, as I will find out later that same night, they are loud, play music (guitar), cuss a lot, smoke, do drugs, and nobody really bothers them. It is apparent they would use force to maintain their superiority. They are a pack unto themselves. For some reason I was drawn to want to be a part of their group since I sensed a protective unity with them, but, after seeing their behavior later that same night, I realized it was good I kept a low profile and hung with the older, less noticeable peers. The alpha group is more like a harmless gang within this community.)

The younger women are usually in groups of five or more with the younger men. I ask a man if this area is a safe place to sleep. He says, "It's pretty safe, but the cops will kick you out if you don't hide. He tells me they feed us in the evening time. I ask, "Who?" He says, "A Catholic man comes in the evening every night to feed us." No wonder there are so many here. I ask his name. He says, "Steve." I say, "I'm Bob." We shake hands, and I say, "Thank you," and walk away.

I hear a woman singing. She's alongside of the building about 100 feet away. I walk that direction. She's looking upward to the sky, eyes closed, with a hand radio and ear pieces in her ears. Three fortunates walk by me, one on his cell phone. I get the "he's homeless" look. Funny how when I started out, in my two-mile walk to this area I was so ashamed because of the way people looked at me. I was really feeling self-conscious. As the hours passed I realized I'm not ashamed anymore. I have bigger fish to fry then my ego.

I get the look, but I don't care anymore. I walk in front of the singing woman as she sits on her blanket on the grass about fifteen feet from the sidewalk where I just passed the fortunates. I stop, but she doesn't see me because her eyes are closed. A man is asleep next to her on a large blanket. They are both black and about forty years old. She sees me after about fifteen seconds. I say, "You have a nice voice." She says, "It's damaged and I'm trying to get it back. Too much yelling at people." She says, "See that red-haired girl down there? I just told her off."

Her conversation was colored with curse words. *She continues, talking about the red-haired girl. She becomes angry and starts rambling about why she is upset at the girl. I just listen and wonder how I'm going to get away from this. She is really working herself up, and I'm not saying a word now. When I sense she's breaking to catch a breath, I say, "Well, I can't blame you. I hope you get your voice back." This calms her and she says, "You seem like a nice person." I say, "You seem nice too," although I'm obviously not thinking that. I ask about the Catholic man. "You mean Sammy?" she says. "You can get clothes from him too on Saturday mornings." I'm thinking to myself,* What about tonight? It's going to be cold, and I'm going to freeze. *She says, "Tomorrow there will be feasts all day. People bring food two or three times on Saturdays. It's the best day." I thank her and find out her name is Dolly before moving on.*

I think about the Catholic dinner provider coming later, and I'm relieved to think I can get a meal if I want one. But I'm going to go downtown and try to earn a meal the honest way. Tonight is still my biggest worry. How safe will it be? Nobody knows where I am. And I have no ID on me. I am writing now, and I keep looking over my shoulder. I can't shake the feeling I might get mugged as I'm writing. It's been overcast all day, and a breeze is bringing on the cold.

I walked a little ways and now I'm in a square between city buildings, where more fortunates walk by. There are only four homeless here. I see three older men, all with backpacks, sitting on a bench. There is one bicycle and, next to it, a separate spoked wheel with no tire on it. A fortunate sits close by on another bench talking on his cell phone and dressed nicely. I talk briefly with the three men. They are not very friendly, but they do give good information to my questions. I ask if anyone wants to join me going to town to try to earn some money by offering to work. They decline. I ask, "What do you guys do for money?" Two of them say they get social security. One doesn't, but he doesn't offer up how he gets his money. I say, "I'm too young for social security. I'm only forty-eight." One man says, "You have to wait for it like we did."

Now, I'm on a bench next to a very old, overweight, and hunchbacked woman. I've walked a ways toward a main street where I'm going to look for work. She has all her belongings in a shopping cart. Her whole life is in that cart. I sit on her left side and notice her left ankle is wrapped and swollen twice the size of her other one. I say, "Hi." She is silent and gets up to walk away. It is obvious she doesn't like my presence. She pushes the cart very slowly across the street. Minutes ago I had crossed that same crosswalk in front of a police car. He gave me the look also. I'm going to get up and offer to help the old woman.

That didn't go very well. She just looked back and shook her head side to side when I offered to push her cart for her. I left. I'll head into town for work.

I walked quite a few blocks between these writings.

I've gotten to an area of town where there are lots of stores. I'm really feeling depressed, and I want to end this now after only about four hours into it. But I'm not giving up. I've planned this for years, and I'm not giving up and failing now. I'll never forgive myself if I call this off this early. My plan is to earn some money or return to the park for food if I fail to do so. I'm feeling the cold again and it has me worried. I wish I had brought a jacket. Maybe I was a little too ambitious coming out here with just the shirt on my back. I'm *all in now. Every two hours feels like about eight. Time moves very slowly. This is going to be the longest night of my life. Moving on.*

I wonder if I look too homeless as I'm in such bad, stained, and ripped clothes, and my hat is pathetic. I need something to cut off the ripped and hanging parts of my hat. I try to cut them with a partly sharp rock but to no avail. I'll get help from someone to cut the pieces off. At this point, I can't even see where I'm walking anymore.

I stopped by a dress shop where they make wedding gowns. No one was in there. I called out a few times but no one answered. Seemed odd. The store next to it was an extension of that store and I found Evonne. I asked if I could borrow scissors to cut the drooping brims off my hat. It was really getting hard to see where I was going. The pieces are falling to the floor and there are little straw pieces everywhere.

She must be wondering, What have I gotten myself into with this homeless guy? *I thank her and leave. Two girls were handing out flyers in front of their store and when I passed they didn't offer one to me. What would be the point of handing one to a homeless man? He has no money. I was treated as worthless to them. At least worthless to the cause of them being able to make any money off me.*

I sit writing again. Evonne looked nervous when handing me the scissors. She was alone in the shop, and she was handing me a weapon. But she trusted me, although hesitantly. I will go back next week and do something nice for her. I've decided that. Maybe just because of the sympathetic look she gave me—like she cared. Anyway, it left an impression on me.

I pass by numerous shops and ask each if I can work an hour of labor for them for three dollars. A flower shop, a travel shop—no luck. A 99-Cent store, where they tell me to ask at the clothing shop next door. The clothing shop has boxes of jeans and shirts everywhere, and three guys are moving them around. I ask if I can work for three dollars for one hour. One guy jokingly says, "Do you know how to file a lawsuit?" Water runs from the ceiling above down on top of some of their boxes. At first I'm thinking that moving heavy boxes is going to do a number on my back, but I'll do it. Actually, they decline my offer, even when I lower the price to two dollars for an hour's work.

This ceiling leak onto their boxes of jeans has them pretty mad. I stray from my promise this one time without realizing I've done so. I say, "I have some plumbing experience and maybe I can fix the leak, but I have no tools and you'll need to get the parts for me." They all pause and look at each other. One of them says, "Here's the ladder, but we don't have a flashlight. I climb the ladder and look through the drop grid ceiling. It smells terrible, and I immediately recognize it is a sewer line leak. This is going to be ugly, and I don't really want to get sick. They say that they will call the manager and that this has happened before. I happily depart from this situation and realize I am not supposed to offer any skilled labor as part of my commitment to myself. I guess I was feeling desperate and didn't realize it when I was in the moment. I tried a couple more shops—no luck. No one is going to hire me. I'll walk back to the park and get the free food. How depressing.

I just finished a long talk of about an hour or so with a new friend, Dale. He's fifty-three, white, male. He was adjusting the spokes on his bike wheel, since it was rubbing badly. It took him over an hour to do it. He's in no hurry. I stayed with him the whole time and made a new friend. These people are my friends now, I'm realizing, because the fortunates aren't going to help me. That was obvious from my city experience.

One thing I learned from this is that people will gravitate to other people who can help their cause, at whatever level that may be. I was gravitating to my homeless friends because that's all I had. And I was welcoming any help I could get at this point. These are my notes after I left Dale. Notice they are in past tense because I was with him for some time and it felt more like a past experience by the time I wrote.

I asked about a safe place to sleep. Dale said he thought it was going to rain and the parking structure is the best place during a rain. I asked about it being all concrete though. He said, "Don't you have a mattress or pad? Where are you from?" I said, "I'm new to this area. I'm from Long Beach, and I'm down on my luck." Dale was quite helpful. He told me how to get in with the groups and make friends. He taught me about 'canning.' I said, "What's canning?" His voice was hard for me to hear. It was quiet, without an edge to discern the consonants, and my hearing isn't what it used to be. He told me canning was digging for cans in the trash. He said it was getting very competitive now.

His hands were cracked and dirty, with cuts on the fingers. His right wrist was red and puffy and scarred. I asked him what happened to his wrist. He said he was in a fight, and he was banned from the civic park by the police. He said, "I've had so many cuts on my hands from digging in the trashcans. I don't pay attention to them anymore." He returned to his complaints about how canning has become so popular and that everyone is doing it now. "Times are tough," he says.

Wow, a sign of our economic times—even hits the homeless—I never saw that one coming. How eye-opening is that?

Dale told me he's made forty bucks in a day canning before. Then he says, "More like ten or fifteen dollars now because the trashcans are getting picked over." But when he gets enough money together he'll get a motel room and get a good shower, a bed, and watch TV for the night. I asked how often he gets a motel room. He said about twice a month. He tells me his wife is over there on the grass on a blanket with their group. There is a dog there with them. It's a beige poodle—as happy as can be—running around with a home-less girl about forty years old. I think, Funny, dogs don't know poverty. Only humans. *That dog is as happy as any rich dog. Maybe more so—he's got the whole park with no fences. This really strikes me as eye-opening—the homeless dog—makes me think long and hard about that truth and the fact that if you don't know you're an unfortunate, then you really aren't.*

Dale's friend walks up, also white, about my age, late forties. He has long hair. Dark red tanned skin, leathered look. Smokes a cigarette. He enters the conversation. Dale introduces me, and I'm accepted. I never find out the new man's name after he tells me he's a parolee from a double murder and got out on a double-homicide conviction. This is the first time I'm thinking, I'm in over my head here. (One of these days Susie will read this, and I'll be hearing it from her.) I decide that befriending Dale may not be in my best interest, as his parolee friend will come with the package.

I see Dale roll some tobacco into a paper and make his own cigarette while he breaks from his wheel spokes' adjustment. I don't think much about it except maybe it's pot because it has the joint look, but it doesn't smell like pot. About twenty minutes into our conversation I notice another homeless man rolling a cigarette with the same-looking tobacco holder and paper. I ask Dale why he doesn't buy a pack of cigarettes instead. He tells me a pack is five dollars, and you can buy the tobacco and paper for less than half that. You can even roll your own and sell them for a quarter each and make a few bucks.

This fascinates me. I realize that at every level of our society there are ways to save money and improve on the current system. Capitalism finds a way to thrive no matter what. People will always find solutions to making money, saving money, and making money go further. In a free society, at every level there is capitalism going on—in ways I've never thought of.

Dale has found an easy way to improve on the standard system and do the same thing at a lower cost. Sounds like a Fortune 500 company to me. I wonder if the quality control is any better.

I'm at a new location now. I'm sitting on a concrete bench in a small park about a quarter mile from where I met Dale. I'm kind of lost now. But figure I'll get oriented at some point. There are some tall buildings at the city hall area where I started out, and I should be able to find them. I just observed a game of cards where they used smooth stones as their money. There was a big pile in the center, and the winner was quite happy with his take. This also fascinated me. At another table I stopped to observe a game of chess. One guy has just won, and a new opponent sits down. I notice the new guy sets up his queen on the wrong color opposing the champion's king. I don't say anything but I fight off the urge to. I almost say something at one point but figure they'll notice. Afterwards I see that my decision for silence was a wise one because I realize they are only speaking Spanish and I can't understand much of what they are saying. They don't talk to me, and as I leave I hear them talking about the strange newcomer, but I don't know what they are saying, just that I'm sure it is about me. They never do see the queen error. I walk away thinking, Does it really matter? And then I think how often it probably really doesn't matter when I do open my mouth about most things. Four other Hispanics play quarters by seeing who can flip one closest to a large crack in the sidewalk. They never exchange the quarters—just play for fun. One rolls near my foot and I point to it. He looks at me strangely, and I feel that I don't fit in at this park very well, at least from their perspective. The language barrier doesn't help me either. This is the first place I feel unaccepted. I'm moving on.

I just stopped to think about what my next move is. I'm a long ways from the civic center now, and it's starting to get dark. The heavy overcast makes it seem like darkness has been coming for hours now, but the last ten minutes have really made the transition become reality. My most feared time is nearing—night. I'm looking upward trying to find one of the tall buildings that will steer me in the right direction of the feeding park. It must be getting close to feeding time. I see a North American Title building. Funny, I think to myself, They are the largest client of my good friend Dave. *A couple of years ago I finished building a 1,700-square-foot wine cellar under his custom-built home that houses his 3,000-bottle wine collection. Funny how it seems much more extravagant to me today. Right now I have nothing, and I'm not seeing things from that side of the equation anymore. That North American building reminds me of my real life. I am an insider looking out, and I don't want to see it the other way now. I want to feel the real experience. I want to hurt, and I want to suffer just like my friends have to. And I know I've got two nights and another day to go through. I'm moving on now toward what I think is the northwest.*

I've arrived at the feeding park just in time. The police are here. Dolly is arguing with them about something. I can't get involved, although I want to help her. The Catholics have just pulled up on the street, so my timing is good. I won't go hungry tonight.

There are about eighty people in a line to get food. A van pulled up with four Catholic workers. Steve sees me and says, "You've come back for food!" *He tells me that if we help set up tables and put the food trays out we can go to the front of the line. I help carry food trays and tables to set up, but I feel that I can't eat before all these hungry unfortunate souls get to eat so I'll forego my place at the front of the line.*

Helping the Catholics set up gives me the opportunity to learn more about them. One of them carries a mail carton and I ask, "What's that about?" *She tells me they deliver and mail letters for the homeless. I find this very odd. Who are they writing to? Do most of them even know how to write? I don't witness any letters changing hands, and the mail experience still seems odd and out of place. To me, there are much more pressing concerns than mail, like food and medical care, but they offer the service anyway. It is nice to see it offered, though, as if the Catholics are letting them know that they are a full-service help outlet.*

The food smells good, and I'm not too proud to have a meal with my new friends. About half have been fed now, but the line has grown back to its original length and even longer, maybe over 100. I admire the Catholic helpers. I really do think that at one time they were in this line themselves. I don't ask, but I do ask how long they've been helping. "Six years," she tells me. I say, "Every day for six years?" "Yes," she says. I'm amazed at her dedication. What a great person I'm in the presence of. I think about how big her crown is going to be in heaven.

The police are still present but quiet. This must be a regular round for them at dinner time. People are quiet as they eat. It is very quiet, except at the table where they are serving. I'm starting to feel less like an observer and more like one of them now. My comment to the helper, "How long have you been helping us?" makes me realize that I didn't say, "How long have you been helping them?" These are my friends, and the people serving us are our saviors. I see familiar faces, and I like these people's souls. I've been bonding with them, and twice now I've been close to tears in how much it hurts to see the poverty. Then I get a glimmer of hope as I see someone show the same joy from something simple and priceless, as it has no intrinsic value, but it has great value to them. Just like the man throwing the quarter close to the crack or the man who won the pile of stones. Their joy is as great as mine when I have moments of happiness. They do it with much less than me, though.

Many eat their meals on tops of street-side news stands or lying down on the grass. All have Styrofoam plates provided by the helpers. Car traffic is heavy on the street as if it's rush hour, but it feels later to me. The overcast day has messed up my ability to sense the time. But it's just another hour for us here. Time does not have the same meaning. Others eat along a four-foot-high concrete wall. There's a construction zone next to us—dirty and trash-littered and chain-link fenced-off areas. A radio plays, and all is well for us during this time of eating. I'm having a moment of real feeling and connection to God right now as people are fed. It is as if God is watching over us and making sure we're taken care of. He has planted his grace in these people's minds to be our caretakers. I hear the John Lennon song "Imagine" on the radio. I think to myself, How fitting and how beautiful at this moment. I'll never hear that song again without placing myself in that exact moment and feeling those feelings.

Day turns to evening now. Only about thirty people are left in line, and

I'm still waiting to make sure they're fed first. A heavy white woman who's been in the same place all day has two plates of food and yells at someone from a distance. She eats from one plate while balancing another on her leg. She has lots of belongings—a bicycle, flashlight, blankets, backpacks—she seems to be a fixture here. You can tell who the leaders and veterans are and who the followers are, but one thing's for sure—if you're nice to people, they're nice back.

The line has only a few people left, and I go over now. The food is literally gone as the last person goes through. They've done this so many times, I figure they've got it down pat now. Only a few cookies remain and some juice and scraps from the fruit trays. I realize I'm not going to eat tonight, but I'm not disappointed. I know I'll have food again in the near future. I've somewhat lost my appetite, maybe knowing I'm not going to eat. I don't know, but I'm glad food isn't controlling my thoughts. The night is, however, and it's here now. I help the Catholics load up the empty trays, and we take the tables down. Hardly anyone helps out on the cleanup. This bothers me a little because they've been so good to us. I think it has come to be expected now and not appreciated enough by the homeless. That's sad also. I make a point to tell the Catholics how much they're appreciated and how great their cause is. It's been many hours since I've eaten anything, and only one sip of water at the library earlier. I had made a point of not eating the day I started the experiment and, in fact, had not eaten since lunch the day before I started. Now it is the evening some thirty hours after my last meal, and it is obvious I'm not going to eat tonight.

The streetlights come on now, and I sit with my back to a dumpster as I write. Two fortunates walk toward me, and one pushes the other toward my legs causing him to jump over me. The pusher laughs. They don't know I'm privy to their little ridicule. I can't care less what anyone thinks of me now. But I feel sorry for them—their actions tell me they have a lot to learn the hard way, especially when it comes to others.

I was amazed at how much previous anxiety I had over the unknown nighttime coming, but how calming it is now that is has finally come and I feel no fear anymore. It makes me think about how we always worry about the unknown, and then it never turns out like we think it's going to anyway.

I see a woman washing things at a drinking fountain, but I'm not sure what it is she's washing. I walk that way, and she starts to brush her teeth at the fountain. She's about fifty years old, dark hair with silver streaks, Mexican, and I ask if she knows a safe place to sleep. Her name is Silvia. This is one of the few times I'm writing as I'm talking, and she continues to brush her teeth. She offers to take me around the block to some benches where she says she likes to sleep.

I follow her to an area that is literally next to a side street where cars do come by but not very often. It is quieter, and there are six benches in three groups of two. All but two are occupied by homeless who have staked out their places for the night. Silvia already has her place as a regular there. I take one of the open benches and thank her for her help. A man comes up within a few minutes and takes the last one, the one next to me. The benches touch at one end so it's like having a bunk mate at the same level. There is good tree coverage above us, and it does seem like a good place to spend the night. There is a strong smell of urine here, and I'm wondering whether or not I can endure this for the whole night. Not to mention the health factor.

The man next to me is old, about seventy, white, and unshaven. He starts to smoke, and the smoke blows heavily onto me. I'm writing this now as I experience it. The smoke is drowning out the urine. That's one benefit. But the combination of the two for three or four minutes makes me decide to find another home for the night. I don't like being this close to the street either— seems dangerous. I'll move on. I'm going to thank Silvia first before I leave. She was kind to me. No one really has an ulterior motive here other then to just get through the day and night, and then do it all over again.

I walked in a new direction now, toward the west for the first time.

I'm really getting tired now. I must have walked over fifteen miles today. And they've been an exhausting fifteen miles, a very slow-paced fifteen miles. And the constant writing doesn't let my mind have much time to rest. That's probably a good thing. I've found a lit area near a commercial store where I can write.

I said goodbye to Silvia when I left the benches. That place had special meaning to me for some reason—I'm not sure why, but it left an impression. Maybe it was just her. Maybe it was the smoke and urine. I don't know, but it's on my mind as I stop to write again. I looked back as I walked away and thought, "I'll never see her again. I hope she'll be okay."

I'm going to continue walking toward the west and explore a new area. I figure if I stay closer to the busy street areas at night it will be safer, and I'll find a place to sleep along the way. I'm feeling like the night really isn't any worse than the day. In fact, it quiets down and feels good, and it has not turned as cold as I feared it would. It was colder during the late day for some reason. But now I'm feeling as if I've accomplished something by making it into the nighttime and facing the unknown. Like I've survived what I feared.

I walked a long ways, past a stadium where a football game was being played. I started to think the area was probably improving, but then I came across a series of bail-bond shops. There were about eight of them. I must be close to the jail to see so many of them. Most of the signs are in Spanish, and now I see some fast food outlets, the first ones of the day.

I'm in a Jack In The Box now taking a rest. I look pretty pathetic and I'm wearing thin. The lack of food and water with the long walking today has me feeling somewhat deranged and my brain is not thinking very well. All of the sudden I'm not writing very good. I can't focus on the paper, and I'm just scribbling, almost unreadable now. I will find a place to sleep now.

I've walked a few more blocks and found myself in the first potentially dangerous situation. I was on the busy street, and there were three younger Hispanic males on the sidewalk in front of me. As I got closer, I saw them separate, one on one side and two on the other side. I didn't think much of it as I was very tired. But the one on the street side had his hand on what looked like a knife as he slipped the instrument into his front pocket. By the time I saw this, I was practically next to him and between the other two. Our eyes met, and he knew that I knew something didn't look right. I continued through the situation watching cautiously, and nothing came of it, but I still think something was up. I felt lucky to be out of it as quickly as it felt I had gotten into it. And it made me more cautious from that point forward.

A few blocks later now, I'm sitting on a plastic chair next to another man in front of a donut shop, and it's getting late. Must be 10 p.m. or so. I'm so tired—I'm just resting my head against the ragged block wall behind my chair. I'll rest and then find my place to sleep. I looked for a place along the way, and the only thing that looked decent was a vacant lot. But I realized it had quite a bit of dog poop all over the place. Too bad I realized that about half way in. I could see better on the way out as the street lights, at that point behind me, helped me to better dodge the newly discovered obstacles.

I find myself back on a main street again, and there is a Denny's type restaurant on the corner, but it has a Spanish name. There is car repair shop next door and then residential homes that start going down the side street. I sit on some stacked tires to rest and notice there are many old tires on this asphalt side yard to this car repair shop. It is dark here, and I suddenly realize this may be a good place to sleep. Even though the ground will be hard, I can stack the tires around me and make a little shelter, and no one will see me now.

There is no shame at this point. I'm dead tired, I'm no longer thinking straight, and I'm desperate to do whatever it takes to sleep.

I'm lying on my back looking up between the tires on my left side and at my feet and head. A block wall is on my right side. The tires are about three feet tall around me. I've taken off my left shoe to use as a pillow. I lie on the dirty asphalt in the dark. Above me is a thick electrical wire that hangs along the side of the building. It is cold, but not too cold to endure. I think about what it would be like to do this every night. I know I'm not capable of enduring the mental capacity necessary to live this way, and that's because I know what it is like to not have to live this way. This bothers me also. It is easier to accept something if you know of nothing better. There's a sadness to this realization. I fall asleep.

It is morning, and I know I've barely slept as my mind was constantly on alert throughout the night. It is very early, but the sky is light-blue even though the sun has not risen. I'm just glad it's morning. I'll get up and start walking now. But to where? Another day just like the last one? Now I want the time to pass quickly even though I know it won't. At least the rising sun will bring warmth, and it looks like there's no cloud cover, so that's a good sign. The season is fall now. I would not have tried this in a cooler time of year. I can only imagine being homeless in the winter. How?

As the morning progresses I have no ambition today, as if to say I've learned enough and all I want to do is sit around and let the time pass and get it over with. I'm tired of writing, and I don't want to be depressed reliving yesterday's experiences all over again with slightly different twists. Maybe one of the twists today will be another situation with a knife, and I may not be so fortunate. I start wondering if I should press my luck with another night out here. For what purpose? It doesn't scare me anymore and, in fact, I'm looking forward to the nighttime today. What a change from yesterday.

I've walked a ways back toward my original starting place yesterday. One thing I've learned is that there is no color out here with the homeless. Black, white, Hispanic, whatever, it doesn't matter—they treat each other well out of necessity—no one turns down a helping hand because it's the wrong color. Brothers are brothers and sisters are sisters because survival removes the discrimination from them. Sad, but they are one up on the rest of society in this area. I'll bet there would be no racism if everyone went homeless for a night or two. So far, and maybe I've been lucky, I've seen no violence, no hostility—other then stern words toward a red-haired girl—no contention, no worry about the stupid little things in life we fortunates worry about. Out here there are bigger concerns: a place to be warm, a place to sleep, a place to call your own, and enough food to get by. No ice cream, no candy, nothing to add a little extra pleasure to our lives. Just enough to get by.

I sit and write again about what I've learned—trying to make sense of it all. Like I've said, there is little pleasure out here other than what you can conjure up in your mind or in a game for stones or aiming at a crack in the sidewalk. But there is also no stress. There is no ambition and no goal, and therefore no feeling of failure. We're not striving for anything, and therefore there is no shortcoming in our goals because there are no goals. Survival isn't a goal, it's a must. Failure is not an option, and getting through the day I know will just become commonplace. No goal, no worry, no nothing. Not even the contemplation of what could be. Without opportunity the mind doesn't think in the same way as it does with opportunity. Out here, it's just about making friends and getting through the day. The only difference is that, as a homeless person, I appreciate the little things a lot more.

I suspect it is after noon now. I haven't written much today. Just sitting around observing the same old thing and doing a lot of soul searching. All of the sudden I feel a euphoria come over me. I realize I don't have to do this again tonight. I suddenly entertain the thought of ending this now, and it feels right to me. I think I'm going to call it good and go home to my first meal in over two days and sleep in my bed tonight and be happier than ever. I'm supposed to do this for another night, though. But somehow I know this is over now. My mind is almost made up before I even think further. I've learned what I set out to learn. I feel wonderful all of the sudden. I think I'm going to *go home. Everyone is still out of town. I'll sit tonight alone in my warm home and give God thanks for all my blessings. Maybe that's a better use of my time—praising God rather then thinking about survival again. But my little bed of tires doesn't seem that scary either. I'll think further about whether or not I'm done now with my experiment.*

I'm back at the place where the Catholics feed the homeless. This is the best place and, for some reason, the most comforting. This is where most of the homeless in this area congregate, and there is a feeling of community that is comforting. The police allow us to be in this area, and there is usually no trouble here. I could just hang out here again today. I see so many familiar faces now—in just two days.

After further thought, I'm going to go home now. I'm going to look around for a little longer and soak in the feeling—so that I never forget my new friends, so that I never forget my new experiences. I want my new wisdom to stay with me forever. I will stay around and soak it all in until I know it is permanent. And then I'm leaving with mixed feelings of happiness for how fortunate I am and sadness for how little I can do to change things. And I know how small of a scale what I have experienced is when compared to the rest of the city and then the country, a country that is the richest on earth. And there are so many countries that have it worse off than this. This would be a step up for them.

I cannot dwell on that without feeling great shame and sadness. This is why there has to be a God who will be just in the end. Otherwise, one cannot find happiness. It is my belief in my God, that He has a perfect plan for all of this to make sense, that allows me to be able to endure it. Maybe it is part of His plan to have me more involved now. I will explore this through new eyes. And I will be a better person for what I now know. Few things in one's life are felt as being one of the best things you've ever done. This was definitely one of them for me. Writing about it now has solidified the experience in my mind and soul. Now, what will I do? How will I be different? What will I change? I don't know, but I'm open to it.

It is Sunday, September 14. My fingers hurt from so much typing yesterday, but I'm still so excited to write about my experiences, and I think about them and my new friends very often throughout my day. Church had a sweet feeling to it today. I was very excited to be celebrating my God, appreciating things at a different level. What was important to me before had a lesser degree of seriousness about it. I was calmer, slower to react, and felt wiser. Hearing God's Word had more power than ever today. I know how lucky I am and how undeserved all my blessings are. I know how incredible my God is for shining down so much grace on my life. I hope I can keep my newfound wisdom and that life's responsibilities don't let me forget how I feel right now. My short time with my new friends has left a real impact on me.

After church I felt compelled to drive back to my new friends and see how they were doing. I thought about them all day yesterday. Rarely did two minutes pass that I did not find myself staring into nothingness, thinking about my experiences, and wondering what my less-fortunate friends were doing. I would ponder, and I would feel so lucky to be given all that I've been given. Why me? I could just as easily be one of them, as I was for thirty hours. And still a part of me is. And I believe it will always be a part of me now. Today, I drove back. I parked nearby and checked my wallet for money. I had not planned on going back today, but I was very compelled to drive there after I left church. I found I had $360 with me. Three hundreds, two twenties, and some miscellaneous small bills. I took the three hundreds and the two twenties out.

I found Silvia first. She didn't recognize me since I was dressed nicely, having come from church. Just nice jeans and a collared shirt, but certainly worlds apart from the man she helped two days ago. Also, I was clean-shaven now and my torn straw hat was no longer my most prominent standout. I said, "Silvia, do you remember me?" She still did not recognize me. I said, "You helped me two days ago in this spot right here, and you took me to the place where I could sleep in the benches around the corner."

"Oh yes," she said, "the man in the straw hat."

"Yes," I said. "I have something for you." I handed her a hundred-dollar bill. Her eyes lit up like it was Christmas. I said, "You were so nice to me that I wanted to do something nice for you." She was so thankful. As I walked away, I turned back around and said, "Silvia, keep doing nice things for people, and I'm going to do the same." She was smiling as big as ever.

I had to walk a couple blocks to the feeding grounds, where I hoped to find Steve. I asked a couple familiar faces where I might find him. No one recognized me as the man from two days ago. One person said Steve was across the street. I searched but was unable to find him. I came across my original starting place where I sat between the roots of the tree. I saw Dale's friend, the parolee, sitting on a concrete bench watching a chess game. I said, "Do you know where Dale is?" He said, "He's at Birch Park." He pointed in the direction I somewhat remembered.

I said, "Hey, I think I owe you something. I handed him a twenty.

He had a confused look on his face, then looked at me and said, "You were the one in the straw hat. I remember you."

I said, "Yes, Dale was kind to me, and I have something for him also."

As I walked away, another man said, "That was cool, man!"

As I walked back to my truck I saw a familiar face, but I couldn't place it. I stopped and said, "I know you." Then it hit me. It was Dolly. I said, "Do you remember talking to me a couple days ago?" She didn't. I said, "Right over there under the tree. You told me about the Catholic man, Sammy, and the clothes giveaway on Saturday mornings."

She said, "Bob, the man in the hat."

I said, "Yes. Thank you for being so friendly to me. This is for you." I handed her a twenty. The same reaction of confusion and joy the others displayed.

I returned to my truck while asking a few more people where Birch Park was and got some vague answers. I couldn't really remember other than the general feeling of southeast from where I currently was. I had walked at least eighteen to twenty miles that day and night. I found Birch Park after circling a few blocks. It was farther south then I remembered. I had walked far.

I was so excited to see that Dale was there. I approached him. He remembered me immediately, but showed no reaction to my nicer appearance. That seemed odd to me. I had spent the longest amount of time with Dale over any other person I befriended. He recognized me right away. I told him I had something for him and gave him a hundred-dollar bill.

He seemed less joyous about the money and said, "Did you get a job?"

I said, "Yes, I have a job. And I want to thank you for all your help and for taking me in as a friend." Dale was the one who said he knew he was going to heaven because he accepted Jesus into his heart. I said, "I'll see you again in heaven very soon." I left.

Except for the fact I was unable to find Steve, I had one more person I really wanted to see and to thank. It was Evonne, the only fortunate who helped me by letting me use her scissors in the dress shop. I was pleasantly surprised to find it open on Sunday, unlike the clothing shop with the sewer leak and all the wet boxes. I walked into the dress shop and I was very pleased to see Evonne. There were two other women with her. I said, "Do you remember me." She did not. I said, "You lent me your scissors the other day, and I cut the dangling straw-hat pieces from my hat right there on the floor. This is for you, for helping me." I handed her a hundred-dollar bill. She looked at her friends and then back at me in amazement, with a look that said, *This couldn't possibly be the same person.*

But she said, "Yes, Bob," and then immediately began to tell her two friends in Spanish what had happened. Her English was weak, and after they talked back and forth in Spanish for a few sentences, her friend, who spoke fairly good English said, "She says she can't take your money because you need it more."

I said, "No, it is hers now for being so nice to me. God is shining down on her for her kindness." I insisted, and handed it to her and left, both of us with big smiles. The look on Evonne's face was one I will never forget. It was as if she thought I was an angel of God when, if fact, she was the angel.

The only downer was that I didn't have more money with me. Today, I wanted to help everyone. All of my friends, not just the close ones who had been nice to me. My incentive wasn't in trying to make myself feel good, even though afterwards I did, but I wanted to help them because I really cared about them. It was as if I had friends now whom I knew were suffering, and I knew I could help. The money seemed so much more valuable in their hands than in mine. It had real worth to them. So often it has real waste in mine. How enlightening.

It is a week later now, the following Sunday, September 22, when I've come back to writing about my experiences again. I went back to see my friends again after church today. My perspective was already weakening from last week's work grind, and I wanted to return to see how they were doing. I found and talked with Silvia and Evonne. I couldn't find the others today. I really am helpless, as one person, to help these people. I know that soon I'll go on with my life and will probably never see them again. But they have left an impression on me, and I won't forget them.

If I could sum it all up in one sentence, it would be this: Don't be surprised if when you face God some day, and we all will, there will be a much less fortunate person held in higher regard in God's eyes and standing elevated to you and me. Why do I know that? Because God says so:

"But many who are first will be last; and the last, first."

JESUS, MATTHEW 19:30

Chapter Twenty-two

RAISING CHILDREN

"Let thy child's first lesson be obedience,
and the second will be what thou wilt."

BENJAMIN FRANKLIN

YOU'RE PROBABLY THINKING: *On what authority is he going to tell me or anyone else how to raise my kids, or any kids, for that matter? And another Ben Franklin quote? Come on!* Sorry, but Ben seems to do a great job of putting God's commandments into human terms.

I'll admit this won't be a long chapter. Honestly, I'm no more qualified than the next parent to give advice regarding the proper methods and psychologies of raising any particular child. On occasion, I still wonder if I'm qualified to comment on the raising of my own three children. Admittedly, without my wife, Susie, having taken on the main role—that is, the daily routine of making our children her number-one priority, her full-time job, and without her incredible guidance and support in raising the children—who knows how they would have turned out? Thanks to her, we've raised children who are genuinely good citizens. That being said, I want to give my brief opinion on this topic.

This topic is so vital because the next generation will determine the direction for our civilization and for its next generation. I know it sounds idealistic, but major changes in the way society acts and sees things can happen very quickly—in one generation or less. In fact, so quickly—think of ten-year periods—even society has named the decades: the Roaring Twenties, the Depression Thirties, the Stylish Forties, the Hip Fifties, the Experimental Sixties, the Fashionable Seventies,...you can coin your own from there...the Eighties, the Nineties—personally, I'd go with the "Spoiled Generations" for the Eighties and Nineties. You get the picture.

Things do change quickly, and our society seemingly has gone from one of order to one of disorder and chaos in almost every form of art. Think music—from the timeless classics, to jazz, to rock, to rap. Can you imagine some curse words and some murder threats thrown into a nice Baroque piece of the 1600s? I can't. Don't get me wrong, I try to respect all types of art, but are these newest forms really art anymore? They may be freedoms of expression, and I believe in First Amendment rights, but merely going for the shock value is like comparing a prostitute to a classy woman.

I think most people can appreciate any art form if the delivery has decency in its makeup. But what outrageous new style will be next? If it doesn't shock anymore, then it has no value to these young so-called artists. How about reaching the soul from a gentle perspective instead? We've come a long way—from the portraits of Rembrandt, the impressions of Monet, and the youthful expressions of Picasso, to a statue of weird shapes glued together, to a white canvas with a red dot in the center, to another canvas with smeared feces and signed in the artist's dark, yellow-stained urine. The problem is, someone is raising these kids.

Business has had the same evolution—from trying to make enough to take care of one's family to trying to make enough to buy a football team and, of course, a private jet to travel in. I'm not putting capitalism down. It has made this country great, and I'm all for it. But the perspectives of so many of our children being raised in today's society are becoming very skewed.

The art forms, the music forms, along with business and many other forms, and certainly the raising of the next generation, are all becoming more chaotic and less organized as time passes. We have to stop this cycle. We need to talk about raising our children for the next generation. We have to teach them about the beauty and importance of the past arts and their histories and get those art forms back into their minds and souls so they can pass them along to their children.

But, more importantly, we need to raise good children with good morals. And raising a kid with a conscience is a good place to start. Let's teach children about class and style and give them an appreciation for the timeless classics. I really do think most of our past forms of art can help accomplish this. In the old days, people may have had the same thoughts as people do today, but they didn't voice them or have instant access to a large public audience. Now, there's a thought—just keep your mouth shut. Today, everything has to be said.

I've come to a conclusion about what makes a good child, and here it is: Respect. If children respect their parents and deeply care about what the parents think of them, they will turn out well. Children will still do the things children do when they are experimenting with life, but they will keep redirecting themselves in line with what they think will please their parents, whom they respect. It is truly a form of obedience. That's why I couldn't resist another quote by Ben Franklin under this chapter's title. How true it is! If the child is obedient, if he cares so much about what the parent thinks that he stays in line, then it really doesn't matter—let the second lesson be anything you want and he will follow. I know this to be true. But the problem is how to achieve that obedience.

Let's see if we can come up with something that makes sense about how to get obedience and respect from our children. First off, if the parent's own morals are off-balance, then having a child respect them could prove counteractive to the raising of a good child. Respect for the parent by itself is not enough. It must be accompanied by a good teacher. The child is going to listen to what the parent says and see what the parent does, and if the two are not consistent then respect is already undermined. Consistent actions have to follow the words. This is what will teach the child. Words are just words unless there is an action that backs up those words.

Let's face it. None of us knew what we were getting into when we had children. Usually, if all is going well, it is calm and quiet the night before your child is born, assuming the wife is not already in labor. But the next day, you have a baby and your learning curve becomes very steep. There is no turning back. Your life changes forever. And, no, it's not quiet anymore—that pretty much lasts forever too.

Don't get me wrong, it's a beautiful change. But not an easy one. All of a sudden, you have an infant who dictates to you. Your flexibility is greatly diminished, not to mention your sleep. The list of new responsibilities goes on and on.

The list of new joys also goes on and on. Raising children teaches one to be less selfish and more selfless. In this selflessness is the desire to raise your child into a better life, with hopefully more opportunity than you had. But, more important, is the desire to raise the child with the proper outlook on life—a philosophy that will bring happiness. All the opportunity and money in the world will be meaningless if the child does not learn to find happiness by appreciating all the little things in life that money can't buy.

It is imperative children be raised with good morals. I happen to believe in Christian morals, and that is what we try to teach our children. But it doesn't mean they are going to turn out to be godly kids. They must decide in their own hearts. It is their free will to choose. My children have chosen to become Christian and to follow Christian ethics, but there are other forms of religion and non-religion that follow good morals and have high standards for living in a decent manner.

Having children seems wonderful some days and dreadful on others. But children are the bond that helps to form a family's unity in ways that cannot otherwise be accomplished. And when times get tough, and they always do, the likelihood for a married couple to stay married is much higher when kids are a part of the equation. Too many married couples without kids just give up, drift apart, and move on. Having children sets a unique bond between a husband and wife. Without that special bond, society as we know it would be very different and much diminished in many respects.

Many states in our great union have recently put on their ballots a redefinition of marriage to include people of the same gender. In my opinion, this is a mistake. Society should give all people the freedom to form partnerships with whomever they choose. And those partnerships should have the same legal rights and tax implications because that is merely treating others as you would want to be treated. But what are we teaching our children here? Redefining the most sacred of all unions between a man and a woman has no possible upside to it—especially if all the other advantages to marriage have already been agreed to by forming another type of union. If no one can come up with a better argument than that, then how about this one: God did not intend for it to be that way. We need less chaos, not more of it. Both extreme sides could come closer to the middle on this one. Is this so difficult that we need to waste so much time and money on it? That's called chaos in my book.

With that in mind, the importance of the family bond and the raising of children to be able to pass along a less chaotic world to your own children is essential. This starts with looking at what made former generations so impressive. The answer is: They had so little and yet accomplished so much through hard work, commitment, and a good foundation. Trouble was more difficult to find back then. You could find it if you went looking for it, of course. But today, it is all around you all the time. It will find you, and you must have the strength to say no and stay grounded, just as your parents and grandparents did. But the temptations are much more prevalent and accepted in today's society.

The Internet has brought a world of wonder and accomplishment alongside a world of potential immediate trouble. If you want to find trouble, it is only a click away on your computer. It is constantly knocking on our doors. The reason is simple—because it sells. It comes in all the forms already mentioned, like temptation, vice, escape, and addiction, just to name a few. The free market knows how to make a buck, and it has seized the opportunity to take advantage of all of our weaknesses. Gambling, shopping for sex, and multiple scams flood the Internet. You name it, it's all there. You need extreme self-control to stay away from these forces because they have moved past your front door and are now available on a twenty-four-hour basis.

Self-control is necessary. You must know what is right and wrong and stick to a plan that keeps you away from the wrong. And then you must instill this concept and practice into your children. If you haven't figured out how to be successful in this, then you will be a failure at passing it along to your children. It's that simple.

> *"I'm starting to wonder what my folks were up to at my age*
> *that makes them so doggoned suspicious of me all the time!"*
>
> Margaret Blair, as a child

The quote by Margaret Blair rings with truth, and thus the humor—because we know what kids are up to. We were kids. We know how they think because at one time we thought the same things. And, thus, we now know our parents knew more about us than we thought they did—because they also had thought it and lived it.

What we don't know is how this present age has changed the way our kids think because we didn't grow up in a cyber society. We didn't have cell phones interrupting our every thought. What once was private, in my opinion, has become too connected.

I can barely have a conversation with my daughter without someone interrupting us with a text message. To the point where Susie and I agreed that Bree only gets her phone at certain times and after all her homework and responsibilities are completed. We saw how addicting her phone was to her. It is hard enough to recognize what is bad for ourselves and to stay away from it, and at the same time we have to teach our children good behavior and be models for them. No wonder we, as parents, feel as if we're failing half the time.

But then we see a glimmer of light when our child makes the right choice, and we think, *It's worth it. We're raising a good kid.* I'll never forget the day my oldest son, Paul, only about thirteen at the time, came to me and said, "I've taken StarCraft away from myself. It's ruining my life." He was addicted to this video game. As much as we'd tried, just as with our daughter and her phone, Paul loved to play this game in his spare time. He was on a baseball team and he was active in other things, but, if he could, he'd spend twenty-three hours a day on StarCraft. It was also a good tool for us to use as punishment. No homework? No StarCraft. Bad grades? No StarCraft. So, we tried to use it to an advantage also. But one day he realized in himself, without our input, that his addiction was hurting him and he hated what it was doing to his life. It's a good thing when pain makes a person change his behavior. So, he cut himself off. He boxed it up and put it on a shelf, and that was the last time I ever saw him play StarCraft.

Those are the days that make it all worth it. A parent couldn't be prouder of a child when the child learns to be his or her own best monitor. And I'd like to think our steadfast parenting and our consistent behavior of rewards and punishments was the reason. In other words, that we parented him to the best of our ability and it paid off.

As I write this, Paul is nineteen years old. As recent as last week, we felt he was making some bad choices and being influenced by some friends we thought might not be good for him. We voiced our opinion and also let him know that he's an adult now and can make up his own mind. But I reminded him he's still living at home and there are certain things that won't be tolerated in my home. If he wants to pay for his own car insurance and his own food and a roof over his head, he can make that choice to go out on his own at any time. Then I let him know how much I love him and how I'll always be there for him, but I won't financially support bad decisions and ungodly actions. It's funny how he has chosen to stay with all the nice things I provide for him over total freedom to make his own choices.

Paul will be finishing out his last two years of college at UC Berkeley away from home this year, and then he really will be on his own. I don't know what he plans to do, except that I told him, "Paul, this is a partnership, our sending you away to college. You've maintained good grades and made good choices up until now, and you deserve to have your college paid for by your parents. But I expect you to treat college as your job. I want you to enjoy the college experience while you're away. But I want you to use your head. Don't drink and drive. Don't risk an unwanted pregnancy. Don't hang out with trouble. Enjoy the experience, and keep up your grades, and learn what it is you're in college to learn. And learn it well. Put yourself above others by being exemplary in all you do. Carry forward what your mother and I have taught you, and be successful on your own now. I agree to finance you if you agree to graduate safely, timely, and educated." I also made it known that timely meant to be done in four years, to take full loads and make that his work. Otherwise, he could take whatever loads he wanted, and pay for everything himself after four years. I said, "My way is free for you. The other way will cost you."

Now, I think that is reasonable and fair. And I'm happy to work extra hard to send my child out into the world prepared. But will I be done parenting? We all know the answer to that. I'll never go to sleep completely free of wondering, "Are my kids okay?" But the beautiful part is that I'll never go to sleep not feeling so incredibly happy they are a part of my life.

Raising a family is as wonderful as it is difficult. It is as rewarding as it is taxing. It is also necessary for society to flourish as a godly society—more than any other thing. We must pass down good morals to our children. Morality is taught to us through different channels, but all of them come from God. And the best channel is from a parent to a child.

It all starts with children respecting parents. Gain their respect by earning it. Earn it by being consistent. And stay committed. The future generations are at our mercy. Let's teach. And let's teach rightly in the eyes of God.

"If the past cannot teach the present and the father cannot teach the son,
then history need not have bothered to go on ..."

RUSSELL HOBAN

Chapter Twenty-three

OTHERS

*"In everything, therefore, treat people the same way you want them to treat you,
for this is the Law and the Prophets."*

MATTHEW 7:12

IF GOD ONLY HAD ONE WORD to use in which to tell us His greatest desire, I believe the word would be "others." Of course, His first commandment is for us to love Him. Many might say "love" would be the word. But then one is left to wonder about the broad and mysterious definition of love. "Others" says it all in one word. And there is a reason it is the focus in the sentence used by Jesus in His Golden Rule.

The meaning of the Golden Rule is obvious and uncontested—to treat another as you would want them to treat you. A simple concept? Yes. Easy to follow? No. And then there is the dichotomy—if a man's true measure is the way he treats others, then why did God make us instinctively selfish? Or did He? Maybe the instinct for self-survival and selfishness is a learned behavior. Whether the behavior is learned or innate in man's nature is not what we should be concerned about, unless anthropology is our interest. What is significant is this: The visible measure of a man or woman, above all other things—what others see and measure you by—is how you treat other people. I call it your "walk in life." And your walk is what makes you great. Don't think God does-n't see it because, after all, it is His Golden Rule. The invisible measurement of rating yourself in how you treat others is also important even though it is not what others will see. So there are two things in play here. The way you treat others and how you think you treat others. But both are measurements of your heart.

There really isn't anything like the feeling you get when you help someone else. I think that is why so many people are charitable in their walk. Yes, one could say it takes away from the selfless act somewhat if, by helping someone else, there is an overabundance of pride. But there is nothing wrong with the joy that comes from helping others. Feeling proud about doing the right thing is the kind of pride God wants us to have. The ability to feel His innate calling in our souls is the connecting of God with our God-given spiritual awareness, which is His gift to us. It is that little voice inside that says, "This is the right thing to do."

Like any other gift, it must be nurtured to be useful and valuable. Many people possess talents that are never realized because they are never developed. I believe God has given every person the ability to connect to Him spiritually. Whether or not we decide to develop that form of communication with Him is our own choice. I believe being still with God and spending time talking with Him is the most effective method. The essential thing is that we sense His calling to help someone else. That little voice telling us to do good should not be ignored. This is one of His ways of asking us to be there for someone else. And there are times He will ask someone else to be there for us. Yes, they, too, may ignore His call, and we may go without help. We are called to put others ahead of ourselves. In doing this we please God in a way that is far above any other form of expressing communication back to Him. We are also acknowledging we are happy and willing to be used in His perfect plan. And we are saying thanks to God for all the times we have been helped. All these things are happening when we listen to His spirit talking to us and we make the decision to be there for someone else.

Helping others can take many forms. That is what makes it so great—we can pick our own method of charity. It can be through financial support or through the giving of time or through meeting the need of another. It can be in service of the needy or the disabled or the elderly. It can be a friend or a family member. It can be anyone who needs anything.

The personal spiritual growth one gets from helping others is so valuable and rewarding. And that is by design. God would not have His Golden Rule command us to act a certain way without showing us how that way would have its rewards. And He does this by blessing us in all sorts of ways. Sometimes spiritually, sometimes financially, but usually in ways we are not even aware of until later when we look back and it becomes clear how He put us in a situation or position that was beneficial to us even though we couldn't see it at the time. Again, this is what makes it so incredible. Certainly the act of helping others has numerous gifts in both directions, especially when the act is done without expectation of anything in return. The truth is, people who are adept at assessing others' feelings make better decisions. That's worth repeating—if you practice "others" as your daily walk you'll make better decisions that will affect your life positively.

We have a God who loves to work in surprising ways. He loves to reward those who remain steadfast in their walk. He loves to reward those who don't give up. He loves to reward those who are humble. And He loves to do the impossible for those who believe it is possible. Remember, we are made in His image. Like us, there is no excitement in doing something for someone with a ho-hum unappreciative attitude. He feels the same way. He wants to sign up winners even when the winners think they're going to be losers. Half the people in the Bible whom God used in miraculous ways were men and women who said, "Why me, God? Certainly I'm not the right person for the job." Moses said, "I'm not the right person because I'm not good with words." Jeremiah said, "I'm too young." Most, if not all, of Jesus' apostles were misfits. But they were misfits in whom He saw great potential. Jesus wasn't looking for rock-solid men who were confident and set in their ways; He was looking for men of clay He could mold.

Since God sees our hearts when we are helping others, it is important that we learn to help without expectations. We help because we feel compelled to do so. We help because we know this will please God. We help because He has commanded us to help. If our hearts are not completely in it for the other person, then we are in it for the wrong reasons and with the wrong frame of mind, and our charity is better off left until it can be given with the right heart.

The ultimate form of giving to others is when we are down. When there isn't much to give. When we are so absorbed with our own worry, our own goals, and our own well-being. It is much harder then to look around and see an even greater need in someone else. But that is when it will be the most rewarding, not necessarily in what you will get in return but by how clear the meaning of life will become to you. That is when one sees the value in life and the lack of value in so many things that normally appear to have value. Material things will be seen for what they really are, and relationships will be seen for what they really are. Time with a friend or with your mother or with a son or daughter will reveal its true value, along with the frailty of the moment. You'll have an awareness the moment is here and then gone and the experience with that special person will only be a memory. But what a powerful and valuable thing a memory is—an experience that can never be taken away, unlike a material thing, which we all know will eventually be taken away.

Too often, and especially when we are down, we exchange the everlasting spiritual experience for the temporary material experience. We focus on the activity more than the person we are sharing the activity with. When we feel down is when we can achieve and receive the greatest gift. God jumps at the chance to reward us when we look away from ourselves, especially when we are hurting and feeling the need to look only after ourselves. I speak like this is easy when I know how difficult it really is. I am the first to say, "Forget that; I'm hurting here." This is when it is so hard, when we must stop and be quiet for a moment—be still and look to God for His strength and direction.

Others. This is His one word that says it all. If our walk was about others all the time, then this would certainly be a different world. Only one person has consistently walked the earth with others as His daily goal, and that was Jesus. It is true, only perfection could walk this way every day of His life without distraction. God doesn't expect perfection in us, His little imperfect beings. But He does expect that we think about it often and that we accept others with all their faults, knowing we also expect them to accept us with all of ours.

> *"Therefore, accept one another,*
> *just as Christ also accepted us to the glory of God."*
>
> ROMANS 15:7

Chapter Twenty-four

FORGIVENESS

"I think that if God forgives us then we must forgive ourselves.
Otherwise it is almost like setting up ourselves as a higher tribunal than Him."

C. S. LEWIS

WHY IS FORGIVENESS SO SIGNIFICANT? Because it is what we expect and even rely on from our God every day of our lives. If we don't rely on it, then we are discounting one of His greatest gifts to us. He gave His Son for this one thing—to pay the price for our sins so He could forgive you and me and establish a pathway that is pure and cannot be altered. If we expect Him to forgive us for every single wrong step in our life, then we ought to be able to say," I forgive all who have wronged me." If we want His forgiveness then we must forgive others. And, more importantly, if we want God to forgive us, then we need to confess our shortcomings and ask Him for that forgiveness. Asking God for forgiveness without repentance is worthless. This may sound harsh but it is true.

When one thinks of forgiveness, it is usually about forgiving another person. And this is what God has commanded us to do. How can we expect Him to forgive us when we cannot forgive another person? But, as the quote above states, it is important for us also to forgive ourselves. Let's talk about that first.

Forgiving ourselves is a process of conviction and self-acceptance for our actions through self-talk in order to realign ourselves when we get off track. We say to ourselves, "I made a mistake that I know was wrong, and I know now what the right course of action is. I must forgive myself for going in that direction and get back on track." Usually this follows the act of already asking God to forgive our actions, but this step is also needed sometimes. It is a way of cleansing our minds and starting over. If we have wronged someone else, then we need to ask for their forgiveness also. And then forgive ourselves.

On the other side of the equation is the act of forgiving someone who has hurt us. This is harder to do because we may feel resentment. We have been treated unfairly, and this other person deserves to be punished, or at least not to be forgiven. But then the time will come when we are in that person's shoes and we are not worthy of forgiveness, and yet we need to have it given to us just the same. That is why we must also forgive. Forgiveness and others are tied together. They are a part of the Golden Rule, and they go hand in hand. God asks this of us, and He expects this of us. We cannot expect God to show us mercy when we have wronged another if we cannot show mercy and forgive when we have been wronged. It is that simple.

Then why is it so hard to forgive another person? Because when we have been wronged we feel the defects in another person in a powerful way, and we are far less capable of looking at our own defects, especially when we were right in our actions during the offense. Think about driving in traffic. How many times has someone done something really stupid that sets you off? You may have thought, *What a jerk! I would never do that.* And then you remembered: *Oh yeah, I do remember going through that red light one time as my mind was wandering*, or *I remember bumping into that other car because I wasn't paying attention*, or *I remember letting my car door get away from me and hitting the car next to me. Even worse, I don't want to leave a note on the car because maybe they'll be mean about it and then I'll have really opened up a can of worms. I'll just let it go. After all, it happens to my car door all the time and nobody ever leaves me a note.* I know this is hitting home. Admittedly, I was guilty of this just recently. The list goes on because we, too, are not perfect. But we're pretty perfect at forgetting to remember our own transgressions. And so is the next guy. We need to be aware of this and practice a little more patience every time we think someone else isn't worthy of our forgiveness.

It helps not to expect someone else to forgive us. This makes us more likely to ask for it sincerely and to have the request received in a more favorable manner. We are much more likely to be forgiven when we act in this manner. Whether we are forgiven or not is another matter. But asking for it with sincerity is imperative.

The degree of how wronged someone has been is also a factor in how hard it will be to forgive or ask for forgiveness. In some cases, especially when death has occurred and especially when it was premeditated, this becomes very difficult, and I cannot speak from experience. But it needs to be addressed, even if the personal answer is to ask God for the permission not to forgive, at least for the time being. There are times when God allows your unwillingness to forgive another person because He knows your heart cannot come to terms with it at that moment. But you are communicating this to God. It is the communication with Him that sets apart what He wants you to do from what He knows you are capable of doing at that time. And He is patient and will not only wait for it to be right for you but will assist in making it turn out right for you.

Your act of communicating to God the fact that you cannot forgive someone else is the bridge to having Him continue to forgive you while you work through it together. In a way, it's like a loan from God. He understands what is in your heart and honors you for sharing it with Him while asking for His help to get through the situation. At the same time He continues in His unlimited capacity to forgive you when you ask for it with repentance. If you've lost a child or a spouse to an unforgivable act by another then you understand this. You may think you can never forgive that person. God will understand if you communicate your feelings to Him. And He can change you over time.

Forgiveness comes in the following forms: The act of God forgiving you when you confess your sins and shortcomings to Him. The act of forgiving others when they have wronged you. And the act of forgiving yourself and asking for forgiveness from others when you have wronged them.

We need to ask for God's forgiveness continually, and it needs to be prefaced with our admission of shortcomings and failures. There is an order—we confess and repent, and He listens to our hearts and forgives. If that sounds too easy, it is. Just like eternal life—it isn't earned—it is asked for and then followed by faith and acceptance.

Don't confuse or mistake *free* for cheap. God's greatest gift to us is free but very far from cheap. If you don't believe this, then ask yourself about the greatest gift you are able to offer to another—your love—which is free. So is forgiveness.

"…but the free gift of God is eternal life in Christ Jesus our Lord."

ROMANS 6:23

Chapter Twenty-five

THE IMPORTANCE OF PRAYER

*"Prayer projects faith on God, and God on the world.
Only God can move mountains, but faith and prayer move God."*

E. M. BOUNDS

PRAYER IS ABOUT HAVING a relationship with God and nothing else. A bold statement? Maybe, but a correct one. Although, admittedly, prayer more often seems to be about asking for something or needing something rather than discussing everyday life with God. And many prayers are simply saying thanks to our God, and He certainly deserves that. But what He wants more than anything is the relationship. He wants us to share everything with Him.

Lately, I felt a real disconnect from God, and I didn't know why. This happens rarely to me but when it does I know He is shaping me in ways I cannot understand. In a previous chapter, we discussed the book of Job and how God sometimes allows bad things to happen to us. At least, they seem bad at the time, but we often look back and see His incredible plan for us forming itself into a good outcome. God gave the devil free reign to call the shots with Job for a while, and thus there was a divine change that occurred between God and Job. This disconnect was only-one sided. Job sensed God had left him for some unknown reason, but concluded it was God's plan to do as He wished. God hadn't really left Job; in fact, He was using Job as an example for all mankind to learn from. He used tragedy to lift Job to be one of the greatest figures of all time. To have a book in the Bible named after you is not tragedy but the ultimate favor in God's eyes.

If you think about it, there was a time when God even disconnected from Himself. Sound impossible? When Jesus hung on the cross, He cried out, "My God, why have You forsaken Me?" God the Father allowed God the Man in human flesh to experience what separation in man's mind felt like. He did this so He could feel what Job felt. He did this so that He can feel what we sometimes feel. More importantly, He did this so we would know His was a genuine life experience as a man of flesh and blood on a cross. God doesn't disconnect from us. We disconnect from Him. And this is my point—I have realized in myself this disconnect comes only from my side of my relationship with God. Sometimes He uses space through separation to teach us wisdom and give us direction.

"I have been driven many times upon my knees
by the overwhelming conviction that I had nowhere else to go.
My own wisdom and that of all about me seemed insufficient for that day."

ABRAHAM LINCOLN

Lincoln really pours out the state of his mind at that moment, and the current state of my heart also. I haven't been able to find direction lately. The problem is I have slipped back into a very easy trap to fall into. I've been relying too much on myself. I felt comfortable with my change in career, and it made me a little complacent. Nothing too right and nothing too wrong, nothing wonderful, but nothing going bad in my life. So, I haven't been appreciating the little things as much as I was, and therefore I haven't been trying to connect with God at the same intimate level as before. Not to find wonderful things all around us every day is wrong. I think God has let me settle into my own little rut because I've created it for myself, but fortunately He has lots of patience.

Lately, He has allowed me to be hurt in numerous ways, and He has gotten my attention, attention I should never have let subside in the first place. I allowed our relationship to slip, and He loves me too much to let me get away with it. It is like a friend who gets mad at us because we haven't been paying attention to him or her, and deservedly so. Why should it be any different with God? Doesn't He have the right to get angry when we stop looking to Him for guidance? And especially when we stop sharing the little things in life with Him? All I can do is thank Him for allowing me to get hurt. It's His way of saying, "Hey Bob, where are you? I'm still here." Why do I take Him for granted so often? It really is wrong. And this brings me to where I want to go with this writing—how to get in touch with God and how to stay in touch with Him and, even more vital, how He wants us to effectively communicate with Him.

First, we must have faith. We need to believe in God with all our heart. We are placing our trust in something we can't see, hear, or touch. Who would do such a thing? Who would want to put so much effort and trust and faith in something our mortal senses cannot connect with? The answer is: those who have faith. They know the reward is so much greater when they give unconditionally. That is what faith is—the unconditional trust in someone or something that cannot guarantee success by answering to our five senses. And our senses are the only things we have besides faith that tell us what to do and what not to do in our daily life. That is why faith is such a great leap for man and why God honors it above all the things we can offer to Him. That is what prayer is—faith in a relationship with an almighty God, whom we cannot feel, touch, hear, taste, or see. But only through our soul. This is where our mind has to take us when we pray because it is the only place that connects us to God—through our faith. Prayer is simply the communication of our faith to God.

So, communicate it with the confidence that says, "I believe in You, God! I have faith in You, God! I love my relationship with You, God!" And, "I miss talking with You, God!" Just say what's on your mind. Don't sugarcoat it and don't be dishonest. He knows your heart and your mind better than you do. Tell Him how you feel about things and tell Him when you're mad at Him. Tell Him when you don't understand something and ask for wisdom to get through your hard times. Acknowledge He is in control, and don't be afraid to ask for direction. But, then, here is the catch: You need to be prepared to go in that direction when it is apparent He is giving you a signal. Don't read into it, but feel it with your heart and soul and mind. This is how He will communicate with you. If you actually hear a voice, then you're one up on most of us. But, if you ask Him for direction and you feel the answers are truly from Him, then follow His direction. That is what I recently prayed for—direction, with the promise I would follow His lead. This way I'm letting His plan meet its perfect ending, without my resistance. He honors that.

Do you realize He already has it planned out? He knows what is going to happen before it happens. So, why should you and I stress over future outcomes that are already determined by His ultimate authority? I constantly do this, and then, hopefully, I find the wisdom to stop and be still for a moment. This helps me realize I'm not in control of it all, and I say, "It's Your plan, God, and I'll be happy with it. Just give me clear direction, and I'll follow Your lead." This is the type of relationship He wants to have with us. But it takes two to have a relationship, and, as I've said before, He gives free will to every person to make the choice for a relationship or not.

Here's how to pray in order to have that relationship and honor God in the highest way. Pray when you are ready, willing, and able to give God all your attention. Not when you're thinking of something else or trying to solve the problem of the day. If you need His council on the problem, then stop, be still, and ask Him to take control. Get all the other things out of your mind so you can be open and clear about talking with Him. If you can't get into that state, then wait until you are able. Going through the motions just to feel like you did your job, such as mumbling through the same quick prayer every time before a meal in order to satisfy tradition is not honoring Him. This is doing Him an injustice. When you pray, mean it. Talk to Him because you are excited about talking to Him. And believe in your heart He is right there with you, listening and answering and loving every moment with you, because He is. With this type of communication you will be giving Him the greatest gift possible—a close and intimate relationship. It is what He wants most from you.

Don't forget to pray with thanksgiving in your heart. Prayer isn't all about your needs and my needs. It's about God's needs too. God is not stoic, without feelings, and they can be hurt in much the same way we can be hurt. Remember, we're made in His image. Give Him thanks for all that you have and for all that you don't deserve. This is honoring Him properly. For every prayer of yours that asks for something there ought to be at least two given in thanks. If you find yourself always asking Him and never thanking Him, then your prayers are out of balance and He is likely to respond to you accordingly. He made you in His image so He can connect with you. He came into the world in the form a man so He can connect with you, so you know He "gets" it. He knows pain and suffering and hunger and sorrow from the flesh of being a man—so you and I could have confidence He knows us inside and out.

Does God communicate to those who don't ask for it? To those who don't ask for a relationship? Of course, He does. He proved this many times in the Bible and, in fact, used many nonbelievers to perfect His plan. Why would it be any different now? The real question is, "Are you listening to Him?" He wants every person on earth to be in His heaven someday, and He wants a relationship with every one of us. I believe each person will get a chance to accept or reject God in some way before He judges their eternal state. Exactly how He accomplishes that I do not know, but He is a merciful God and, at the same time, a just God. The person who takes the first step toward Him and opens the relationship on faith is far greater than the one who has to be convinced by some miracle first. It takes great wisdom to sense that a higher being often answers people who are not even asking a question. But are you wise enough to hear the answers when they are God-given? Especially when you are not even looking for answers?

Faith precedes prayer, which precedes one's behavior, which precedes one's degree of success in life. I'm not talking about monetary success. Prayer builds character during one's life on earth, but even more so it builds a relationship that will be eternal.

"Prayer governs conduct, and conduct makes character"

E. M. BOUNDS

The above quote is from a well-known author who has written many books on the subject of prayer. Bounds began each day with three hours of prayer. His book *The Necessity of Prayer* is a good source on the importance of praying to our Creator, a wonderful God who deserves to have a relationship with each and every one of us. The sad but true fact is that He does have a relationship with all of us, but many choose not to have one with Him. It is truly sad when one's full potential relationship with God is neither desired nor realized.

"Desire precedes prayer, accompanies it, and is followed by it."

E. M. BOUNDS

Chapter Twenty-six

BE POSITIVE

"The pessimist is the man who believes things couldn't possibly be worse, to which the optimist replies, 'Oh yes they could.'"

VLADIMIR BUKOVSKY

WITH SO MANY THINGS out of one's control, here's one we can control. So, why not do it, especially with so many benefits that come from having a positive attitude? This is one thing we can make into a reality simply by going through the motions even if they're not genuine when we start. It's like laughing. We can make something funny by starting to laugh first. It is one of the few things in life that can work in reverse, unlike most—where we need one thing before the other can happen. It takes money to purchase an item. Trying to buy something without money doesn't create the money. But having an outwardly positive attitude, even forcing it when it is not genuine, will bring on an inward positive nature and a much better chance at a positive outcome, thereby forming a genuine positive attitude.

We can create it from nothing just by the effort of our mind. How many things can be created with only the effort of one's thoughts? It really is incredible. We are all in need of picking ourselves up at times, often daily, and getting a grip and seeing good when we are in the mood to see bad. This takes effort— to see the good when we want to see the bad. Then, to take that negative impulse and force ourselves to make it a positive influence on our minds and then our actions. That is the art. If we practice it we can get good at it, and it will change our lives for the better. Some days we may say, "Forget it. I'm in the mood to see the bad, and I'm going to see the bad." Occasionally that can be healthy in order to understand what really is bad. But, all too often, we are negative on a daily basis, and, quite frankly, that is much too often.

Sometimes when I am in a great mood, for some reason, I find myself saying, "Uh oh, something bad is probably going to happen to spoil it all." Isn't that terrible? And then I catch myself and think, *What am I doing? Why am I ruining something good?* The answer is because I'm protecting myself from potential disappointment in case things don't turn out so wonderful in the end. But my pessimism may end up being the cause of my ruin. As soon as I realize this, I say, "Okay, I'm in a good mood. Things are going well, but I'm also going to be realistic." That is when I need to look to God and be thankful for my positive situation. That is when it is important to once again be still with Him and say, "Thank You, God. I know You can let my joy turn into sorrow at any moment, and You're more likely to let the natural progression of earthly happenings do just that if I'm not thankful when I should be. So, here I am, God. I'm pouring out my heart of thanks to You, and I'm trusting it all into Your hands. I'm going to continue in my positive attitude, confident things will turn out for the best." Now, that's a prayer of thanksgiving with a positive attitude. Wouldn't it be a much better world if people constantly had such an outlook?

Optimism is a practice. Wake up with positive goals to reach every day, and be happy about them. Feel good about making progress toward them, even if it is only a little progress. It will add up each day of your life. And before you know it, you'll have something concrete to add value and character to your life and its accomplishments. But you need a good attitude about it. If you can't have the right attitude about a specific task, then stop doing that task if possible and find something productive you can be positive about. It is better to be positive about a very small goal and not make it happen than to be negative about a very big goal even though you may accomplish it. Success, in a big way, is about how you act on the way there. We all have stories about the person who achieved something quite grandiose but stepped on others and left a trail of bitterness. What kind of success is that? What kind of message does it send? The person who walks with a positive attitude and projects it to others around them will be seen as successful in the eyes of others, whether or not they ever reach their goals.

Now, what do you do when negativity surrounds you? What do you do when your boss is pessimistic or moody or a friend has nothing positive to say? Or a parent tells you you're a disappointment for some reason? Ask them, "What can I do to make it better?" This one sentence will catch just about anyone off-guard because it isn't expected. Negative people expect negative feedback, not positive problem-solving questions. Especially when the question involves improving things. It is up to them to tell you how they want to be helped. Wow, talk about turning the tables. They won't know what hit them. And you've done it in such a positive way they'll probably feel ashamed to stay in a negative mode to answer you. If they do have the gall to say, "Nobody can help me; the situation is helpless," then say: "I want you to know I'm here for you when you need me. For now, I'm going to do the best I can with what I have to work with. That way I can feel good about knowing I did everything I could." Sometimes you need to let the person have some time and space to absorb it all, and then be there for them with a positive attitude when they're ready for you.

Just the other day, I was driving with my son Paul and he was feeling down about a few negative things happening in his life. I could tell most of the things were really just in his mind and not reality based. So, I said to him, "Paul, do you realize it is easy to find negatives in life? They are all around us. But good things are also all around us. The wise person practices seeing the good around them, not focusing on the bad." Next, I said something and followed up on it. It was one of those things in life that left an impression on me also, even though it was only meant to be a lesson for Paul.

I said, "Watch this. Before I get to the next traffic signal, I'll find five negative things to complain about." I was stopped at a signal, and the next signal was only about five hundred feet away. I thought to myself, *How am I going to pull this off?* But then I went into negative mode: "Look at the trash blowing down the street! And why did I have to get stuck at this signal? And, look, there's a homeless person—how depressing." I hadn't even left the signal yet, and I had come up with three things. I quickly commented on the negative impact of the noise at a construction site across the street, and I had my fifth negative comment about the fact I was going to miss the next green light. I still had plenty of time to find another five negatives. I quickly pointed that out to Paul, and I could see by his reaction he realized how bad it all sounded. Being around someone negative for even a few minutes could bring the world crashing down on everyone rather quickly. Who would want to be with a person like that? Actually, I amazed myself at how quickly I was able to find the bad in everything.

Then, stuck at the second signal, I said to Paul, "Now watch, and before the signal changes back to green, I'll point out five positive things around us: Look how nice the weather is today, a comfortable seventy-five degrees with the sun shining. And I'm really enjoying having quality time alone with you today, Paul (*that is, until we started this whole negative talking*). I'm enjoying this nice song on the radio, which is attached to this nice truck that I'm fortunate to own. And, look, the signal just changed green for me. Everything is going my way." Five positive things that fast. But, like everything in life, it's easier to take the path of least resistance, to find the bad rather than the good, and to make the easy choice rather than the hard one. But the harder choice, the one that takes more effort, pays off with the greatest reward. Finding the positives in life is harder than finding the negatives. It's also much more rewarding.

Remember, you can't change everyone's attitude and you can't feel responsible when someone wants to remain negative and grumpy. We all want to feel negative at times, so let that person have their low moment and offer your support. Stay positive when you are around them, and don't let them drag you down. You bring them up instead, even if it takes time. Hopefully, they'll do the same for you when you fall into your negative rut. Our lows in life are often times for us to rest and to charge our batteries. The trick is to recognize when you're starting to slip into them and catch yourself by saying, "Okay, this isn't good. I see where this is going. What can I change right now to get out of this downward direction?" Then start steering away quickly. Like everything else, it takes practice. But it's definitely worth the effort. I'm no expert at always being in a good mood and staying positive, but I have become much better at realizing when I'm blowing it and letting negativity rule my day. Our goal should be to stop negativity before it starts gaining momentum. And, even better, to turn it around into positive thinking and then into positive actions.

> *"The pessimist complains about the wind;*
> *the optimist expects it to change;*
> *the realist adjusts the sails."*
>
> WILLIAM ARTHUR WARD

Chapter Twenty-seven

SPOILED BY CHOICE

"Virtue is insufficient temptation."

GEORGE BERNARD SHAW

DO YOU WANT TO KNOW how to ruin a perfectly good steak and a great bottle of wine? Have them every night of the week.

This goes for just about everything. Too much of a good thing spoils the good thing. Human beings don't appreciate things that have become commonplace. This single fact is at the root of our great country's undoing. As I write this chapter, early March 2009, it is a time of great concern for most Americans because of the existing recession, home foreclosures, high unemployment rate, government bailouts, and business bankruptcies. General Motors, AIG, and Citibank have all gone from fifty-dollar stocks to around one dollar. Times are tough, especially to a generation that hasn't seen such times. You could say these tough times are forcing us to appreciate what we have now lost. You could say that, having been spoiled, we have allowed ourselves a false reality, which has now come to an end. And you could say that now we will learn to appreciate the little things and really appreciate the big things that are becoming scarce.

I have been fortunate to have been raised in the great state of California, a land of opportunity and wealth in many different forms. It has also made me aware of how spoiled we can become when we have everything. My business has given me the opportunity to work with clients who are well off, so I've been able to observe my surroundings and see how wealth affects people. When I'm honest with myself, I am also able to observe my own tendencies and see some of my own spoiled nature and how it takes away from my happiness. What is true for California is also true for the rest of our nation. Therefore, I'm going to get sidetracked for a moment to make my point about a state that's choosing to be spoiled. This is a place I'm familiar with, a place I've lived for the past forty-seven years.

California is one of the richer regions in the world. It has millions of acres of timberland, oil supplies, and natural gas. It has 1,300 miles of beautiful coastline and a wonderful climate that enables people to enjoy many different activities year-round. The state has two of the world's great ports, located in Los Angeles and San Francisco. Its Gross State Product in 2008 was about $1.85 trillion, making it easily the leading commerce state in the United States with thirteen percent of the country's Gross Domestic Product. Compared with all the other countries in the world, California's total commerce alone would rank in the top ten.

Its higher education system consists of 110 junior colleges, twenty-three state universities, and ten University of California campuses to ensure a well-educated population. It has the world-renowned movie industry in Hollywood, along with one of the world's top wine-producing regions in Napa Valley, and is home to some of the top technology names such as Apple, Google, Intel, and Yahoo.

Millions of tourists come to California to enjoy our world-famous attractions, such as Disneyland and Sea World. Did I mention California's year-round weather tops the charts? As America's richest farming state, California leads the nation in dairy production as well as in fruit and vegetables

It is easy to see that the present generation has enjoyed a head start on their lives through the hard work and investment of its often forgotten predecessors. The same can be said for our entire nation. What is true for California is also true for the United States of America as a whole. Certainly America is great because of its combination of what all of its fifty states have added to the nation. But California is the leader in so many areas of how America thinks and acts, so by bringing its faults to the forefront it can certainly help to steer the entire country away from trouble. And many of these faults—bad decisions, if you will—have occurred in the last twenty years. Now, after building up this great state of ours, let's dissect its current path and talk about its bad decisions—decisions that the rest of our great country should not emulate and that, hopefully, California will correct in the near future.

California has managed to achieve the nation's highest sales tax and income tax rates and also the country's largest annual state deficit. Spending has grown well beyond inflation and its population. Our state-run health programs are out of control. The state is releasing prisoners well before their prison terms are served because the government has mismanaged the budget to the point that it cannot afford to keep dangerous people locked up. Biannual state proposition initiatives often let voters approve additional entitlements and benefits without providing the money to pay for them. Our high schools experience a thirty-percent dropout rate. More than one-half million aliens are caught each year trying to enter the state illegally. We enjoy and want to keep the low wages of our illegal immigrants while complaining about having to pay for their needed services. We seem to want it both ways, yet when paying for things, California has the worst credit rating in the nation. This alone tells me how spoiled we've become. We can spend like there's no tomorrow, but we can't bother to balance our checkbooks. We have the fourth highest unemployment rate and the second highest home-foreclosure rate in the country. Half of our country's 2008 foreclosures are from this state alone. It's no wonder when our country's average home price is 3.2 times the average worker's annual income, compared to California's 8.3 times the value of their annual income. That means the average American who makes $75,000 per year has a home value of $240,000, whereas the average Californian who earns $75,000 per year has a home worth $622,000. Get the picture? We're too spoiled here.

California has the highest labor costs and most complicated building regulations and land-use restrictions, which contribute to its high property costs. I know this firsthand because I've been in the construction industry struggling to pull permits and satisfy inspectors and building officials' busting egos for twenty-two years. This situation has more people leaving our state than ever before. And who can blame them? America, meet California, because you're becoming more like it every day.

Why have I bothered to ramble on about California and its problems? Because our state's problems all come from a very simple concept: When people have it too good for too long, they take things for granted. In my opinion, this recession is good thing. People often behave better in bad times. They appreciate the little things. In my experience, they also treat others better in bad times. We need a cleansing process to take place, and we have one going on right now. Thank God. Embrace it for what it is—getting the bad out and starting over with the good. And this goes for government too. Thank God, we still have those who remember their grandparents' hard work and sacrifice, who didn't over-leverage their homes, who saved a little money while most were spending, who bought a used car even though they could afford a new one, who put money toward their kids' college fund instead of a vacation. Let sacrifice have its day in the sun, and let waste and greed work like their grand predecessors who made this state and country great in the first place. Let the bleeding begin and the bandages come out. Don't think I'm not feeling it too. But this country needs to feel it, and we need to get it through our heads that self-control is a virtue and the lack of respect for it will lead to destruction. That's where we are now. It's time to change our course. At some point, people need to realize they're on the Titanic, and then go to plan B because plan A is going to sink. Yes, this is a generation of spoiled Americans. Californians have again led the country, but this time not in a good direction. We need people who are grounded with the virtues of our parent's parents, who struggled to make ends meet and taught their offspring how to respect a dollar, to once again instill in us the self-discipline and responsibility they proudly practiced in their daily lives.

I look fondly back to the days when going to McDonalds's was an infrequent treat, and to the rare occasion when my mother would buy me a cheap plastic ball to kick around and I felt like I won the lotto. Of course, that was 1968, the year my dad lost his job. How I miss the "good old days" when I had nothing. At least there was the dream then. Now the dream is to get this country back to that mindset and to appreciate the little things again. Like so much of life, they have to be lost before they are truly appreciated. Great things are so devalued when seen through spoiled eyes.

Let's not eat the best steaks and drink the best wines daily. Let's save those things for special occasions. Let us once again appreciate all the great things in life by choosing not to make them commonplace, an everyday event that becomes the norm and not the exception. Even though we can afford to do it, let's choose not to. If we can afford to waste, let's make a greater effort not to waste. If we can afford to squander our resources, let's make an even greater effort not to.

Individuals often feel there is nothing they can do. But it starts with each and every person practicing self-control, along with a collective effort from our families and friends, our communities and our leaders, and ultimately each state that makes up our great nation. Since government can affect our lifestyles and our happiness, it is obvious we need to control it. If you don't think so, ask those who live in North Korea or Cuba.

"To prohibit a great people form making all that they can of every part
of their own produce, or from employing their stock and industry
in the way that they judge most advantageous to themselves,
is a manifest violation of the most sacred rights of mankind."

ECONOMIST ADAM SMITH
IN THE YEAR OF AMERICA'S REVOLUTION, 1776

It is most important that our great nation realigns its compass to point in the right direction again, and this may have to happen at a grassroots level. It wouldn't be the first time greatness came from a people with a passion for great change. This is how our country was founded. The cleansing process we're going through currently is necessary, and with it an understanding that we've become spoiled by our own choices and we need to change our ways. It is never too late, but the longer we wait, the harder it will be to repair the damage.

Let's choose not to be spoiled anymore. We can work hard and enjoy the fruits of our labor without wasting so much. We can enjoy a day off and a drive through the country for the drive itself and not for the car we ride in. We can enjoy a dinner with our family because we're with family and not for what is on our plates. In short, we can appreciate all the little things again. Let's not be a nation that had it all, like California, and lost it because its citizens chose to become spoiled, always wanting more and never satisfied.

Let's be a nation that once again looks to God and says, "Thank You, God, for all the great free gifts You've given us. Let us use them in ways that are pleasing to You and pass them along to our children. And let our children pass along to their children, not just this great country but a great and godly way of thinking about it and respecting it."

This is my wish: That we will choose not to become spoiled. That we will demand our children work hard and appreciate everything they earn. That we won't spoil them, especially when we have the means to do so. I've told my wife many times that one of our biggest challenges with our children isn't in teaching them how to be happy by giving them things, but how to not ruin them by giving them things. Give to them after they've worked hard for it and have learned to appreciate it. Then, and only then, will it have meaning to them and earn its due respect.

This all starts with our own mindset about spoiling ourselves. Man needs to challenge himself with appreciating the little things or else he will not appreciate the great things. God has given us too many incredible gifts to insult Him by being spoiled and not seeing His grace for what it is. It is His free gift to us. He gives us our lives to live the way we choose to live them. Let's choose to honor Him by respecting all that surrounds us and by cherishing all that is His and has been given to us through His grace. Grace is something freely given without desiring anything in return. That is God by nature—a nature that has designed man to be at his best when he's not spoiled.

> "It is better to be humble in spirit with the lowly
> Than to divide the spoil with the proud"
>
> PROVERBS 16:19

Chapter Twenty-eight

Sharing the Christian Faith

"And He said to them, 'Go into all the world and preach the gospel to all creation.'"

Mark 16:15

I HAVE FOUND that most people are not comfortable sharing their faith. This is certainly true for me. Nor do I feel gifted at it. I always got nervous when I had to talk in front of groups, and I certainly did not feel qualified to be any kind of expert in biblical study.

On Thanksgiving Day 1985, I had planned to help out at a Christian mission for the homeless. I envisioned myself serving turkey and mashed potatoes to a line of homeless people. But while the volunteer help was being assembled, one of the directors asked if anyone would be interested in witnessing about their Christian faith to the people as they ate. Of course, no one volunteered, myself included. After a few moments in the drop-dead silence, something compelled me to raise my hand and say, "I'll do it." At the same time, I was standing outside of myself saying, "Who is this person who just volunteered for something he knows nothing about?" And yet the silence was as if God was feeling the pain of no one going to bat for Him. It felt wrong, and I had to do something about it.

So, there I was, the only volunteer, feeling the horror in my own mind while seeing the relief on everyone else's faces. And yet I knew I was attempting to do something great in God's eyes. What happened in the following hour I'll never forget. I bombed. I walked away that day feeling so bad about how I represented my faith. No one showed any interest in hearing about Christianity, and I never felt more rejected in my life. I thought, *Certainly this is not my talent. Certainly there can be no joy in this type of endeavor.* I couldn't help but wonder, *What was I thinking when I raised my hand?* There was a great lesson to be learned that day, and yet I wouldn't discover it until many years later.

Here is the lesson: It is not about *you* when you share your faith. It's about God. You are sharing His Word and His truth, not your words and your truths.

When one comes from a place of sharing someone else's good news, it comes across much more believable because there is no gain for you, and that is very evident to the listeners. If they think you have a motive then they will be suspect of what you are saying. When you speak on behalf of what God wants for others with no selfish motive or interest, then gaining someone's trust becomes effortless. Even if they don't believe what you say is the truth, they will certainly believe you believe it. And that's what sharing your faith is all about—an example of how much you believe in what you are saying. The rest is up to God and the individual you are sharing with. It is their relationship, not yours. You are merely introducing them to each other.

Why is it so important we share our faith? Can't we get to heaven by our own faith alone? Why do we need to open our mouths and proclaim Christ to others? The reason should scare all of us. Jesus says, "If you won't go to bat for Me in front of others, I may not go to bat for you in front of My Father." Here it is in His own words:

> "Therefore everyone who confesses Me before men,
> I will also confess him before My Father who is in heaven."
>
> MATTHEW 10:32

Now, He hasn't said you can't get to heaven without proclaiming Him, so I will leave it up to you to interpret. But it is a strong statement. He's saying, "If you really have faith in Me, you'll be excited to share the truth with others." It should be a joy to share if you really believe. If you have doubts, you probably won't be too motivated to share the gospel. That is convicting. But don't share out of fear. Share out of excitement about your faith and what you know is the truth. That is the kind of faith God wants you to have. Not the kind that says, "I'd better share because I might not get to heaven if I don't." Sharing your faith may not be an obstacle to God receiving you into heaven, but it is important to Him because it shows your true heart—all that really matters to Him. Although sharing one's faith may seem difficult to do, it cannot come from fear. It must be motivated by love.

I think sharing my faith is one of the hardest things for me to do. First, I need to be in the right mood, and that doesn't seem to happen very often. Secondly, I'm not a hard sell, and frankly I'd rather live my faith by example than by proclaiming God's Word. It's easier and there isn't the risk of rejection. Honestly, I hate the thought of having to evangelize others. It is a terrible thing to say, but it is the honest truth. And here is another truth—I've never felt so good as when I was the tool God used to bring another person into His eternal kingdom. I've always thought I would be the last person who could ever learn how to effectively share my faith. It didn't happen overnight, but a few events in my life made me into a type of Christian I thought I would never become. But I am also ashamed to admit, most of my close friends don't even know this about me—that I love my Lord as much as I do. This is something I need to correct.

It was within a year or two after my Thanksgiving episode that I heard about a piano teacher named Brian who might be willing to teach me the piano. I was twenty-five years old, and I had always wanted to learn how to play the piano but I had never taken a lesson. Brian attended the same church as my sister, and that was our connection. I called Brian, and he said he didn't give piano lessons, but he had heard through my sister I used to play the trombone in high school and his church orchestra really needed a trombone player. Brian was the orchestra leader. He said, "I'll tell you what; if you join our church orchestra as our trombone player, I'll take you on as a piano student." After hearing Brian play jazz on the piano, I was sold. Brian was a great jazz player and I wasn't going to find a better teacher, so I agreed. That was the beginning of a great friendship with Brian. He was about five years older than I and a fine Christian leader. I wasn't very active in church at the time. My life was more about making money, and I worked God in when I could find the time. Sad, but true.

During one of our lessons, Brian asked me if I would be interested in joining a new class he planned to teach at the church. It was called Evangelism Explosion (EE). I had never heard of it, but he said it would be a couple of evenings a week for about eight weeks. I agreed. Thoughts of my initial attempt at evangelizing that Thanksgiving came to mind, but then I thought, *What do I have to lose?* That course was a changing point in my way of thinking about my faith and also in being able to share it properly. It was a fantastic course. It was organized, and it was clear, and it was the truth. I learned it, but I didn't really practice it enough to be effective at it, and the reason was that I didn't want to be good at it. I didn't want to evangelize, even though I was equipped with EE and it was a great tool. But it was not something I looked forward to ever practicing in real life. The knowledge was good enough for me. Funny,

God didn't see it that way. He let me go on my way without giving me any sign otherwise.

Twelve years later, I was at one of my job sites and I had hired a welder that day. His name was Jim. He did a great job for me, and occasionally I'd hire him to do a day's work. One day Jim asked, "Are you a Christian?" And I said, "Yes, what made you ask?" He said, "Because I could tell by the way you carried yourself and by the way you treated your employees and by the way you have been treating me." It was one of the nicest compliments I ever received. It meant I was walking the Christian walk, and it even made me feel all the more like I didn't need to tell people about my faith and I didn't need to evangelize to others because my walk was enough. After all, if someone asks you if you are Christian you must be doing something right. I was filled with pride, to a fault.

We talked about what churches we attended and shared some stories, and then Jim said, "Have you ever heard of Evangelism Explosion?" I said, "Heard of it? I took the course many years ago!" He proceeded to tell me about how his church was implementing EE and how fast it was growing. I now lived in Orange County and attended a local church, not really getting too involved, but going to services and trying to keep my eye on God, while focusing mainly on my future financial goals and raising my family, which had grown to three children. Jim challenged me to start EE at my church and be a teacher. I kind of let the suggestion go in one ear and out the other, and rather quickly. I couldn't really even remember most of EE, and, certainly, I could never teach the program.

I would hire Jim on average about once every five months, and every time he saw me he would say, "Have you started EE at your church?" And every time I answered, "No." I always had a good excuse. There was no way I was going to start teaching EE. Our work relationship continued, and so did Jim's consistent question, "Have you started EE yet?" One day, after about the sixth or seventh time and after about two years of his persistence, I thought to myself, *The next time he asks me, I'm going to say yes.* And I followed through.

I asked my pastor if I could use his office during his off hours to teach the class to anyone who was interested. He said, "Why don't you get up in front of the congregation on Sunday and present your class to the church, and we'll send a signup sheet around that day?" I reluctantly agreed. I hated getting up in front of groups, especially large ones and especially about topics I knew very little about. What had I gotten myself into? But I had gone this far; I might as well see the thing through. I stood up nervously in front of my church and presented the class outline to about 125 people. Only two signed up. That was a relief to me because I didn't know what I was going to do with the class anyway.

I got my head into the original EE manual and relearned the course—even better this time because I was going to be teaching and I couldn't fake my way through it. Jack and Rene were my two students. I learned a lot about how to lay out the course for them. In essence, I had to figure out how to teach starting from scratch. It was challenging, but it was rewarding, and I learned how to refine my style to be better for the next class. I taught a larger class after that, and then another one after that, and I was refining my skills as I taught. I was learning more from teaching than I ever did as a student. It was very rewarding.

But let me caution you about something I found out as I taught the class. It seemed that during the times I was teaching and going to bat for my God negative things seemed to happen in my life. I am convinced the teaching of God's Word is one of the biggest targets of Satan. When he catches wind that you are out to help build up what he detests more then anything, he comes at you with a vengeance. So, if you're going to stand up for God, you have to pray to God for His protection before you go into battle. I think God let's this happen to some degree in some people because He wants to see how far they will go for Him. At least, that's what I think He did with me. So, I always pray before I attempt one of my classes and ask God for His protection. I know the victory will be there in the end, but it is hard to see sometimes when you're on the battlefield. And Satan's battles are fierce ones. But he's no match for God.

Now, let's talk about how to share the Christian faith by using the Evangelism Explosion method. This course was developed by Dr. D. James Kennedy and is now being used in every country in the world. I will present my own summary of it here in a condensed form, but I encourage you to find a class in your area and take the complete course. It is so much more effective when it is learned properly from a qualified teacher, focusing on one particular area each week. EE is a powerful evangelizing tool and also a great way to share your own faith with confidence and biblical backing.

The presentation begins with two diagnostic questions designed to find out if a person believes he is going to heaven and, if so, why. These questions should be worked into a conversation:

QUESTION #1: "If you died today, do you know for sure you would go to heaven?"

How people answer this question tells you whether or not the second question even needs to be asked. If they say, "I'm a good person," or "I've done good things," or "I've raised a good family," or "I've attended church all my life," then they are relying on their works as a means to be saved. We know biblically this is not what God promises. If they say anything that isn't based on the fact they are trusting in Jesus Christ alone for their salvation then they are not following God's Word on the way to receive eternal life. It really is that easy and that precise. Now, if they aren't answering with Christ alone as to their means to heaven, then there is no reason to ask them question two. But, if they answer, "I think I will go to heaven because I am Christian or because I believe in God, then more clarification is needed. That is the purpose of the follow-up question.

QUESTION #2: "If you died and were standing before God and He said to you, 'Why should I let you into my heaven?' how would you reply to Him?"

You have taken this to its final level to determine if Christ is their answer. The Bible says in John 14:6 in Jesus' own words, "I am the way, and the truth, and the life; no one comes to the Father but through me."

Since the Bible is very clear about how to be with God for eternity, the purpose of EE is to find out if people are already relying on Christ for their salvation, and, if not, then to convince them the Bible is the true Word of God. The EE outline is easy to memorize because it is broken into five categories, with two main points and Bible verses to back up each point.

A. GRACE

Heaven is a free gift! It is not earned, and it is not deserved.
Ephesians 2:8–9 goes with the earned part, *"not as a result of works, so that no one may boast."*
Romans 6:23 goes with the deserved part, *"For the wages of sin is death, but the free gift of God is eternal life in Christ Jesus our Lord."*
What we deserve is death.

B. MAN

Everyone is a sinner.
Romans 3:23 *"For all have sinned and fall short of the glory of God."*
Conflict: Man cannot save himself.
Matthew 5:48 *"Therefore you are to be perfect, as your heavenly Father is perfect."*

C. GOD

He is merciful.
1 John 4:8 *"God is love."*
But He is just.
Exodus 34:7 *"He will by no means leave the guilty unpunished."*

D. CHRIST

Who is He?
John 1:1, 14 *"In the beginning was the Word, and the Word was with God, and the Word was God.*
And the Word became flesh, and dwelt among us."
What He did. Died on the cross as payment for our sin.
Philippians 2:5–11.

E. FAITH

What it isn't:
It is not intellectual
James 2:19 *"You believe that God is one. You do well; the demons also believe, and shudder."*
It is not temporal (of this earth):
Matthew 8:29 *"What business do we have with each other, Son of God?"*

What it is:
Trusting in Christ alone for your salvation. Act 16:31
1 John 5:11–13 *"And the testimony is this, that God has given us eternal life, and this life is in His Son. …"*

This is how the Bible defines faith:

> *"Now faith is the assurance of things hoped for,*
> *the conviction of things not seen."*

HEBREWS 11:1

In summary, and it really is this simple:

1. **Grace**—God's ultimate desire for all of us is to accept His grace, eternity in heaven.
2. **Man**—The problem is man's nature doesn't allow us to get there on our own.
3. **God**—The conflict is between man and God. God wants us to have heaven, but He is a just God and will not accept us into His perfect heaven unless we are perfect in His eyes.
4. **Christ**—Jesus is the doorway to heaven. Christ came to earth—God in the form of man—and died for us so we can be seen as perfect, without sin, if we accept Him as our Savior and our pathway to God.
5. **Faith**—Faith is the key to opening the door (Christ). Through faith in Jesus Christ we are saved. Christ is the answer.

> *"I intend to go anywhere, sponsored by anybody, to preach the Gospel of Christ,*
> *if there are no strings attached to my message."*

BILLY GRAHAM

Chapter Twenty-nine

INVESTING IN WHAT YOU BELIEVE

"I am the way, and the truth, and the life;
no one comes to the Father but through me."

JESUS, JOHN 14:6

THIS CHAPTER, although one of the shortest, is the most significant. All the other topics, as important as they may be, only help to make life easier, more structured, and hopefully happier. But life will be short on this earth, and eternity is long—very long! What do I believe? In what will I invest? What do you believe? In what will you invest?

The following is what I believe, and this is what all these years of writing and making sense of it all mean to me. Hopefully, it can add quality to your life. But even more meaningful to me, would be if these writings could help to take some of the responsibility of your "purpose" away from you and turn it over to our great God. Give Him a chance to have total control. Be still, and let Him be your God.

To summarize, I believe:

Most of us, Christians or not—pick any religion, it doesn't matter—most of us are not living as if God truly exists. I'm not judging anyone, just stating a fact. And the fact also rings true about my life too much of the time. How many things in life, when you don't know what to expect, do you do nothing about? Not much. Most of us try to figure out what we don't understand if we think it is going to hurt us by not understanding. But we don't seem to want to do this with God. None of us know if there's going to be an earthquake or a fire or a flood large enough to wipe out our homes, and yet we carry insurance for the unknown because we don't want to risk being wrong.

What about God? Isn't He bigger than an earthquake or a fire? Apparently not, for so many of us. If we truly believe God exists and has a heaven waiting for us, wouldn't we start investing in it? If we knew that doing a kind act for someone else would give us more favor in God's eyes when we get to heaven, wouldn't we start living differently here on earth? Wouldn't we invest in doing more kind acts and spend less time making money? If our time on earth is just a blip in time, whereas heaven is for eternity, wouldn't we put all of our investment into eternity? I'm sure the answer to all these questions is yes, but only if we knew, only if we had complete faith in God. We don't, or we would be living differently. If you can't admit this is the truth, then you are lying to yourself. The reason you invest so much in this world is because you don't know if God exists, at least not with enough certainty to act on it.

The truth is that I'm tired of investing in this world. I'm tired of not living what I truly believe, that all the stuff is just that—stuff. I get no satisfaction out of building anymore because I see no real value in it. I had to do it first to understand it, eventually losing my desire to spend so much time shaping the temporary molecules around us. I am no saint simply because I've gained a better understanding. I just want to invest in what I believe in. I want to invest in God and in the things that will please Him. I want to invest in His perfect plan, not mine. I want to invest in what will last for eternity. I'm not motivated by a higher place in heaven or more comfort in the afterlife. I'm motivated by a feeling in my soul that God truly exists and He wants to give His grace over fully to all of us who have faith in Him and live for Him.

God exists in our lives and we live inside His perfect plan, whether we like it or not. He created the heavens and the earth. He has a perfect plan that will happen exactly as He intended from the very beginning—before the earth was created and long before you and I were born. But we were in the plan from the very beginning. Our wonderful God planned you and me from the very first moment of all existence. He also designed us to have free will to make choices and to decide how willing we are to open ourselves up to be used by Him. That doesn't mean our big part will happen while we are alive on this earth. In fact, many who have sown their great seeds here will have their reward later on in heaven. That reward will last for eternity, while many who have walked this earth in comfort will come behind those who had nothing during their short stay here.

I believe in the Bible's teachings; however, I think man's interpretation of those teachings, although close, can have fault, as with all things from man. It is not God's intention to have us figure it all out while we are on earth. To worship a God who is completely understood would be impossible for mortal man. This will come in heaven.

"For now we see in a mirror dimly, but then face to face;
now I know in part, but then I will know fully just as I also have been fully known."

1 CORINTHIANS 13:12

While we may not understand all of God's teachings at this point, most are very obvious and well-written so there would be no misunderstanding. We have freedom to accept these as truth or to deny them. We must each make this decision in life. We must openly declare ourselves as believers in our God, or it will be understood that we are not. We cannot sit on the fence and wait until God appears, thereby proving Himself to us, and then make our decision. God operates and responds through our faith. Faith only comes when we do not have proof and yet still believe with all of our hearts. This is the key to eternity in heaven with God.

Faith is the key. Christ is the doorway to heaven. The key unlocks the door. We will only get to the Father through the Son. God is clear on that. We have to believe this to be the truth or declare that it is not. Or simply do nothing, whereby we declare it is not the truth.

What do you believe? Are you willing to take a stand? Are you willing to be still and let God be God? Are you willing to say, "God, it's all Your plan. I'm so thankful to be a part of it. I want my wishes for my life to be Your wishes. May I simply be used to help achieve Your great and perfect plan, which I believe You laid out from the beginning. I don't want it to be my plan but Yours. I put my life and my commitment through faith into Your hands, and I'll be happy and accept whatever You have planned for me. Use me however You will. I trust You, and I love You. Lord Jesus, thank You for coming to earth as God in the form of a man and dying on the cross for me, for cleaning me up and saving the world from sin, for making us perfect in Your Father's eyes and creating a pathway to heaven for us to be with You for eternity. Although at times I may be weak, I will trust in You forever, and I will be your humble servant in faith." That's what I believe. That's where I make my stand.

I challenge you to make your stand. Invest in eternity and make your stand for God. Too many of us think, *If God is full of grace and mercy, then He won't keep me out of His heaven, especially since I've been a pretty good person.* But that's my point, He's already shown His grace and mercy by giving you a whole lifetime to make a choice for Him. What are you going to say when you die and you're face to face with God and He asks you, "Why should I let you into My heaven?

Why haven't you made a stand for Me?" Are you going to say, "I need more time to figure it out?" Don't do that.

I challenge you to make a decision, and then live for that decision. If you choose the world, then you'll be investing in the world. If you choose God, then invest in God. We make commitments all the time to people, we sign contracts, we stay committed to goals, and we resolve to be successful at our endeavors. But we sit on the fence with the most important decision we'll ever have to make to the most important Being in our lives. There is something wrong when we are that blind to what is right in front of us for our entire lives and we continue to ignore it because it hasn't given us our sufficient proof that we demand. The decision will be made by each and every one us, whether we admit it or not and whether we consciously make it or not.

Don't be smart in life but foolish with eternity. Let us all take the necessary time to research and learn with open minds and open hearts so that we can make this most important decision. Then, all that is left to do is to confess it with our mouths, believe it in our hearts and live it in our daily lives.

"That if you confess with your mouth Jesus as Lord,
and believe in your heart that God raised Him from the dead,
you will be saved."

ROMANS 10:9

BIBLIOGRAPHY

Bounds, E. M., *The Necessity of Prayer*, Grand Rapids: Baker Books, 1991.

"In the silence, God reveals the answers I seek," *Daily Word*, Unity Publications. (May 19, 2002).

Franklin, Benjamin, *The Autobiography of Benjamin Franklin*, New York: W. W. Norton & Co, 1986.

Kennedy, D. James, *Evangelism Explosion*, Third Edition, Tyndale House Publishers, Wheaton, Illinois, 1970, 1977, 1983.

McDowell, Josh, *Evidence that Demands a Verdict*, San Bernardino: Here's Life Publishers, Inc., 1979.

McDowell, Josh, *More Than a Carpenter*, Wheaton: Living Books, Tyndale, 1977.

Osteen, Joel, *Become a Better You: 7 Keys to Improving Your Life Every Day*, New York: Free Press, 2007.

Piper, John, *A Godward Life*, Colorado Springs: Multnomah Publishers, 1997.

Pollock, Robert, *The Everything World Religion Book*, Avon, Mass.: F & W Publishers, 2002.

Prager, Dennis, *Happiness is a Serious Problem*, New York: Regan Books, Harper Collins, 1998.

Tyner, Christopher L., "President Abraham Lincoln Simplicity Helped Make Him the Greatest Communicator," *Investor's Business Daily, Inc.* (February 20, 2001).